Palgrave Studies in Compromise after Conflict

Series Editor
John D. Brewer
Queen's University Belfast
Belfast, UK

This series aims to bring together in one series scholars from around the world who are researching the dynamics of post-conflict transformation in societies emerging from communal conflict and collective violence. The series welcomes studies of particular transitional societies emerging from conflict, comparative work that is cross-national, and theoretical and conceptual contributions that focus on some of the key processes in post-conflict transformation. The series is purposely interdisciplinary and addresses the range of issues involved in compromise, reconciliation and societal healing. It focuses on interpersonal and institutional questions, and the connections between them.

More information about this series at
http://www.palgrave.com/gp/series/14641

Ray Nickson · Alice Neikirk

Managing Transitional Justice

Expectations of International Criminal Trials

palgrave
macmillan

Ray Nickson
Fresno Pacific University
Fresno, CA, USA

Alice Neikirk
Australian National University
Canberra, ACT, Australia

Palgrave Studies in Compromise after Conflict
ISBN 978-3-030-08538-4 ISBN 978-3-319-77782-5 (eBook)
https://doi.org/10.1007/978-3-319-77782-5

Printed on acid-free paper

This Palgrave Macmillan imprint is published by the registered company Springer International Publishing AG part of Springer Nature
The registered company address is: Gewerbestrasse 11, 6330 Cham, Switzerland

For Cynthia Sue and Edna Bonnie

General Editor's Introduction

Compromise is a much used but little understood term. There is a sense in which it describes a set of feelings (the so-called 'spirit' of compromise) that involve reciprocity, representing the agreement to make mutual concessions toward each other from now on: no matter what we did to each other in the past, we will act toward each other in the future differently as set out in the agreement between us. The compromise settlement can be a spit and a handshake, much beloved in folk lore, or a legally binding statute with hundreds of clauses.

As such, it is clear that compromise enters into conflict transformation at two distinct phases. The first is during the conflict resolution process itself, where compromise represents a willingness amongst parties to negotiate a peace agreement that represents a second-best preference in which they give up their first preference (victory) in order to cut a deal. A great deal of literature has been produced in Peace Studies and International Relations on the dynamics of the negotiation process and the institutional and governance structures necessary to consolidate the agreement afterwards. Just as important, however, is compromise in the second phase, when compromise is part of post-conflict reconstruction, in which protagonists come to learn to live together despite their former enmity and in face of the atrocities perpetrated during the conflict itself.

In the first phase, compromise describes reciprocal agreements between parties to the negotiations in order to make political concessions sufficient to end conflict, in the second phase, compromise involves victims and perpetrators developing ways of living together in which concessions are made as part of shared social life. The first is about compromises between political groups and the state in the process of statebuilding (or rebuilding) after the political upheavals of communal conflict, the second is about compromises between individuals and communities in the process of social healing after the cultural trauma provoked by the conflict.

This book series primarily concerns itself with the second process, the often messy and difficult job of reconciliation, restoration and repair in social and cultural relations following communal conflict. Communal conflicts and civil wars tend to suffer from the narcissism of minor differences, to coin Freud's phrase, leaving little to be split halfway and compromise on, and thus are usually especially bitter. The series therefore addresses itself to the meaning, manufacture and management of compromise in one of its most difficult settings. The book series is cross-national and cross-disciplinary, with attention paid to inter-personal reconciliation at the level of everyday life, as well as culturally between social groups, and the many sorts of institutional, inter-personal, psychological, sociological, anthropological and cultural factors that assist and inhibit societal healing in all post-conflict societies, historically and in the present. It focuses on what compromise means when people have to come to terms with past enmity and the memories of the conflict itself, and relate to former protagonists in ways that consolidate the wider political agreement.

This sort of focus has special resonance and significance for peace agreements that are usually very fragile. Societies emerging out of conflict are subject to ongoing violence from spoiler groups who are reluctant to give up on first preferences, constant threats from the outbreak of renewed violence, institutional instability, weakened economies, and a wealth of problems around transitional justice, memory, truth recovery, and victimhood, amongst others. Not surprisingly therefore, reconciliation and healing in social and cultural relations is difficult to achieve, not least because inter-personal compromise between erstwhile enemies is difficult.

Lay discourse picks up on the ambivalent nature of compromise after conflict. It is talked about in common sense in one of two ways, in which compromise is either a virtue or a vice, taking its place among the angels or in Hades. One form of lay discourse likens concessions to former protagonists with the idea of restoration of broken relationships and societal and cultural reconciliation, in which there is a sense of becoming (or returning) to wholeness and completeness. The other form of lay discourse invokes ideas of appeasement, of being *compromised* by the concessions, which constitute a form of surrender and reproduce (or disguise) continued brokenness and division. People feel they continue to be beaten by the sticks which the concessions have allowed others to keep; with restoration, however, weapons are turned truly in ploughshares. Lay discourse suggests, therefore, that there are issues that the Palgrave Studies in Compromise after Conflict series must begin to problematize, so that the process of societal healing is better understood and can be assisted and facilitated by public policy and intervention.

In this volume in the Series, Ray Nickson and Alice Neikirk focus on what has become perhaps the most significant and popular process for post-conflict healing and reconciliation, namely, transitional justice. This field is an interdisciplinary space and one where practitioners and theoreticians mix in challenging and fruitful collaborations. It is a burgeoning and exciting field, and there are now many transitional justice research institutes and a very large number of practitioner groups and agencies, ranging from well-funded international bodies to financially strapped local, bottom-up organisations. Transitional justice practices take many forms and such diversity adds to this sense of rapid growth. Its modes and practices range from truth recovery procedures, which are themselves very different in focus and form, criminal courts, legal and public enquiries, demobilisation and demilitarisation policies amongst ex-combatants, support structures for victims, policies and procedures for the management of post-conflict emotions, and structures for victim-perpetrator dialogue, amongst many other things. Advocates speak strongly for the effectiveness of these practices in delivering healing, reconciliation, and recovery after conflict.

One of the limitations of transitional justice, however, is the level of expectations surrounding the claims about its success in delivering justice, truth recovery and healing, or what Jon Elster once called 'closing the book' after conflict. Nickson and Neikirk refer to this as the problem of expectations—and the expectations of transitional justice outcomes are very great indeed. They thus caution against the expectations that various stakeholders naturally develop and offer a useful and timely corrective to these 'great expectations'. They concentrate their arguments on the role of international criminal courts, focusing in depth on two case studies, the former Yugoslavia and Cambodia.

Comparison of these two cases is in itself interesting for generating cross-national comparative work on war crime trials, but the focus is primarily on what the cases tell us about transitional justice as a field. It addresses the key question: can it deliver what people expect of it? In answering this question, their arguments are based on careful and detailed documentary and content analysis, interviews with a variety of stakeholders who have invested in the outcome of international criminal courts, and media coverage. It is a thoughtful and insightful analysis of transitional justice as practiced by international criminal courts, and as Series Editor, I very warmly welcome this new edition to the Series.

Belfast
January 2018

John D. Brewer

Acknowledgements

We are very grateful to John Braithwaite for his guidance during this research project and the production of this manuscript. We are also grateful to the Regulatory Institutions Network at the Australian National University for supporting this research and fieldwork. Thanks are also due to Rod Broadhurst, Thierry Bouhours, Jennifer Llewellyn, Elizabeth Stanley, and Michael Savvas who all provided feedback on various aspects of this research at different stages.

Note on Spellings

This study deals with two cases, one from the Balkans and another from Southeast Asia. Because the study deals with events and people involving multiple languages, names and places have been given their Romanized spelling to maintain consistency across both cases.

Contents

List of Figures

List of Tables

1
Introduction

On the 25th of March 2016, while waiting for an international flight in the United States, we picked up a copy of *The New York Times* (*NY Times*). The front-page image was striking: the Srebrenica memorial with a grieving woman covering her face. The headline triumphantly stated, 'Justice for Genocide Victims in Bosnia'. Reading the associated article, that appeared eight pages later, it was evident that the conviction for genocide, committed by probably the highest-ranking figure convicted at the International Criminal Tribunal for the Former Yugoslavia (the Tribunal), war-time president of Republika Srpska, Radovan Karadzic, was viewed as a crucial moment. This was a moment not only for victims but the broader aspirations of an international justice system. The article also hinted that Karadzic's conviction might aid reconciliation and bring closure to "the bloodiest European conflict since WWII" (Simons 2016, p. A8). It was further suggested in the article that the conviction would act as a deterrent: preventing alternative versions of history from fuelling future atrocities in the region. Despite these high hopes for what due process and a guilty verdict could achieve,

R. Nickson and A. Neikirk, *Managing Transitional Justice*,
Palgrave Studies in Compromise after Conflict,
https://doi.org/10.1007/978-3-319-77782-5_1

expectations of victims had been disappointed. According to victims quoted in the article, the 40-year sentence was viewed as lenient. The article flagged Karadzic's role in the deaths of 8,000 Muslim men and boys in Srebrenica to underscore the victims' sense of injustice. While the author of the article hoped the judgment would propel reconciliation, the victims expressed discontent, and it was reported that there was at least one protest in Serbia against the sentence.

The *NY Times* coverage of the conviction revealed a deeper conundrum for transitional justice: an expectation dilemma that exists between anticipated benefits and likely outcomes of transitional justice trials. This echoed what we found in wide-ranging interviews with people involved with the Tribunal and the Extraordinary Chambers in the Courts of Cambodia (the Chambers): that various groups, from local stakeholders to international jurists and diplomats, hold a diversity of expectations for transitional justice. These expectations frequently did not align with the likely contributions a given transitional justice mechanism may make. In transitional justice endeavours, expectations of speedy reconciliation, that court determinations regarding recent history will be accepted, or that prosecutions will symbolically satisfy victims, are laudable intentions but often reflect almost impossible expectations to achieve. Yet beyond an immediate determination of guilt or innocence, trials do hold wider significance. They can aid in documenting history, compelling social action, or encouraging societal self-reflection. It is not unreasonable to hold high expectations for international criminal trials, particularly in the context of transitional justice.

This book is a story about expectations, but it did not start out that way. Initially, the focus of our study was the construction of historical records in international criminal trials and their role in collective memory. Once in the field, participants consistently raised concerns about the need to manage the expectations people held of the Tribunal and Chambers. It was remarkable how frequently this concern was expressed. Nearly half of participants directly stated that unrealistic expectations were a problem for transitional justice, with eight participants using the term "managing expectations" in initial interviews. A greater number discussed managing expectations in other terms. It was something that we had not encountered before fieldwork and by the time we reached Cambodia, our final fieldwork site, it was clearly a significant issue for the majority of participants. An expectation dilemma was such a dominant concern for participants that it would have been difficult for the research not to respond. Participants constantly lamented that their work at either the Tribunal or Chambers was saddled with expectations they could never reasonably be expected to fulfil. This was not merely a problem of unrealistic expectations held by members of affected communities—the international communities that fund (and often champion) the courts also attached lofty expectations to the institutions. Participants recognized these layers of expectations and several speculated that one factor that impacted in expectations was the media. Despite many participants observing problems concerning expectations and transitional justice, there was no consensus as to what appropriate expectations would be. Participants did agree, however, that expectations needed to be managed. This raised innumerable questions. What were these expectations? How did they impact on transitional justice? How could they be managed? And was managing them the best or only response?

An Expectation Gap

The significance of transitional justice—the process that seeks to address the abuses and crimes of prior regimes or conflicts in transitions to more democratic polities—spans national and international spheres. At a national level, transitional justice may be of fundamental importance for communities in the wake of violence. It is one way that can serve to address their particular needs as survivors, victims, perpetrators, and as a society. Internationally, transitional justice plays an important role as well. Localised conflicts frequently have a destabilising effect well outside the immediate zone of hostilities. For instance, other states are often required to accept refugees fleeing the violence that engulfs their homelands. Conflict zones may help to fuel extremism around the world. In a time when nations are increasingly concerned with the threat of terrorism, external states may be eager to end hostilities and seek remedial steps to address their causes and consequences.

Transitional justice has blossomed as a field of study in a relatively short period (Bell 2009; Posner and Vermeule 2004). Indeed, the last 30 years has seen a proliferation of transitional justice activities. The end of the Cold War provided numerous opportunities to perform transitional justice activities in former Eastern Bloc nations as they transitioned to democracy. Majority rule in South Africa and the end of apartheid is perhaps the most well-known African example of transitional justice. Yet conflicts in other parts of Africa—Rwanda, Sierra Leone, Liberia, Uganda, Sudan—have seen transitional justice processes (frequently judicial and prosecutorial). Older conflicts have also been examined in contemporary transitional justice enterprises—most obviously the trials of Khmer Rouge leaders in Cambodia that form the second case of this study. Elsewhere in Asia, judicial and non-judicial forms of transitional justice have been employed to address the wounds of conflict in Indonesia and many other countries (Braithwaite et al. 2010; Braithwaite et al. 2012).

Despite a burgeoning literature on transitional justice, little has been written about the expectation issue. Nettlefield (2010) has made one of the more direct acknowledgments of the problem, noting that the Tribunal had often been assessed unfavourably. In these assessments the Tribunal had been examined in light of its stated goals, which Nettlefield (2010, p. 10) claims, "are primarily the policy pronouncements of architects of the court, used in times of crisis to justify its creation at a point when not all of those supporting it had honorable intentions." The pessimistic view of the Tribunal is the consequence of judging the Tribunal against inappropriate (essentially unrealistic) standards. These standards were premised upon the contributions the Tribunal was expected to make in the former Yugoslavia. For Nettlefield (2010, p. 6), the expectation problem cuts deep: "[a] gulf exists between the often unrealistic expectations … and the output of the court on any given day." This is unsurprising, given that the Tribunal was the most high-profile response that directly sought to address the crimes committed during the Balkan conflicts. As the work of the Tribunal and Chambers has progressed, it became clear that most expectations were channelled and focused primarily on these single official institutions. Participants recognized that the responsibility to perform all the task of transitional justice largely rested on the courts. This led to discussions about the possible need for more transitional justice mechanisms and greater diversity in conducting transitional justice. The isolated nature of these institutions led some participants to question whether single institutions, and particularly single institutions that were criminal courts, was the best way to undertake transitional justice.

This research sheds new light on the expectation gap: the space between what it is hoped transitional justice will achieve and what transitional justice most frequently can deliver. In this way, the study investigates the place of expectations in transitional justice. It then seeks to understand how well a single mechanism response to transitional justice contributes to the aims of transitional societies. We will see that a constant refrain in interviews was that expectations had to be managed. That is, expectations needed to be controlled so that they better reflected what the mechanism could provide. This is an important part of the issue, but only one part. Informing stakeholders about the likely contributions a trial (or other mechanism) can make is a prudent policy in transitional justice. It goes some way to ensuring that the contributions of the mechanism are judged fairly. It may also serve to better satisfy people with those contributions. But this begs the question: What is to be done with the remaining expectations? How are those expectations that were deemed unsuitable to the mechanism addressed? Are they inappropriate or unrealistic by virtue of their perceived unsuitability? For example, is it unrealistic or inappropriate to expect repair to one's home (destroyed during ethnic cleansing), in transitional justice efforts despite the adoption of trials? We argue that this is an entirely valid expectation (though it may never be satisfied). Transitional justice must be more responsive to the diversity of expectations that are held for it. We argue for a more central role of expectations in the design, establishment, and work of transitional justice.

Methodology

We set out to examine two different jurisdictions: the former Yugoslavia and Cambodia (the establishment of both the Tribunal and Chambers in response to conflicts in these regions is later covered in detail in Chapter 2). While the differences between the Tribunal and Chambers

Table 1.1 Number and role of interview participants

	Prosecutors	Defence	Registry	Judges	Outreach	NGO	Total
Tribunal	6	7	1	3	8	4	29
Chambers	3	0	1	2	2	20	28
Joint/Cross	0	0	0	0	0	1	1
Total	9	7	2	5	10	25	58

are many, there was one crucial similarity between the two selected cases: there had been no other official institution of transitional justice in either country. It was significant that the Chambers or Tribunal was, to date, the only official transitional justice institution for either conflict. The importance of this fact became apparent as participants raised the issue of expectations.

This study consisted of two data-sets: interviews with transitional justice practitioners and stakeholders; and a content analysis of news articles discussing the Tribunal and Chambers. Interviews sought to include participants with some intimate role with the court: judges; prosecutors; registry staff; outreach staff; court media officers; defence counsel; and justice-oriented NGOs dealing with the courts. Table 1.1 displays the number of interviews conducted, and the relevant groups that interviewees belonged to.

Fieldwork began in January 2011, with initial interviews conducted in The Hague. This was selected as the first destination, as it is the site of the Tribunal, as well as hosting a cluster of other international courts and transitional justice organisations. From The Hague, fieldwork shifted to the Western Balkans. With a base in Sarajevo, we shuttled to Belgrade and Zagreb, interviewing Tribunal staff and NGOs in Bosnia, Serbia, and Croatia. After visiting the former Yugoslavia, fieldwork was conducted in Cambodia, primarily in Phnom Penh. During days when participants were not available to meet, we visited sites of atrocities from the conflict and spoke with the curators of museums that commemorated victims of the Khmer Rouge regime or the wars in the Balkans. We also attended proceedings at the courts and collected locally available materials relevant to this research.

Given that participants considered the influence of the media as significant, this role was also studied. A content analysis of media coverage was included as part of the data collection. This sought to answer how expectations were expressed and framed in the media: What expectations are communicated about international criminal trials? How are these expectations represented? And what might influence, and be the influence of, such expectations? The decision to include a content analysis was the result of a need to analyse the way the media reflects and influences expectations regarding the Tribunal and Chambers.

Given the near impossibility of comparing local newspapers for the entire period of the study, it was decided that a newspaper with international credentials and maximum international readership across all groups would be most suitable. For this reason the *NY Times* was selected as the source. The advantages of the *NY Times* were manifold. The *NY Times* had covered, in sufficient quantum, both the Tribunal and the Chambers (not to mention the conflicts that necessitated the creation of these judicial institutions). It also employed correspondents in all the relevant locations for each case and has a proximity to the United Nations that was relevant as the institution responsible for creating (or in Cambodia, co-creating) the courts. Further, the conflict in the former Yugoslavia and the Khmer Rouge generated large numbers of refugees that resettled in the United States, as well as other countries where the *NY Times* is syndicated. These diasporas, though outside the "local" context, would also have hopes and expectations that are potentially influenced by the media.

In total, 665 articles were analysed. The start date of articles relating to the Tribunal was the day the Tribunal was created—25 May 1993. For the Chambers, it was decided that articles should be collected from the day that Cambodia's joint Prime Ministers sent a letter to the UN requesting assistance in undertaking trials of the Khmer Rouge—21 June 1997. Had the subsequent date of the creation of the Chambers been selected the important communications about early hopes for trials, speculation regarding a trial of Pol Pot, and the negotiations to institute the Chambers, would have been omitted. The end date of articles for both courts was 31 December 2011. Because the research question sought to explore how expectations might feature within communications, it was decided that *themes*, defined by Holsti (1969, p. 116) as "a single assertion about some subject", would constitute the recording units. When coding themes, the researcher is primarily searching for the expressions of an idea (Minichiello, Aroni and Hays 1990). In this way, coding themes permitted us to unitise and analyse expressions that were relevant to expectations, such as commentaries on impunity, peace, reconciliation, or crimes. Themes were coded for their appearance in each article. This permitted the use of such measures as absolute frequencies of themes (how often a theme appeared over the course of the study), and relative frequencies, such as the percentage of the appearance of a theme in comparison to all themes (Krippendorff 1980). Such frequency measures are often utilised in content analysis as indicative of importance, attention, and emphasis (Holsti 1969). Although themes were created inductively from sources as a whole, some were specific to either the Tribunal or Chambers.

There is, of course, the potential for an imperialist bias in selecting the most influential daily newspaper of the world's greatest power. While conducting the content analysis in English presented certain limitations to the study—largely because proximity to the local communities would be reduced, with other sources created for a different or wider audience—it benefitted the validity and reliability of the study, as the content analysis was conducted in the researchers' first language. Additionally, there have been several content analyses (for example, the volume edited by Dzihana and Volcic 2011) of Balkans media coverage of the Tribunal already (though not directly looking at the issue of expectations). Indeed, it is worth recalling that the Tribunal and the Chambers were not created for a purely local audience, but also an international one. International expectations are also examined in the research and indeed are an important part of it.

Book Layout

This book begins by looking at the expectation problem as it has been represented in previous studies. Chapter 2 builds upon the work of others who have argued that (1) transitional justice is currently dominated by legal responses and theory that limit the many ways it can make meaningful contributions; (2) trials and prosecutions have become a favoured response to mass violence; and (3) trials and prosecutions are suited to performing only a handful of functions well. The chapter provides a brief background to the establishment of the Tribunal and

Chambers. Significantly, this permits a more nuanced understanding of the context in which many expectations may have been generated. It also highlights how compromise, or a lack of compromise, in the creation of these institutions contributed to an expectation dilemma later. Both the Tribunal and Chambers have specific expectations attached to them. In addition, it is obvious that a great deal of overlap in expectations occurs between both institutions.

What did participants have to say about expectations and transitional justice? After all, it was their insights that shaped the direction of research toward this issue. The voices of participants echo throughout Chapter 3, expressing concern about expectations for, and of, the Tribunal and Chambers. Three overarching groups of expectations were observed in the data: expectations regarding the scope of justice; expectations for answers; and forward-looking expectations. According to most participants, these did not reflect the institutions that had been created to respond to justice needs following the conflicts in the former Yugoslavia and Cambodia. Chapter 4 examines the need to "manage expectations", discussing how some expectations were conceived by participants as inappropriate or unrealistic. The necessity of managing expectations was stated by a large number of participants who worked for, or with, the Tribunal and Chambers. Their frustrations largely reflected the view that expectations did not correspond to the contributions that institutions such as the Tribunal and Chambers could realistically make. What participants frequently omitted to consider was whether institutions should, or could, reflect expectations. The chapter questions this paradigm and asks whether it is appropriate to consider designing transitional justice responses that better reflect stakeholders' expectations.

Given participants' concerns about the role of news media, Chapter 5 examines how news media reported on the Tribunal and Chambers. In particular, it analyses how coverage could reflect, advance, ignore, diminish, reject or advocate for particular expectations. Chapter 5 presents data from a content analysis of *NY Times* coverage of the Tribunal and Chambers. This content analysis was designed specifically to examine expectations in media coverage. Results demonstrate that news media are an unreliable partner for transitional justice institutions. Connections between the media and expectations of transitional justice are observed in a preponderance of assertions that people are guilty of crimes before or during trials which may fuel expectations for convictions; the need to include elements of drama in stories about otherwise mundane legal proceedings, which can reinforce or alter expectations; and a constant refrain regarding the *number* of victims and the graphic details of their victimisation. The chapter argues that news media are limited in what they report, and that expectations may be distorted by this coverage.

The many threads of previous chapters are woven into a cohesive analysis in Chapter 6. Here issues are teased out and the foundations for the normative proposals of Chapter 7 are laid. Chapter 6 asks that we reconsider the labelling of certain expectations as wrong—a view proposed by many participants in our interviews—and that we more actively consider their context in this assessment. The limitations of trials in addressing the great variety of expectations are discussed. The chapter then invites us to imagine institutions designed with expectations in mind. It arranges expectations into three categories: expectations that can be achieved, that could be achieved through an alternative or complementary mechanism, and expectations that cannot be achieved. Understanding expectations in this way helps to better direct efforts to satisfying or managing expectations as appropriate. Proposals for a more expectation-inclusive approach to transitional justice are made in Chapter 7. Three steps to addressing the expectation problem are proposed. The first is to develop more robust expectation management strategies. This would involve active identification of expectations, preferably before the creation of transitional justice institutions. The next step is to develop shared aims. Through collaboration and dialogue, shared aims are developed that reflect informed expectations of all stakeholders. These shared aims should then inform the design of institutions in transitional justice. In this way, mechanisms to address mass violence should both reflect as well as respond to shared aims in their design. The third step recommends that we broaden, deepen and lengthen our conception of transitional justice. We broaden by considering the plurality of ways that justice might be delivered. We deepen by providing greater opportunities for meaningful engagement in transitional justice. By lengthening all these efforts we allow for people to participate when they are ready: the exile who returns years after the conflict ends; the mother who cannot testify in the immediate aftermath as her grief is too acute; the perpetrator who is in jail but wants to make a reparative gesture to his victims. Finally, the chapter adopts a transformative lens from peace studies and argues that such a lens provides a helpful view for how to perform transitional justice.

The working title of this research was *Great Expectations*. But in truth, the expectations observed in this research were not great or extraordinary. Survivors sought to know what happened to loved ones and to have their suffering acknowledged. There were expectations of punishment for wrongdoers and reparations for victims. It was expected that courts might communicate lessons from and about the atrocities, conflicts, and transitions. As will become clear, there were a great number and diversity of expectations. Most expectations were ordinary, regular, and all too mundane. They were concerned about what assistance might be given in a transitional society, frequently by a well-funded international body. These are valid expressions of the desires and aims for processes supposed to aid in moving forward and beyond violence. They are invested with hope. These are ordinary expectations in extraordinary circumstances. Responding to these expectations is a great task; it is not an insurmountable one.

References

Bell, C 2009, 'Transitional justice, interdisciplinarity and the state of the 'field' or 'non-field'', *International Journal of Transitional Justice*, vol. 3, no. 1, pp. 5–27.

Braithwaite, J, Braithwaite, V, Cookson, M and Dunn, L 2010, *Anomie and violence: Non-truth and reconciliation in Indonesian peacebuilding*, ANU E-Press, Canberra, Australia.

Braithwaite, J, Charlesworth, H and Soares, A 2012, *Networked governance of greedom and tyranny: Peace in Timor-Leste*, ANU E-Press, Canberra, Australia.

Dzihana, A and Volcic, Z (eds) 2011, *Media and national ideologies: Analysis of reporting on war crime trials in the former Yugoslavia*, Media Centar Sarajevo, Sarajevo, Bosnia and Herzegovina.

Holsti, OR 1969, *Content analysis for the social sciences and humanities*, Addison-Wesley Publishing Co., Reading, Massachusetts.

Krippendorff, K 1980, *Content analysis: An introduction to its methodology*, Sage Publications, Beverley Hills, California.

Minichiello, V, Aroni, R, and Neville Hays, T 1990, *In-depth interviewing: Principles, techniques, analysis*, Longman Cheshire, Hong Kong.

Nettlefield, LJ 2010, *Courting democracy in Bosnia and Herzegovina: The Hague tribunal's impact in a postwar state*, Cambridge University Press, New York, New York.

Posner, EA and Vermeule, A 2004, 'Transitional justice as ordinary justice', *Harvard Law Review*, vol. 117, no. 3, pp. 761–825.

Simons, M 2016, 'Bosnian Serb leader Karadzic convicted of genocide and war crimes', *The New York Times*, March 25.

2

Courting Justice in Transitions

Over the past twenty-plus years, transitional justice has emerged as a field with a principal focus on institutions, mechanisms, and processes for revisiting past human rights abuses and violent conflicts. As the field has developed and grown, so to have the various understandings of transitional justice. Yet Bell (2009, p. 7) explains, all understandings "view transitional justice as the attempt to deal with past violence in societies undergoing or attempting some form of political transition." Generally, that political transition is conceived as a move from totalitarian or authoritarian regimes to democracy, and/or conflict to peace. Teitel (2005, p. 38) adds a further element to Bell's summary of transitional responses by noting that it is a justice "characterized by legal responses to confront the wrongdoings of repressive predecessor regimes." This reflects a key theoretical critique of transitional justice: the dominance of legalism. However, responses are only *primarily* legal (not exclusively legal) in their approach to addressing past abuses. There are many calls for transitional justice to expand beyond traditional legal responses (for example, see McEvoy 2008). Nevertheless, there is no consensus that the primacy

R. Nickson and A. Neikirk, *Managing Transitional Justice*,
Palgrave Studies in Compromise after Conflict,
https://doi.org/10.1007/978-3-319-77782-5_2

of law and legalism in transitional justice is a negative, though the quality of transitional justice scholarship and practice has been diminished by its legalistic preoccupations has been suggested (McEvoy 2007).

Beyond the theoretical underpinnings, criticism has also been levelled at the goals and impact of transitional justice. While transitional justice mechanisms may perform vital work, the impact of such work may be hampered for numerous reasons. For instance, individualising guilt may also contribute to a belief in collective innocence (Fletcher and Weinstein 2002); the selection of defendants for trial may not correspond with community needs for healing (Akhavan 1998); members of affected communities may be unwilling to accept determinations and findings of fact (Leebaw 2008; Hodzic 2010); and the assessment of blame is often premised upon a moral order that does not conform to the one in place during conflict (Aukerman 2002). Further critiques have argued that transitional justice institutions often exhibit structural problems that include politicization; insufficient resources; and impunity for wealthy countries (Call 2004). Call's (2004, p. 103) critique that transitional justice currently "replicate[s] structural deficiencies of the global order" is mirrored by Leebaw's (2008) view that because transitional justice institutions promote histories that focus on local accountability, the role of the Cold War is removed and replaced with predominantly local responsibility (Leebaw 2008). This in turn "contributes to denial regarding the role of Great Power interventions in local conflicts" (Leebaw 2008, p. 111).

This chapter will illustrate that although there is no definitive agreement regarding the fundamental goals of transitional justice, there is much agreement among scholars on the value of specific goals to transitional societies. Transitional justice scholars have recognised that not all goals will necessarily be desired by each and every society in transition. Most importantly, if we understand that certain institutions (such as courts) or certain mechanisms (such as prosecutions) are best suited to providing only some of the goals, then we can understand that single institution or mechanism approaches to transitional justice will likely fail to adequately address many goals. This in turn, may lead to unrealised hopes and disappointed expectations of transitional justice. In studying the Balkan and Cambodian cases of transitional justice, it is important to be aware of their distinct contexts as well as the literature regarding the expectations associated with transitional justice efforts.

The Goals of Transitional Justice

Given the critiques of transitional justice—both theoretically and as praxis—a fundamental question is "What does transitional justice seek to achieve?" Teitel (2005) and Bell (2009) have shown that transitional justice refers to efforts that address prior wrongdoing in situations of political and social transition: from conflict to peace or dictatorship to democracy. Call (2004), in defining a broad conception of transitional justice, gives us further insight into what these efforts attempt to produce and explicitly refers to two goals that are widely attributed to transitional justice. The first is reconciliation and the second prevention (where prevention may include deterrence, rehabilitation, and incapacitation). It is significant that this understanding of transitional justice (as it is implemented) is so closely associated with what it seeks to achieve. Rather than understanding transitional justice as merely the process of dealing with past atrocities, this conception sees transitional justice as the process of dealing with past atrocities for the goals of reconciliation and prevention. However, definitions that posit or impute specific goals for transitional justice may be problematic. This is because a prescribed rubric may stifle the variety of goals that transitional societies may prefer when employing transitional justice mechanisms. Indeed, an immense variety of goals and purposes have been ascribed to transitional justice.

Across the literature, the goals proposed for transitional justice include the following: education (primarily of society, but often on different topics, such as recent history or human rights norms); deterrence; truth-telling; (closely related to truth-telling) establishing a historical record of past abuses; ending violence; creating peace; fostering reconciliation; building the rule of law; retribution and just deserts; securing new governments; promoting democracy; rehabilitation (usually of society, but also of victims and offenders); incapacitation (preventing a dictator from rising again, or from obstructing peace and reconciliation); denunciation; restoring the dignity of victims; restoration of society more generally; contributing to memory and memorialisation; engendering respect for human rights; disarmament; demobilisation; reintegration; justice; liberalisation; nation-building; confronting denial of atrocities; acknowledging the suffering of victims; challenging the legitimacy of prior political practices; fostering dialogue; individualising guilt; reform (particularly of institutions); moral transformation. This list should not be seen in any way as exhaustive and similar lists have been compiled by Schrag (2004), Reisman (1996), and Balint (1996). Some may be understood as mechanism specific. That is, the goals are attached to a particular way of conducting transitional justice: punishment from a prosecution; societal healing from a truth commission; institutional reform through lustration. Often though, goals have a much wider scope. There appears to be no consensus about what are the precise, or even appropriate, goals of transitional justice endeavours. As many goals for transitional justice may exist as there are hopes for societies undergoing transition. What this list does demonstrate is that a variety of goals may be sought during transition.

Although different goals are attributed to transitional justice, some are more prevalent in the literature than others. Accountability is a goal consistently invoked. In fact, the original conception of transitional justice placed accountability at its centre (Bell 2009). Accountability, however, can be addressed in a variety of ways. Closely related to the goal of holding perpetrators of human rights abuses accountable for their conduct is retribution: just or proportional punishment of offenders for their crimes. This has been stated as a primary goal of the ad hoc tribunals (which have been important mechanisms of transitional justice) (Luftglass 2004), and it is often more "politely described in terms of combating impunity or bringing perpetrators to justice." (Aukerman 2002, pp. 58–59). The future orientated goal of deterrence is strongly associated with both retribution and the ad hoc tribunals (Luftglass 2004). Iyer has stated that the prosecution of individual human rights abusers "should be seen as providing one of the strongest safeguards against future similar wrongdoing" (Iyer 2007, p. 8). However, the effectiveness of deterrence as it relates to transitional justice has been criticised in much the same way as it has been in domestic contexts (for example, see Meron 1993a). Deterrence remains a controversial justification for punishment, with the capacity of criminal sanctions to deter offending frequently debated (see Villa-Vicencio 2000, for a sound critique).

Another goal is truth-telling. Truth-telling may be seen as both a category and a mechanism—when used to describe institutions such as commissions of inquiry that seek to discover and publish the truth—but also as a goal in itself. Truth has been described as an "imperative" (Bassiouni 1996, p. 24) and "essential if traumatized societies are to begin resolving their … conflicts through democratic processes" (Aukerman 2002, p. 47). Yet, what constitutes truth may be hotly contested in many transitional societies. For this reason, Braithwaite's (2005, p. 291) "high-integrity truth seeking" may offer a more realistic alternative to discovery of "the truth" as an essential goal of transitional justice:

> What matters is not so much revealing an objective truth as a process that all the stakeholders in an injustice see as a high-integrity process for revealing what may end up being multiple truths—where the victim's truth may be different from the perpetrator's for example.

Truth-telling often appears to correspond with the related concept of establishing a historical record, which is also cited as a goal of transitional justice.

Other goals that appear frequently in the transitional justice literature are peace and reconciliation. Meernik suggests that peace and reconciliation are "intangible, long-term and intended goals of most judicial institutions" (Meernik 2005, p. 275). Peace, however, may mean a wide variety of things (Bassiouni 1996). Johan Galtung (1969) influentially distinguished between negative peace (the absence of personal violence) and positive peace (the absence of structural violence). Consequently, in academic discussions, peace is usually divided into peace where there is no direct violence (negative peace) and peace where structural and cultural violence has been addressed (positive peace) (Kong 2008).

Unfortunately, when peace is invoked as a goal of transitional justice, it is often unclear as to exactly what type of peace is being sought, or considered possible by those advocating it. Reconciliation is also subject to various conceptions within the literature. According to Crocker (1999), there are at least three meanings of the term reconciliation. These range from "simple coexistence" to more developed conceptions of social harmony and interaction (Crocker 1999, p. 60). Philpott argues for "reconciliation as a concept of justice" that encompasses "a restoration of right relationship" with numerous practices to "redress wounds of injustice" (Philpott 2012, p. 49).

The Relationships Between Transitional Justice Goals

Frequently, goals are placed as responsible for, dependent on and premised upon the success of other goals. These connections are by no means consistent. By way of example, Meernik (2005, p. 275) suggests that the goals of peace and reconciliation are established "through many small and large acts of deterrence, truth-telling, retribution, and development of the rule of law." Scharf (1996) and Akhavan (1998) agree that truth—or a record of mistakes—and its acknowledgment will contribute to deterrence. Additionally, Fletcher and Weinstein (2002, p. 586) assert that "[t]ransitional justice scholars largely agree that a necessary foundation for healing a society that has experienced mass violence is learning the truth about what happened." Crocker (1999, p. 50) takes the importance of truth a step further: "without reasonably complete truth, none of the other goals of transitional justice … are likely to be realized." While others believe, or observe the belief, in such connections as: individualising guilt with reconciliation (Cassese 1998); or between accountability, deterrence, rule of law, and democracy (Olsen et al. 2010). Certainly, there are many other connections between the goals of transitional justice that are asserted in the literature; this is merely a sample to highlight the perceived interconnectivity between goals.

The difficulty with such assertions regarding the interconnectivity of goals is that connections are often assumed without evidence for their relationship. Connections may appear common sense, but require greater examination. For instance, what sort of truth is required for the promotion of other transitional goals? And how is truth to be achieved? That is, we must determine not only how the truth will be ascertained to satisfy these pronouncements (an already difficult task), but that same truth will need to be accepted as such by the affected communities. Other problems exist with mere assertions of connectedness between goals. For example, why is deterrence linked to democracy? Is it not possible that totalitarian regimes attempt deterrence as well? What is the effect if some goals are not done well? What will their impact be upon others? Some transitional justice mechanisms may be better at achieving certain goals than others. What then is the impact for single mechanism efforts at transitional justice on the various goals that are sought?

According to Aukerman (2002, p. 15):

> [s]cholars of transitional justice distinguish between the repair of relationships that will suffice for a society to move forward and unrealistic expectations of transformative interactions between victims and perpetrators.

That Aukerman characterises some understandings of reconciliation as "unrealistic expectations" is important. Such a statement is a critique of how the goal of reconciliation is understood. Expectations and their appropriateness are a major theme of this study and Aukerman's statement is an explicit recognition of this problem. Given the scope of goals and the various ways that the foundational concepts are defined, compromise between stakeholders—including direct stakeholders such as victims, offenders and other members of transitional communities, as well as indirect stakeholders such as international jurists—is at once inevitable and fraught. It is not merely the promotion of many, and often engorged, goals that might contribute to unrealistic expectations regarding what transitional justice will provide. Expectations among communities in transitional societies may understandably be high, particularly with the promise of international institutions designed to address their suffering in some way. Similarly, the overselling of transitional justice institutions by leaders is common in efforts to secure support and funding. These all contribute to expectations that often do not match what can realistically be offered by institutions and mechanisms of transitional justice. That expectations are raised in relation to transitional justice has been recognised previously (Nickson 2017). McEvoy (2007, p. 426) points out that:

> [t]he 'overselling' of the capacity of major legal institutions to deliver forgiveness, reconciliation or other features associated with post-conflict nation-building may well encourage unrealizable public expectations and ultimately an unfair assessment that such institutions have 'failed.'

Braithwaite et al. (2012) similarly noted in a study of peacebuilding in Timor Leste that UN Secretary-General Annan had oversold the capacity of transitional justice to provide for certain goals.

Particular goals are best achieved by particular mechanisms. Hence, a greater understanding of goals and motivations should inform the selection of mechanisms (trials, truth commissions, lustration, etc.) that are employed. This will in turn enhance the effectiveness of transitional justice. Of course, what also needs to be considered is that different mechanisms will have different cultural and contextual impacts: a trial will not necessarily be seen to perform the same tasks from one society to the next. It is Aukerman's (2002, p. 45) contention that transitional societies are entitled to decide for themselves what they would like transitional justice to provide:

> If transitional societies themselves have the right to decide, then we must recognize that different societies will have differing goals. Some societies emerging from mass trauma will demand retribution, while others will focus on compensation. Still others may concentrate on rebuilding a shattered economy or on strengthening democratic institutions.

Increased honesty when explaining the motivations for punishing human rights abusers will assist in clarifying what transitional justice can achieve and improve the chances of achieving it (Aukerman 2002).

Some mechanisms may be conducted quite differently between societies, so that what passes for a trial in one cultural context is different in important ways from a trial in another. A basic example of that difference would be between adversarial and inquisitorial trials. Such factors must also be accounted for when designing transitional justice.

Expectations of Transitional Justice Institutions

Transitional justice is directly concerned with institutions such as international and hybrid criminal tribunals. However, criminal trials are seen as particularly problematic when it comes to expectations. It has been suggested that because international tribunals had such large ambitions initially, they have become foci for "disappointment and even cynicism" (Hafner and King 2007, p. 92). Drumbl (2002, p. 18) claims that, "criminal trials may offer the lure of the easy solution to the complexities of mass atrocity. But this lure may create unrealistic expectations and, in the end, lead to disappointing results." The result of (often unrealistically) high expectations raised by prosecutions may be "a serious backlash against democratic institutions" (Landsman 1996, p. 85). And Humphrey (2003, p. 181) cautions that if the law reaches "beyond what it is capable of achieving [it leaves itself] open to criticism for raising expectations too high and hence failing to attain justice." Trials are perhaps best suited to achieving only a few goals of transitional justice well. It is possible then to extrapolate that many of the goals and hence expectations of trials are ill suited to a prosecutorial transitional justice mechanism. Other mechanisms in conjunction with trials may better address multiple expectations and goals.

Trials are now, however, a dominant feature of transitional justice: internationally there is an increasing consensus for investigations into and punishment for human rights violations (Theissen 2004, p. 4). It is observed that among international lawyers and activists "trials of selected individuals, preferably undertaken at the international level, constitute the favoured and often exclusive remedy to respond to all situations of genocide and crimes against humanity" (Drumbl 2002, p. 7). Similarly, such trials are said to have "gained normative currency" among the aforementioned groups (Drumbl 2003, p. 265). Fletcher and Weinstein (2002, p. 582) have remarked that "events of the [1990s] suggest that many diplomats and human rights advocates conceive of international criminal trials as the centrepiece of social repair." This corresponds with earlier discussion about the dominance of legalism in the field of transitional justice: trials are a fundamental expression of legalism in the practice of transitional justice.

The ascendance of prosecutions and trials is due to many factors. Meron (1993b), rather critically, has suggested that the tribunal is the preferred solution for the promotion of justice and international law because the international community has been unable to bring to an end conflict and atrocities. Unfortunately, this does not adequately explain why prosecutions and trials currently possess such normative currency in transitional justice. One explanation may be found in the proposition that states are obliged under international law to investigate and punish war crimes and crimes against humanity (Orentlicher 1991; Theissen 2004). Alternatively, the assumption that prosecutions are preferable has encouraged an attitude that other mechanisms are inferior (Aukerman 2002). In this way, the focus on trials is also self-perpetuating: the more that trials dominate the transitional justice landscape, the more they will be seen as an essential element of any transitional justice enterprise. The position of law(yers) in both the practice and theory of transitional justice has promoted judicial and legal responses to questions of transitional justice and contributed to entrenching trials with the normative currency they now hold. Finally, the role of NGOs in calls for an end to impunity and the punishment of war criminals (often above calls for other forms of reckoning with the past) further cements trials as a dominant—if not *the* dominant—tool of transitional justice.

The focus of this study is on two attempts at transitional justice that have employed single judicial mechanisms—trials—as the official response to past forms of mass atrocity. The first is the International Criminal Tribunal for the former Yugoslavia. The second, created over a decade later, is the Extraordinary Chambers in the Courts of Cambodia. As an examination of how these experiences highlight broader lessons about goals and expectations for transitional justice, it is necessary to examine the creation of these courts, particularly as they reflect the compromises required for their establishment.

Conflict in the Balkans, Compromise in the UN

The wars in the former Yugoslavia have been well-documented. Books, such as *The Fall of Yugoslavia* (Glenny 1996) and *Yugoslavia: Death of a Nation* (Silber and Little 1997) chart the disintegration well. More personal accounts of the conflicts are also available, such as *Zlata's Diary* (Filipovic 2006) or *My War Gone By, I Miss It So* (Loyd 2014). The detailed history of these conflicts will not be covered here—that is outside the scope of this project and has been done admirably by others. Instead, it is useful to chart, albeit briefly, the creation of the Tribunal.

While war was raging in the former Yugoslavia in the early 1990s, the international community was searching for a way to respond to the reported atrocities. As Scharf (1997) describes in *Balkan Justice*, responses by the international community to the conflict in the former Yugoslavia—ranging from initial inaction to eventual creation of the Tribunal—reflected divergent motivations of the international actors. According to Scharf, the United Nations Security Council (UNSC or Security Council) were unwilling to act decisively in the early stages of conflict and so their initial responses had little effect. These included a lopsided arms embargo, a resolution permitting military intervention that was not employed, ineffective economic sanctions, a no-fly zone that was unenforced for years, and the creation of "safe areas" that were anything but safe for those who sought protection there. In other circumstances, these responses may have been more effective. They were, however, compromised as a result of negotiations between UNSC members, who did not want to upset fragile peace negotiations, expose their own military personnel to risk, or compromise existing relationships with other states.

But, in light of the atrocities occurring in the Balkans the UNSC was forced to act lest it risk compromising its own integrity. As indicated above, these actions were piecemeal, beginning with a resolution that established the individual accountability of persons committing or allowing the commission of war crimes, and another that sought the cooperation of the international community in gathering evidence of such war crimes. Of those responses, the most prominent and enduring was the Tribunal. The Tribunal set a modern precedent for transitional justice through criminal trials—the first of a new wave of international tribunals and courts established to address human rights abuses and war crimes. But this was not a ride on the easy wave of success for the Tribunal. In fact, the Tribunal was subject to much hostility (some of which endures): from nations that helped to establish it, as well as from nations it sought to exercise jurisdiction over. While the Tribunal steadily built credibility, that credibility was sorely lacking at its beginning: it faced inability to secure the arrest of those it indicted, and while a lack of cooperation was expected from regional states, limited international cooperation hampered its early progress. Not only were those conflicts and compromises integral in shaping the Tribunal, but they also influenced the expectations that were held of it. Because of its context, the Tribunal would become a repository of many hopes and expectations. In fact, these expectations were often immense and at times in conflict with each other. This contributed to an expectation gap—between anticipated and delivered outcomes of the Tribunal.

Tribunal Goals

As we have seen, the transitional justice literature is full of claims regarding its goals, intended outcomes and anticipated contributions. The literature and public statements surrounding the Tribunal have been no different. Given that the wars in the former Yugoslavia were the first major European conflict in 50 years and that the Tribunal was the first international war crimes tribunal since Nuremberg, high hopes were held of the Tribunal. Indeed, Teitel (2005) suggests that because—unlike Nuremberg—the Tribunal was established while the conflict was ongoing, its aims were more ambitious. And Hazan (2004, p. 5) described the Tribunal as "an antilogy, the bearer of all hopes and contradictions."

The Security Council saddled the Tribunal with some specific objectives: to re-establish international peace and security (Hazan 2004). Nettlefield (2010b, p. 88) has distilled the following stated purposes from the Tribunal's website: "'holding leaders accountable', 'bringing justice to victims', 'giving victims a voice', 'establishing the facts', 'developing international law' and 'strengthening the rule of law'." It has also been observed that judgments at the Tribunal frequently cite deterrence and retribution in their justifications during sentencing (Orentlicher 2010). Table 2.1 collates various statements from the Tribunal's website and connects them with the expectations they reflect. While some of the language is measured—using words such as "contribute" and "help"—other expectations are more explicitly related to the work of the Tribunal. As Table 2.1 demonstrates, a diverse number of expectations are connected to the operation of the Tribunal. Significantly, the Tribunal's website supports the dominance of legalism and prosecutorial responses in transitional justice: "The Tribunal has laid the foundations for what is now the accepted norm for conflict resolution and post-conflict development across the globe, specifically, that leaders of mass crimes will face justice" (International Criminal Tribunal for the Former Yugoslavia, accessed 16 March 2013).

While the goals in Table 2.1 may represent the more commonly recognised "official" goals of the Tribunal, examining the literature produces a much longer list. The following goals have all been ascribed to the Tribunal: contributing to the historical record, establishing the truth and truth-telling (Wilson 2005; Leebaw 2008 [quoting Madeline Albright]; Saxon 2005); providing justice for victims (Akhavan 1993; Joyner 1993; O'Brien 1993; Ivkovic 2001); facilitating, aiding and promoting reconciliation (Clark 2009a; Akhavan 1993, 1998; Meron 1993a, b; O'Brien 1993; Ivkovic 2001; Saxon 2005; Hodzic 2010; Scharf 1997); promoting and maintaining peace (Akhavan 1993; Meron 1993a; Ivkovic 2001; Hodzic 2010; Scharf 1997); deterring both human rights offences in the former Yugoslavia and war crimes globally (Akhavan 1993; Joyner 1993; Meron 1993a; O'Brien 1993; Scharf 1996, 1997; Ivkovic 2001); advancing international law (Joyner 1993; Meron 1993a, b); incapacitating war criminals (Akhavan 1993; O'Brien 1993); punishing war criminals (Ivkovic 2001); ending cycles of violence (Ivkovic 2001); ending impunity (Akhavan 1998); educating (mostly about the conflict or of human rights standards and norms) (Akhavan 1998); transforming values (Akhavan 1998); and promoting the rule of law (Hodzic 2010; Scharf 1997). Some commentators and scholars felt that the Tribunal would strongly achieve certain goals from the above list: for example, Akhavan wrote forcefully about the capacity of the Tribunal to establish the truth and to perform a truth-telling role (Akhavan 1998). Others, however, merely observed the existence of the goal. The great majority of goals were points upon which advocates campaigned strongly for the perceived beneficial roles of the Tribunal.

Table 2.1 Justice expectations from the Tribunal's website

Expectation	Statements on the International Criminal Tribunal for the Former Yugoslavia's website[a]
Ending impunity	"the Tribunal has shown that an individual's senior position can no longer protect them from prosecution."
Accountability	"[the Tribunal] has now shown that those suspected of bearing the greatest responsibility for atrocities committed can be called to account."
Historical record/Truth	"The Tribunal has contributed to an indisputable historical record ..."
Acknowledgment	"The Tribunal has contributed to ... combating denial ..."
Healing	"The Tribunal has contributed to ... helping communities come to terms with their recent history."
Individualise guilt (to aid reconciliation)	"[The Tribunal] has shown that ... guilt should be individualised, protecting entire communities from being labeled as 'collectively responsible.'"
Efficiency	"The Tribunal has proved that efficient and transparent international justice is possible."
Impartiality	"[The Tribunal] takes no side in the conflict and does not attempt to create any artificial balance between different groups."
Due process/Fairness	"The Judges ensure a fair and open trial, assessing the evidence to determine the guilt or innocence of the accused."
Incapacitation (of war criminals' continuing influence)	"Undoubtedly, the Tribunal's work has had a major impact on the states of the former Yugoslavia. Simply by removing some of the most senior and notorious criminals and holding them accountable the Tribunal has been able to lift the taint of violence, contribute to ending impunity and help pave the way for reconciliation."
Deterrence	"By bringing perpetrators to trial, the ICTY aims to deter future crimes ..."

(continued)

Table 2.1 (continued)

Expectation	Statements on the International Criminal Tribunal for the Former Yugoslavia's website[a]
Provide justice to victims	"By bringing perpetrators to trial, the ICTY aims to … render justice to thousands of victims and their families …"
Peace	"[the Tribunal is] contributing to a lasting peace in the former Yugoslavia."
Transparency of proceedings/ Accessibility of proceedings	"Those interested in the Tribunal's proceedings can visit the ICTY and watch trials first-hand. Trials can also be followed through the internet broadcast on this website."
Focus on 'Big Fish' offenders	"The ICTY aims to achieve this [completion of its mandate] by concentrating on the prosecution and trial of the most senior leaders, while referring a certain number of cases involving intermediate and lower-ranking accused to national courts in the former Yugoslavia."
Build local capacity	"This plan [to refer lower-ranking accused to national courts], commonly referred to as the Tribunal's 'completion strategy', foresees the Tribunal assisting in strengthening the capacity of national courts in the region to handle war crimes cases."

[a]ICTY, *About the ICTY*, International Criminal Tribunal for the Former Yugoslavia http://www.icty.org/section/AbouttheICTY (accessed 16 March 2013)

The list is not exhaustive. As with transitional justice itself, the goals that have been expressed for the Tribunal are likely to be as broad and numerous as the hopes that were held for the Tribunal, international law, human rights development, peace in the Balkans, and other relevant concerns. That expectations were high is clear, and it is similarly evident that many expectations or goals have been difficult to achieve.

One of the first studies that looked at attitudes towards the Tribunal was conducted through the Human Rights Center at the University of California, Berkeley (2000). This research interviewed 32 Bosnian judges and prosecutors and found overall support for the concept of accountability but significant participant concerns with respect to the Tribunal. In another study, Ivkovic (2001), interviewed refugees displaced by the wars and found support for the Tribunal as the preferable institution for conducting war crimes trials over local mechanisms. Ivkovic observed considerable support for the death sentence to be imposed by the Tribunal, an expectation that had no prospect of being met, leading Ivkovic to postulate that many respondents would be disappointed by the available sentences. Of course, the imposition of the death penalty would be no guarantee of satisfaction for those respondents either.

Saxon (2005) concluded that the Tribunal had helped in confronting the past but had failed as a pedagogic tool for achieving reconciliation. Clark's (2009b) research pointed to the conclusion that because of the Tribunal's remoteness from the region it was easier to dismiss or ignore its work. In a study focused on the Prijedor region that echoed Ivkovic's research findings about the death penalty, Hodzic (2010) discovered that the most important factor determining perceptions of justice at the Tribunal was the length of sentence convicted defendants received. McMahon and Forsythe (2008, p. 412) concluded that "the ICTY has had thus far little direct [liberalising] impact on Serb leaders and political parties, the rule of law, or civic society." Other research suggested that the Tribunal had the effect of destabilising the liberal democratic transition in Serbia (Spoerri and Freyberg-Inan 2008).

Perhaps the most thorough examination of attitudes towards the Tribunal has been in a series of surveys conducted by the Belgrade Centre for Human Rights. In 2003 and 2004, surveys revealed that a majority of residents in Serbia felt that the Tribunal was biased (Belgrade Center for Human Rights 2004). In 2009 this was still a common opinion: 58% thought judges at the Tribunal were biased (Belgrade Center for Human Rights 2009). Relevant to this study 6% of respondents in 2004 felt that the purpose of the Tribunal was to act as a deterrent while 16% believed it was to provide peace and tolerance and combat impunity: these demonstrate clear expectations about the role of the Tribunal (Belgrade Center for Human Rights 2004). Unfortunately, the overwhelming majority (74%) considered that the purpose of the Tribunal was as part of one or more conspiracy theories, such as blaming the Serbs for all war crimes or promoting the United

States' influence in the region (Belgrade Center for Human Rights 2004). Similarly relevant was that 27% of respondents had formed their opinion of the Tribunal based on the way it had been established, while 24% formed their opinion as a result of actions of the prosecutor (Belgrade Center for Human Rights 2004). In 2009, respondents provided other insights into expectations of the Tribunal. For instance, 76% of those surveyed in Serbia believed that the Tribunal had no impact on reconciliation in the region (Belgrade Center for Human Rights 2009). Fifty-four percent felt that the Tribunal did not provide the truth about the conflict and 45% felt the Tribunal did not provide justice because trials were either too slow, the wrong people were prosecuted, or the sentences were too lenient (Belgrade Center for Human Rights 2009). The latter figure had been as high as 74% in the survey conducted in 2004 (Belgrade Center for Human Rights 2004). Each of these responses relates to various expectations, particularly the scope of justice: how quickly people will be tried; who will be tried; that there will be convictions; and that people will be punished.

Yet the Tribunal has had positive impacts. Orentlicher found that although the Tribunal had disappointed many Bosnians, the existence of the Tribunal was still important to them (Orentlicher 2010). Nettlefield's (2010a) study of the Tribunal and its role in fostering democracy in Bosnia and Herzegovina suggests some positive outcomes. In particular, "the ICTY… has also challenged extreme versions of dominant nationalist narratives and assisted with the development of democratic institutions that bolster the rule of law" (Nettlefield 2010a, p. 273). This may contribute to the goal of reconciliation. Overall, opinions have been mixed regarding the success, to date, of the Tribunal in attaining the goals and hopes that were held of it. Burke-White (2008) argues that the Tribunal has had a positive influence over local judicial institutions in Bosnia and Herzegovina. In respect to the Tribunal's first trial, Scharf (1996, p. 865) argues that it has produced definitive accounts of crimes and the conflict "that can endure the test of time and resist the forces of revisionism." Call (2004) also points to the conviction of killers as having cleared the path for refugee returns in certain parts of Bosnia and Herzegovina. Nettlefield (2010a) observed many positive effects of the Tribunal in her research and concluded that the criteria that many negative assessments employed were wrong.

What is perhaps most significant is that these various assessments of the Tribunal—both positive and negative—generally focus on wider goals, expectations and hopes. These studies rarely consider the success or failure of prosecutions, and only a few look at procedural issues at the Tribunal. Largely, these studies implicitly (and sometimes explicitly) recognise the importance of broader hopes for transitional justice, particularly as the Tribunal has represented them. Goals that are evident in the studies cited include the establishment of a historical record and the truth; rule of law development; deterrence; reconciliation; and refugee return. That studies assessing the success of the Tribunal have focused on these topics further reinforces the view that it is these broader goals for transitional justice that are the most important and valuable.

The Khmer Rouge Regime and the Creation of the Chambers

Again, space does not permit a lengthy historical analysis regarding the origins, metamorphosis, and atrocities committed by the Khmer Rouge (see Kiernan 2004, 2008a). However, a brief introduction can provide context for some the later issues the Chambers would grapple with. Following independence from France and Royal rule, Cambodia was subject to external forces as a result of both the Vietnam War and the wider Cold War. When the military coup led by General Lon Nol and supported by the United States overthrew the Royal government, the King of Cambodia urged his subjects to join the resistance led by the Khmer Rouge—a communist movement dating back to the 1940s (Kiernan 2004). By 1 April 1975, when Lon Nol was forced to flee Cambodia due to the advance of Khmer Rouge forces towards the capital, Phnom Penh, his regime had been receiving almost one million US dollars each day in military and economic aid (Kiernan 2004). Two weeks later, the Khmer Rouge marched victoriously into Phnom Penh and began their four years of rule, underscored by some of the worst human rights abuses of the twentieth century. By the time the Vietnamese had wrested control of Cambodia from the Khmer Rouge in January 1979 (Chandler 2008), it has been estimated that as many as 1.871 million Cambodians had perished under the Khmer Rouge's short rule (Kiernan 2008b). The scale and responsibility for atrocities were enormous, leading some to make comparisons with better-documented atrocities: "individual and collective responsibility for international crimes committed in Cambodia is as great as that of the Nazis" (Marks 1994, p. 17).

Following the overthrow of the Khmer Rouge, there have been several attempts to respond to the atrocities that occurred during their rule. The first followed immediately after Vietnam's invasion, with the establishment of the People's Revolutionary Tribunal, which tried and convicted Pol Pot and Ieng Sary for genocide in absentia, sentencing them both to death (Etcheson 2005). There have also been a number of domestic prosecutions throughout the years of cadres who committed crimes relating to their role in the Khmer Rouge (Etcheson 2005). Multiple attempts were made to invoke the jurisdiction of the International Court of Justice, and there were also attempts to create a truth commission in Cambodia (Etcheson 2005). According to Etcheson (2005, pp. 137–138), the reasons these efforts failed in their attempts to bring transitional justice to Cambodia include the following:

1. disputes over the legitimacy of various Cambodian regimes;
2. irregularities in the various legal proceedings;
3. lack of institutionalized international accountability mechanisms;
4. failure to obtain physical custody of the accused;
5. failure to secure statutory jurisdiction over the accused;
6. capricious selection of persons to be prosecuted;
7. considerations of 'national reconciliation';
8. financial corruption;
9. superpower politics;
10. domestic politics;
11. a general lack of political will.

It would take more than three decades and significant compromise to create an official institution to address the crimes of the Khmer Rouge.

Creating the Chambers

The creation of the Extraordinary Chambers in the Courts of Cambodia was long and drawn-out. It began with a joint letter from Cambodia's co-Prime Ministers to the United Nations, seeking assistance in trying Khmer Rouge leaders (United Nations General Assembly and Security Council 1997). In response, a group of experts was formed to explore the possibility for trials (General Assembly Resolution 135 of 1997). In 1999 that group recommended to the United Nations that prosecutorial duties be adopted by the current prosecutor at Tribunals for the former Yugoslavia and Rwanda and that trials be conducted outside of Cambodia. Following the report, negotiations began between the United Nations and Cambodia to create the Chambers (Bertelman 2010). These negotiations were a stop-start affair, with the Cambodian government and the United Nations disagreeing over whether the Chambers would be international or part of the local judicial structure and disputing the level of foreign participation as staff and judges (Bertelman 2010). As a result of disagreements, negotiations were suspended by the United Nations in 2002 but resumed in 2003 (Bertelman 2010). An agreement on the Chambers was signed that year and ratified in 2004, entering into effect in 2005, with the prosecutor's office commencing investigations in 2006 (Bertelman 2010).

Many early commentaries about the Chambers were negative. For example, Klein (2006, p. 550) felt that upon its creation, the Chambers exhibited shortcomings that would affect its operations:

> The features of the tribunal, which present risks to its success, include: (1) lack of judicial independence due to interference by political manipulation of the Cambodian governments, (2) no independent, international prosecutor, (3) the limited number of competent Cambodian judges and (4) a flawed supermajority formula.

Bertelman (2010) agreed, believing that the Chambers' hybrid structure was a risk to independence, rather than a benefit. The establishment of the courts was a series of protracted compromises and the international newspapers covered these—generally unfavourably (this media coverage is discussed further in Chapter 5).

The Chamber's Transitional Justice Goals

As with the Tribunal and other transitional justice institutions, a variety of hopes have attached to the Chambers. Table 2.2 shows how various expectations for the Chambers have been expressed on the Chambers' website. As official statements of what to expect from the Chambers, there is a similar diversity as was evidenced in Table 2.1 regarding the Tribunal. Un and Ledgerwood (2010, p. 1) claim that the Chambers are important for healing in Cambodia, as the Chambers will contribute to Cambodians knowing their history and believing "that there can be justice." The role of history and truth revelation is frequently mentioned as an important role for the Chambers. In this way, the Chambers are also seen to perform a public education role (Un and Ledgerwood 2010). It has been suggested that the Chambers will counter the impunity of offenders in Cambodia and the negative effects associated with it (Ratner 1999). The involvement of victims in proceedings at the Chambers is perceived as a measure that will "contribute to national reconciliation and enhance the effectiveness of the Cambodian legal system in the future" (Boyle 2006, p. 313). The Chambers are also seen as a means to allay victim anger:

> [T]he U.N.-sponsored trials of the Khmer Rouge leaders may make it easier for some Cambodians to let their anger towards the Khmer Rouge 'melt away' and to cope with their suffering and loss. Perhaps the trial will even serve as a symbolic severing of the collective Khmer Rouge 'head'. (Hinton 2005, p. 95)

Table 2.2 Expectations from the Chambers' website

Expectation	Statements on the Extraordinary Chambers in the Courts of Cambodia's website[a]
Fair apply international standards transparent	"The ECCC is designed to provide fair public trials in conformity with international standards."
Justice for Cambodians	"The chief goal is to provide justice to the Cambodian people, those who died and those who survived."
Healing	"It is hoped that fair trials will ease the burden that weights on the survivors."
Education	"The trials are also for the new generation – to educate Cambodia's youth about the darkest chapter in our country's history."
Build rule of law capacity	"[T]he trials will strengthen the rule of law."
Punishment	"By judging the accused in fair and open trials and by punishing those most responsible."
Accountability deterrence	"[The trials will] set an example for people who disobey the law in Cambodia and for cruel regimes worldwide. If criminals know that they will be held accountable, they may be deterred."
Aiding development in Cambodia	"By supporting and learning about justice, we can all contribute to the reconstruction of our society."

[a]ECCC, *Frequently Asked Questions*, The Extraordinary Chambers in the Courts of Cambodia http://www.eccc.gov.kh/en/faq (accessed 16 March 2013)

Somewhat more practically, the hope that the Chambers will serve to increase the number of trained lawyers and judges in Cambodia (a capacity building goal) has also been expressed (Horsington 2004).

The Impact of the Chambers

Given the relatively brief operation of the Chambers, there are few studies regarding the impact of the Chambers in Cambodia. Some observations, however, have been made addressing the contribution of the Chambers. It has been noted that Duch's trial has generated discussion of stories from the Khmer Rouge period: "[It i]s not just that the trial teaches history, but that it generates interest in people to learn more" (Un and Ledgerwood 2010, p. 5). Similarly, the Duch trial has shed light and provided more information to the public about the operation of the Tuol Sleng prison (Un and Ledgerwood 2010). Un and Ledgerwood (2010, p. 9) also found that the Chambers had been beneficial to those victims who had experience with it, with victims claiming "that it was empowering and helped them deal with the suffering they still experience." Such observations run counter to fears at the creation of the Chambers that its proceedings risked re-traumatising Cambodians (Margolis 2007).

There have been two major studies that have examined perceptions towards the Chambers. The first study revealed that despite their involvement in the trial, many civil parties (victims participating in the trial) "lacked understanding about key aspects … including sentencing" (Pham et al. 2011, p. 264). Motivation to apply as a civil party revealed interesting insights regarding expectations: 68% cited justice as their motivation to apply; 43% sought to know the truth; 32% wanted to honour the memory of relatives; 27% wished to tell their story; 17% hoped for acknowledgment; and 15% wanted to confront the defendant (Pham et al. 2011). The opportunity for victims to tell their story was considered by the civil parties interviewed to be a significant positive outcome of the trial (Pham et al. 2011). Unfortunately, the study also found that one in three civil parties felt the trial had not met their expectations (Pham et al. 2011). There were correlations between both participation and knowledge with disappointment: those civil parties who had spent more time at the Chambers and claimed to be more informed were more likely to be disappointed with the trial (Pham et al. 2011). A great deal of disappointment was felt towards the sentence and its perceived inadequacy, but astonishingly, almost half the civil parties interviewed were unaware that Duch's sentence had been appealed (the sentence was later increased on appeal) (Pham et al. 2011). The results of that study led its authors to conclude:

> [V]ictim participation, and indeed trials in general, are unlikely on their own to address the wounds of a society affected by mass atrocities, or bring about healing, closure, and reconciliation to victims or to the larger population. (Pham et al. 2011, p. 284)

The second major study was a population-based survey of the attitudes of Cambodians towards the Chambers (Pham et al. 2009). Respondents in this study did not rate justice as a priority (2%), while the economy (56%) and infrastructure (48%) were major concerns. This research found that many Cambodians had little or no knowledge of the Chambers. Most respondents also stated that their knowledge of the Khmer Rouge regime was poor or very poor. However, people overwhelmingly wanted to know more about the Khmer Rouge regime, and a desire for truth was profound, with 86% believing that establishing the truth was necessary of itself and 64% agreeing that the truth was necessary for reconciliation. When asked what justice meant to them, one of the most common responses was that "justice meant revealing/establishing the truth" (Pham et al. 2009, p. 33). It is possible to conclude from these results that significant expectations existed regarding the extra-judicial contributions the Chambers would make. The study noted that Cambodians had high expectations regarding the Chambers (Pham et al. 2009).

Disappointed expectations both in relation to the Tribunal and Chambers reflect the difficulties flagged in the broader literature of transitional justice. In particular, while trials dominate the transitional justice terrain, prosecutions are better suited to retributive goals than other mechanisms (Aukerman 2002). For reasons such as the scale of offences and the implication in crimes of people from across post-conflict societies, true retributive justice following mass atrocity is usually impossible (Aukerman 2002). Further, "although trials can play a vital role in establishing the truth of individual acts of atrocity … they tend to break down in the face of massive systemic atrocity" (Humphrey 2003, p. 172). It has been remarked that trials, rather than establish truth, provide incomplete histories and may even distort the truth (Simpson 1997). The truth may be distorted when a focus on certain individuals emphasises their role, while diminishing or hiding the role of others or wider complicity (perhaps of industry and businesses as well as individuals); and by not addressing structural aspects that permitted atrocities. Trials are also criticised for the effects that polarisation between guilt and innocence may have on the lessons societies learn from conflict and that their contribution to collective memory is constrained by what it is possible to prosecute (Humphrey 2003).

Conclusion

There is as much scepticism as there is support in the literature regarding the capacity of trials to deliver transitional justice goals. Much of the commentary, both for and against, is unsupported by any direct evidence on the role of trials in transitional justice—though many of the statements make intuitive sense. This does not exclude the possibility that trials can contribute to much wider goals in different ways. Instead, it proposes that trials should be employed when particular goals are sought during transitional justice. If the prioritised goals for a transitional society do not correspond to the goals that trials are best suited to achieve, it is preferable to consider utilising different mechanisms. This understanding also permits the belief that multiple mechanisms may be employed to address as many goals as possible. Unmet or disappointed expectations are almost certainly inevitable to some extent, and can only be mitigated by being fully aware of the potential for an expectation gap and making distinct efforts to bridge it. It is evident that from the initial discussions regarding how to address justice needs, that expectations are being created and influenced. What that justice may look like needs to be considered very early in the process.

A variety of expectations have been specifically attached to the work of the Tribunal and Chambers. Very few of these are what we might consider traditional prosecutorial goals. Instead, they reflect a diversity of hopes and aims that are held for transitional justice. For both the Tribunal and Chambers, there are no other official institutions (or unofficial institutions with as much status or recognition) to share the burden of all these hopes. In these circumstances, the research suggests that many expectations are disappointed. For example, the more victims knew about the Chambers and the more deeply involved they had been in exercising their rights, the less satisfied they were likely to feel. In that scenario, had there been other institutions to address some of the hopes and aims of victims, they may have been more satisfied with the Chambers and with transitional justice overall. When single institutions are required to carry the weight of all hopes for justice, it is very possible that they will buckle.

References

Akhavan, P 1993, 'Punishing war crimes in the former Yugoslavia: A critical juncture for the new world order', *Human Rights Quarterly*, vol 15, no. 2, pp. 262–289.

Akhavan, P 1998, 'Justice in The Hague, peace in the former Yugoslavia? A commentary on the United Nations war crimes tribunal', *Human Rights Quarterly*, vol. 20, no. 4, pp. 737–816.

Aukerman, MJ 2002, 'Extraordinary evil, ordinary crime: A framework for understanding transitional justice', *Harvard Human Rights Journal*, vol. 15, pp. 39–98.

Balint, JL 1996, 'The place of law in addressing internal regime conflicts', *Law and Contemporary Problems*, vol. 59, no. 4, pp. 103–126.

Bassiouni, MC 1996, 'Searching for peace and achieving justice: The need for accountability', *Law and Contemporary Problems*, vol. 59, no. 4, pp. 9–28.

Belgrade Center for Human Rights 2004, *Attitudes towards the International Criminal tribunal for the Former Yugoslavia 2004*, Belgrade Center for Human Rights, Belgrade.

Belgrade Center for Human Rights 2009, *Attitudes towards the International Criminal tribunal for the Former Yugoslavia 2009*, Belgrade Center for Human Rights, Belgrade.

Bell, C 2009, 'Transitional justice, interdisciplinarity and the state of the 'field' or 'non-field'', *International Journal of Transitional Justice*, vol. 3, no. 1, pp. 5–27.
Bertelman, H 2010, 'International standards and national ownership? Judicial independence in hybrid courts: The Extraordinary Chambers in the Courts of Cambodia', *Nordic Journal of International Law*, vol. 79, no. 4, pp. 341–382.
Boyle, D 2006, 'The rights of victims: Participation, representation, protection, reparation', *Journal of International Criminal Justice*, vol. 4, no. 2, pp. 307–313.
Braithwaite, J 2005, 'Between proportionality and impunity: Confrontation, truth, prevention', *Criminology*, vol. 43, no. 2, pp. 283–306.
Braithwaite, J, Charlesworth, H and Soares, A 2012, *Networked governance of greedom and tyranny: Peace in Timor-Leste*, ANU E-Press, Canberra, Australia.
Burke-White, W 2008, 'The domestic influence of international criminal tribunals: The International Criminal Tribunal for the Former Yugoslavia and the creation of the State Court of Bosnia and Herzegovina', *Columbia Journal of Transnational Law*, vol. 46, no. 2, pp. 279–350.
Call, CT 2004, 'Is transitional justice really just?', *Brown Journal of World Affairs*, vol. 11, no. 1, pp. 101–113.
Cassese, A 1998, 'Reflections on international criminal justice', *Modern Law Review*, vol. 61, no. 1, pp. 1–10.
Chandler, D 2008, *A History of Cambodia*, 4th ed., Westview Press, Boulder, Colorado.
Clark, JN 2009a, 'Judging the ICTY: Has it achieved its objectives?', *Southeast European and Black Sea Studies*, vol. 9, no. 1, pp. 123–142.
Clark, JN 2009b, 'The limits of retributive justice: Findings of an empirical study in Bosnia and Hercegovina', *Journal of International Criminal Justice*, vol. 7, no. 3, pp. 463–487.
Crocker, DA 1999, 'Reckoning with past wrongs: A normative framework', *Ethics & International Affairs*, vol. 13, no. 1, pp. 43–64.
Drumbl, MA 2002, 'Restorative justice and collective responsibility: Lessons for and from the Rwandan genocide', *Contemporary Justice Review*, vol. 5, no. 1, pp. 5–22.
Drumbl, MA 2003, 'Toward a criminology of international crime', *Ohio State Journal on Dispute Resolution*, vol. 19, no. 1, pp. 263–281.
Etcheson, C 2005, *After the killing fields: Lessons from the Cambodian genocide*, Praeger, Westport, Connecticut.
Filipovic, Z 2006, *Zlata's diary: A child's life in wartime Sarajevo*, Penguin, New York.

Fletcher, LE and Weinstein, HM 2002, 'Violence and social repair: Rethinking the contribution of justice to reconciliation', *Human Rights Quarterly*, vol. 24, no. 3, pp. 573–639.

Galtung, J 1969, 'Violence, peace, and peace research', *Journal of Peace Research*, vol. 6, no. 3, pp. 167–191.

Glenny, M 1996, *The fall of Yugoslavia*, 3rd edition, Penguin, London.

Hafner, D and King, E 2007, 'Beyond traditional notions of transitional justice: How trials, truth commissions and other tools for accountability can and should work together', *Boston College International and Comparative Law Review*, vol. 30, no. 1, pp. 91–109.

Hazan, P 2004, *Justice in a time of war: The true story behind the International Criminal Tribunal for the Former Yugoslavia*, Texas A&M University Press, College Station, Texas.

Hinton, AL 2005, *Why did they kill? Cambodia in the shadow of genocide*, University of California Press, Berkeley, California.

Hodzic, R 2010, 'Living the legacy of mass atrocities: Victims' perspectives on war crimes trials', *Journal of International Criminal Justice*, vol. 8, no. 1, pp. 113–136.

Horsington, H 2004, 'The Cambodian Khmer Rouge tribunal: The promise of a hybrid tribunal', *Melbourne Journal of International Law*, vol. 5, no. 2, pp. 462–483.

Humphrey, M 2003, 'From victim to victimhood: Truth commissions and trials as rituals of political transition and individual healing', *The Australian Journal of Anthropology*, vol. 14, no. 2, pp. 171–187.

Ivkovic, SK 2001, 'Justice by the International Criminal Tribunal for the Former Yugoslavia', *Stanford Journal of International Law*, vol. 37, no. 2, pp. 255–265.

Iyer, V 2007, 'Of prosecutions and amnesties: Does Fiji's experience suggest a reconsideration?', *Australian Journal of Asian Law*, vol. 9, no. 1, pp. 1–43.

Joyner, CC 1993, 'Enforcing human rights standards in the former Yugoslavia: The case for an international war crimes tribunal', *Denver Journal of International Law and Policy*, vol. 22, no. 2 & 2, p. 235.

Kiernan, B 2004, *How Pol Pot came to power: Colonialism, nationalism and communism in Cambodia 1930–1975*, 2nd ed, Yale University Press, New Haven, Connecticut.

Kiernan, B 2008a, *The Pol Pot regime: Race, power, and genocide in Cambodia under the Khmer Rouge, 1975–79*, Yale University Press, New Haven, Connecticut.

Kiernan, B 2008b, *Genocide and resistance in South East Asia: Documentation, denial and justice in Cambodia and East Timor*, Transaction Publishers, New Brunswick, New Jersey.

Klein, KM 2006, 'Bringing the Khmer Rouge to justice: The challenge and risks facing the joint tribunal in Cambodia', *Northwestern Journal of International Human Rights*, vol. 4, no. 3, pp. 549–566.

Kong, SO 2008, 'Jurisdiction *ratione personae* of the Extraordinary Chambers in the Court of Cambodia: Peace vs. justice', *Forum of International Development Studies*, vol. 37, pp. 149–167.

Landsman, S 1996, 'Alternative responses to serious human rights abuses: Of prosecution and truth commissions', *Law and Contemporary Problems*, vol. 59, no. 4, pp. 81–92.

Leebaw, BA 2008, 'The irreconcilable goals of transitional justice', *Human Rights Quarterly*, vol. 30, no. 1, pp. 95–118.

Lloyd, A 2014, *My war gone by, I miss it so*, Penguin, New York.

Luftglass, S 2004, 'Crossroads in Cambodia: The United Nation's responsibility to withdraw involvement from the establishment of a Cambodian tribunal to prosecute the Khmer Rouge', *Virginia Law Review*, vol. 90, no. 3, pp. 893–964.

Marks, SP 1994, 'Forgetting "the policies and practices of the past": Impunity in Cambodia', *Fletcher Forum of World Affairs*, vol. 18, no. 2, p. 17.

Margolis, JE 2007, 'Trauma and the trials of reconciliation in Cambodia: View from the ground', *Georgetown Journal of International Affairs*, vol. 8, no. 2, pp. 153–161.

McEvoy, K 2007, 'Beyond legalism: Towards a thicker understanding of transitional justice', *Journal of Law and Society*, vol. 34, no. 4, pp. 411–440.

McEvoy, K 2008, 'Letting go of legalism: Developing a 'thicker understanding of transitional justice' in McEvoy, K and McGregor, L (eds), *Transitional justice from below: Grassroots activism and the struggle for change*, Hart Publishing, Portland, Oregon.

McMahon, PC and Forsythe, DP 2008, 'The ICTY's impact on Serbia: Judicial romanticism meets network politics', *Human Rights Quarterly*, vol. 30, no. 2, pp. 412–435.

Meernik, J 2005, 'Justice and peace? How the international criminal tribunal affects societal peace in Bosnia', *Journal of Peace Research*, vol. 42, no. 3, pp. 271–289.

Meron, T 1993a, 'The case for war crimes trials in Yugoslavia', *Foreign Affairs*, vol. 72, no. 3, pp. 122–135.

Meron, T 1993b, 'Rape as a crime under international humanitarian law', *The American Journal of International Law*, vol. 87, no. 3, pp. 424–428.
Nettlefield, LJ 2010a, *Courting democracy in Bosnia and Herzegovina: The Hague tribunal's impact in a postwar state*, Cambridge University Press, New York, New York.
Nettlefield, LJ 2010b, 'From the battlefield to the barracks: The ICTY and the armed forces of Bosnia and Herzegovina', *International Journal of Transitional Justice*, vol. 4, no. 1, pp. 87–109.
Nickson, R 2017, 'Unmet expectations and the legitimacy of transitional justice institutions' in Karstedt, S and Brants, C (eds),*Engagement, contestation and legitimacy*,Hart Publishing, Portland, Oregon.
O'Brien, JC 1993, 'The international tribunal for violations of international humanitarian law in the former Yugoslavia', *The American Journal of International Law*, vol. 87, no. 4, pp. 639–659.
Olsen, TD, Payne, LA and Reiter, AG 2010, 'The justice balance: When transitional justice improves human rights and democracy', *Human Rights Quarterly*, vol. 32, no. 4, pp. 980–1007.
Orentlicher, D 1991, 'Settling accounts: The duty to prosecute human rights violations of a prior regime', *The Yale Law Journal*, vol. 100, no. 8, pp. 2537–2615.
Orentlicher, D 2010, *That someone guilty be punished: The impact of the ICTY in Bosnia*, The Open Society Justice Initiative, New York.
Pham, P, Vinck, P, Balthazard, M, Hean, S and Stover, E 2009, *So we will never forget: A population based survey on attitudes about social reconstruction and The Extraordinary Chambers in the Courts of Cambodia*, Human Rights Center, University of California, Berkeley, California.
Pham, PN, Vinck, P, Balthazard, M, Strasser, J and Om, C 2011. 'Victim participation and the trial of Duch at the Extraordinary Chambers in the Courts of Cambodia', *Journal of Human Rights Practice*, vol. 3, no. 3, pp. 264–287.
Philpott, D 2012. *Just and unjust peace: An ethic of political reconciliation*, Oxford University Press, New York.
Ratner, SR 1999, 'The United Nations Group of Experts for Cambodia', *The American Journal of International Law*, vol. 93, no. 4, pp. 948–953.
Reisman, WM 1996, 'Legal responses to genocide and other massive violations of human rights', *Law and Contemporary Problems*, vol. 59, no. 4, pp. 75–80.
Saxon, D 2005, 'Exporting justice: Perceptions of the ICTY among the Serbian, Croatian and Muslim communities in the former Yugoslavia', *Journal of Human Rights*, vol. 4, no. 4, pp. 559–572.

Scharf, MP 1996, 'The prosecutor v Dusko Tadic: An appraisal of the first international war crimes trial since Nuremberg', Albany Law Review, vol. 60, no. 3, pp. 861–882.

Scharf, MP 1997, *Balkan justice: The story behind the first international war crimes trial since Nuremberg*, Carolina Academic Press, Durham, North Carolina.

Schrag, M 2004 'Lessons learned from ICTY Experience', *Journal of International Criminal Justice*, vol. 2, no. 2, pp. 427–434.

Silber, L and Little, A 1997, *Yugoslavia: Death of a nation*, Revised Edition, Penguin, New York.

Simpson, G 1997, 'Didactic and dissident histories in war crimes trials', *Albany Law* Review, vol. 60, no. 3, pp. 801–839.

Spoerri, M and Freyberg-Inan, A 2008, 'From prosecution to persecution: Perceptions of the International Criminal Tribunal for the Former Yugoslavia (ICTY) in Serbian domestic politics', *Journal of International Relations and Development*, vol. 11, no. 4, pp. 350–384.

Teitel, R 2005, 'The law and politics of contemporary transitional justice', *Cornell International Law Journal*, vol. 38, pp. 837–862.

The Human Rights Center and the International Human Rights Law Clinic, University of California Berkeley, and the Centre for Human Rights, Sarajevo, 2000, 'Justice, accountability and social reconstruction: An interview study of Bosnian judges and prosecutors', *Berkeley Journal of International Law*, vol. 18, no. 1, pp. 102–164.

Theissen, G 2004, *Supporting justice, co-existence and reconciliation after armed conflict: Strategies for dealing with the past*, Berghof Research Center for Constructive Conflict Management, Berlin.

Un, K and Ledgerwood, J 2010, 'Is the trial of 'Duch' a catalyst for change in Cambodia's courts?', Asia Pacific Issues—Analysis From the East-West Center No 95, East-West Center.

United Nations General Assembly and Security Council, *Identical Letters dated 23 June 1997 from the Secretary General addressed to the President of the General Assembly and the President of the Security Council*, 23 June 1997, UN Doc. A/51/135-s/1997/488 (letter dated 21 June 1997 from the First and Second Prime Ministers of Cambodia addressed to the Secretary-General annexed thereto).

Villa-Vicencio, C 2000, 'Why perpetrators should not always be prosecuted', *Emory Law Journal*, vol. 49, no. 1, pp. 205–222.

Wilson, R 2005, 'Judging history: The historical record of the International Criminal Tribunal for the Former Yugoslavia', *Human Rights Quarterly*, vol. 27, no. 3, pp. 908–942.

3

Expectations of the Tribunal and Chambers

It is unsurprising, given the literature on transitional justice, that participants identified a wide variety of expectations. One respondent thought Cambodians held innumerable expectations about the Chambers: "Cambodians overwhelmingly expect justice, the truth, vindication, retribution, healing etc. etc." (Cambodian NGO #9). It was said in relation to the Tribunal that no two groups had identical expectations: "Everyone has different expectations … And even if I just went to one group—like the victims—I would get a different answer" (Tribunal Media #1). Another response was similar:

> For people from the region, there are differing expectations. Some solely want the truth to be brought out through the trial proceedings and others want/need someone to blame for the crimes which took place during the war in order to bring closure. (Tribunal Defence #6)

This plurality of expectations was reflected in connection with the Chambers:

R. Nickson and A. Neikirk, *Managing Transitional Justice*,
Palgrave Studies in Compromise after Conflict,
https://doi.org/10.1007/978-3-319-77782-5_3

> [For s]ome people … the justice is the trial. For example, they see the Khmer Rouge leaders are prosecuted from the ECCC or some people just really want revenge, an eye for an eye. And then some maybe want education—especially in my generation—the younger generation they want an education and knowledge and to learn from, to learn about what happened in the past. That is also a kind of justice, to reconcile between the next generation and the older generation. (Cambodian NGO #11)

These differences in expectations were perceived not simply as local differences between groups and individuals, but also between local and international communities. A judicial officer at the Tribunal felt that quite different expectations existed between local and international communities:

> Generally, people in [the] former Yugoslavia expect us to severely punish the accused belonging to another group. In the West it is expected that we fulfil our duty, establish the facts, pass down well-reasoned, convincing judgments and keep the length of proceedings under control. (Tribunal Judge #1)

There was a clear recognition among participants that not only was there no universal expectation held by everyone but there was a potential lack of consensus among those with a stake in the transitional justice process.

This chapter discusses the various expectations that interview participants identified. The expectations discussed here are not intended as an exhaustive list that may be held for courts, trials, or transitional justice. Rather, they represent the three most common expectations highlighted in interviews. The first is the *scope of justice*. This refers to what will be provided or achieved directly by transitional justice trials. Under this heading are collated expectations about punishment, prosecutions, convictions, reparations, and legal determinations (specifically concerning genocide in this research, but in other contexts the specific legal determination may be different). The second is about *answers*, expectations of which were manifested in three ways. One is that answers to questions of societal importance will be provided about the conflict. The second is that answers to questions of individual significance will be addressed—for instance the fate of loved ones. The third, is the idea that an expectation exists to contribute one's own answers to the larger question of what occurred during the conflict. The final category covers those expectations that are *forward looking*, in particular expectations about education, reconciliation, and prevention. These categories help us understand expectation dilemmas that emerge in transitional justice settings.

Expectations That Reflect the Scope of Justice

It was widely considered by interviewees that there had been expectations of a greater number of prosecutions than could, or was ever likely to, occur at the Tribunal or Chambers. The expectation of more encompassing prosecutions was raised by one interviewee in Cambodia:

> [People want the] Court [to] try all the leaders and a few also want lower people ... A lot of people died during that time and just a few people to be prosecuted is not enough. (Cambodian NGO #11)

An expectation that more people would be prosecuted was also a common remark in relation to the Tribunal:

> There is also that common misconception that we did 161 people. I think most people thought we were doing 10 000, and so when they know that someone in their family was killed by a soldier and they expected us to be there, you know, then we weren't. (Tribunal Outreach #6)

Another outreach officer remarked: "[V]ictims for long thought (and expected) that the Tribunal would try virtually all war criminals" (Tribunal Outreach #2). One respondent recalled the surprise people had expressed when it was announced the Tribunal would begin no new investigations (Tribunal Outreach #2). These expectations may reflect an assumption that well-funded (at least relative to local institutions) international courts will be very powerful and their work all-encompassing. The rhetoric that surrounds such endeavours, where diplomats and U.N. officials tout the salutary benefits of trials, no doubt contributes to this expectation. But this may also have related to an expectation that one's own suffering or victimisation during conflict would be covered by transitional justice trials.

Of course, many victims would have had little or no direct harm caused by top officials but would often have had unspeakable crimes perpetrated against them by low-level offenders. Many participants remarked on the difficulty victims experience co-existing side-by-side with those who harmed them. At both the Chambers and the Tribunal, these war criminals were not often included in indictments. As an NGO worker in Cambodia pointed out "The question was asked, 'why you only just punish a small number? Why not the killer who still survive, and still live in front of my house or in the village, the same village?' That is a big problem" (Cambodia NGO #18). In the former Yugoslavia an outreach officer remarked:

> They [victims and community members] are very much bothered, as they always say, 'you know, it's good to have Karadzic and Mladic and whoever on trial', but they are very much concerned with the small fish, that they say, 'we see them every day on the streets and I know that this particular person killed my son', or whatever. So for them, or they are still working as police officers, or have certain political functions within a certain community. For them it's also very much important that this issue is discussed or at least that the cases are processed, prosecuted, and that those responsible are brought to justice. (Tribunal Outreach #2)

There were clear expectations, then, about the specific or individual nature of prosecutions. The dilemma that interviewees observed was that the work of the Tribunal and Chambers in focusing on trials of senior leaders did not meet many expectations for a more direct or encompassing justice. Such an expectation may not exist only at an individual level. It was also suggested that expectations in respect to symbolic events and crimes during conflict would be given greater prosecutorial attention:

> Croatia expected one big spectacular case for all the, you know, the people who are to be blamed for what happened in Vukovar, for somebody

> really big to be indicted and for their suffering to be recognised and through huge sentences. And it did not happen. And those guys who were indicted for the Ovcar crimes that happened in the vicinity of Vukovar, they were not the highest ranking officials or officers. So it was perceived as a failure of the prosecution and the ICTY as a whole. (Tribunal Outreach #5)

The effect of not meeting expectations was disappointment (Tribunal Outreach #3). The significance of prosecutions was stated by respondents for the former Yugoslavia, Cambodia, and transitional justice more broadly.

An expectation of convictions was also raised by interviewees. Given the experiences of victims it is understandable that many may consider it unimaginable that indictees, especially high-profile ones, could be acquitted. Regarding the former Yugoslavia, an expectation existed "that all those tried will be found guilty as they [the people in the former Yugoslavia] have already made their minds up from the information they have seen in the media" (Tribunal Defence #6). The role of the media is something that many interviewees had strong opinions on and is explored more thoroughly later. In Cambodia, one court official felt that such expectations extended beyond local community members:

> There is this popular opinion that we are just here to sentence people … And this seems to go very deeply, even into the NGO society, that this is an exercise to sentence—not an exercise to try people. So the presumption of innocence is a key challenge. Everywhere we go, people will say, 'Why do we need these lengthy proceedings? There is evidence all over this country about what happened. Why do we need these proceedings? We know they're all guilty'. (Chambers Media #1)

This research did not seek to answer how pervasive this expectation might be. It is possible that the apportionment of this expectation to many members of either society in the Balkans or Cambodia is unfair. However, it does further reinforce the value of communication with affected communities. In efforts to manage an expectation like this, concepts such as "innocent until proven guilty" and "due process" may be further enhanced. This can be particularly important where rule of law capacity is being addressed in a transitional society.

Participants overwhelmingly felt that many people considered the sentences given to convicted persons at the Tribunal and Chambers to be too lenient. As the Tribunal has sentenced a considerable number of people in comparison to the Chambers, it is perhaps not surprising that this was reflected more frequently in discussions with interviewees who worked on the former Yugoslavia. One outreach officer believed:

> [T]he general view is that basically all the sentences are lenient. I would think that people are, the victims are, usually expecting higher sentences in that respect, but it's always, you know, at least that person was brought to justice. (Tribunal Outreach #2)

Similarly, a member of the prosecution staff at the Bosnian War Crimes Chamber (a local war crimes court whose work is intended to complement the Tribunal's) believed that "public perception is that there are low sentences at the ICTY" (BWCC Prosecutor #2). One representative of a war victims' advocacy group in the former Yugoslavia explained that expectations about the severity of a sentence were directly relevant to the satisfaction felt by the victims he represented:

> [T]hey are about how many years an individual is going to spend in jail, which is good; that is exactly what we want and the more years the better ... justice can be measured. People say justice cannot be measured but yes it can: it is how many years the war criminal is going to spend behind bars ... That is what justice is about. It can be counted, you know, quantified. This is the only way to quantify it. (Former Yugoslavia NGO #2)

Another participant, who worked in the victim and witness support units of transitional justice courts, had observed this expectation in operation:

> When the verdict, and if it is a guilty verdict when the sentence is announced, that is when they [victim witnesses] often become quite

> distressed. So if it is an acquittal when they expected a guilty or if it is a guilty and they expected 40 years and the accused gets 10 then these people can become really angry or bitter or frustrated and not satisfied at all. And a group of women once—I represented a group of women—they rang me after. They said if we had even dreamed that it was possible that the accused would get such a small sentence we would never have testified. (Chambers Victims Support #1)

This demonstrates a clear disconnect between the expectations of members of affected communities and the realities of sentencing in international criminal law, an issue that we return to later.

Participants provided several reasons for expectations of sentences not corresponding more closely to the sentencing principles of international criminal law. At least two interviewees felt that it was due to comparisons between the domestic experience of communities in regard to sentencing, and the sentences handed down for international crimes (Chambers Outreach #1, Tribunal Outreach #6). This ought to be considered in light of the understanding that most domestic offences, even murderous ones, are of a less serious nature than the human rights abuses committed during conflict. Although it was remarked (perhaps unfairly) that this was partly because of an uneducated populace (Chambers Outreach #1), it was also evident in relation to people who were regarded as highly educated:

> I do remember a specific question by a very talented assistant law professor, and she was concerned that a person who commits a single murder in Croatia could get 15 years and a person that organised all sorts of atrocities, including multiple murders and torture, gets similar. So yeah, I think there is a concern about sentencing guidelines and discrepancies between national jurisdictions and the ICTY. (Tribunal Outreach #6)

A further explanation was that people expected sentences to be commensurate with their suffering:

> [F]or those people who have lost and been victims they want the suffering of the perpetrator to be proportionate to their own and for them it is

> life and, you know, a child, a parent, a family member, a friend is gone for ever. So no sentence can ever really be enough. (Chambers Victim Support #1)

Lack of familiarity with sentencing frequently led to disappointment: "Generally people don't understand exactly how a decision on sentence is reached. And obviously, you know that after the Duch sentence was handed down people were generally very disappointed." (Cambodia NGO #9). Some respondents saw the disappointment with sentencing as inevitable (Tribunal Outreach #5). This expectation gap—between expected and actual sentences—may well be one area where management is appropriate. If it is accepted that international criminal sentencing guidelines in their current form are just, then certainly efforts to explain those throughout transitional justice trials will be useful. A participant who was involved in "managing expectations", following widespread disappointment with the Duch sentence, felt that little could be done in advance of a sentence (Chambers Media #1). His concern was that outreach efforts to outline possible sentences would be seen to be pre-empting the court's determination. The alternative, as it currently operates, is that communities are frequently dissatisfied with an unexpected outcome. Conversely, dissatisfaction with an expected outcome may be equally as galling to those who have suffered but may possibly be less profound.

Expectations about the provision of reparations were also raised in interviews. This was less common concerning the Tribunal, though it was stated by a representative of a victims' advocacy group that it remained a goal that had not yet been achieved (Former Yugoslavia NGO #2). Because reparations were included within the mandate of the Chambers, the issue was more prevalent in interviews regarding that court. What seems apparent from responses in interviews about the Chambers and reparations is that a great deal of disappointment resulted. It seemed that the Chambers may have unwittingly raised expectations by offering reparations, without fully explaining the scope and limit of those reparations. Representatives of various NGOs shared this opinion, as the following example reveals:

> The civil base—from my observations of the case 001 appeals—the civil parties expressed disappointment over reparations and a lot of them were simple folk who have difficulty understanding what moral and collective reparations are. But that is all the court could ever give them. (Cambodia NGO #14)

Another said that "reparation is a really big issue. I mean that was a really big dissatisfaction with the court: the judges didn't decide on any of the civil party requests" (Cambodia NGO #19). They went on to explain that they were now tasked with managing civil party expectations as a result. By offering reparations—that did not correspond to common understandings of reparations—the Chambers needed to clearly explain what could be provided under this scheme. Expectations for reparations were disappointed when this was not done. A court official agreed with the assessments of NGO workers, saying, "We have to deal with managing expectations of the reparations with civil parties, whether they receive anything or they don't" (Chambers Outreach #1). The Chambers adopted a reparations programme of providing for only "moral and collective" reparations. Unfortunately, the scope of "moral and collective" reparations was not adequately explained to people who sought the benefit of them. This appears to have left many victims unsatisfied and provides a lesson on the value of communication regarding the measures that courts seek to employ in transitional justice.

Expectations for Answers

The second category of expectations was about answers to societal and individual questions as a result of conflict. While interviewees agreed that an expectation for answers existed, there was no consensus about whether trials could satisfy these expectations. Respondents spoke of three types of answers for which expectations may exist. The first type sought answers to societal questions about the conflict. By way of example, this was expressed frequently in Cambodia as a desire to know "why

Khmer killed Khmer?" In essence, this was an expectation for truth or for the trials to establish a historical record of events. A second type was answers in response to individual questions. These questions sought to discover answers to specific questions about loved ones and family members: their fates; whether they suffered; and their current locations. A third category involved an expectation to provide one's own answers to questions about conflict. This expectation reflected the wish of individuals to share their own stories of suffering, victimisation, and survival.

The first type—answers to larger, societal questions—was expressed frequently in interviews. These answers were considered significant in the process of transition. An NGO worker in Cambodia, when discussing what trials might provide responded:

> One is a final judgment. We never had a final judgment through a court of law: Who did this? Who was responsible? And that is important to set the history. It is important to have a final judgment so that we can refer to it and move on. Any final judgment that comes out of the ECCC, it may not please all of us, but at least through a proceeding that is acceptable, that is credible, Cambodia after 30 years, somehow we move on, that would be able to accept and bring a closure and move on with their life to a better future. (Cambodia NGO #5)

This was echoed for the Tribunal as well:

> [I]t is important [the court's historical record] because, I think, particularly to the people in the region. There is a lot of folklore in the Balkans and it's not all correct and I think what you need to do is to keep a record to let people make up their own minds as to what happened and if they have got access to all the records and they can go in and read the documentation, they can then make up their own minds. (Tribunal Prosecutor #2)

These passages enunciate the importance of having such answers in the transitional context. There is a link between the desire for answers and the desire to move forward. This was clear to an interviewee when considering the expectations of younger generations in Cambodia about the Chambers:

> [E]specially the truth is very important, not only for the survivors, but especially for the next generation. They want to know because if they cannot have a clear picture of what happened and why, then it is difficult to move forward. (Cambodia NGO #7)

In this way, answers to larger questions about conflict could satisfy both personal and social needs. The desire for answers was considered profound and widespread:

> What most people ask is why this happened, at least in Cambodia. My impression from travelling around the country and speaking with all kinds of people is that … they also want to know why things happened. Whether they will actually get those answers is too early to say. Hopefully they will get some answers, though probably not get all of the answers they want. (Chambers Media #1)

This sentiment was repeated again and again in Cambodia. Not only did Cambodians "[e]specially want to know why Khmer killed Khmer" (Cambodia NGO #7), it was seen as an expectation that the Chambers would provide the answers to these larger questions about their own history. One interviewee felt that Cambodians "do not really want to know who, but why? Why did they commit the crime? Why did it happen?" (Cambodia NGO #11). In one follow-up to an initial interview, two respondents from a prominent NGO felt that many Cambodians believed the Chambers would provide an historical record:

> Cambodians believe that the proceedings will give Cambodians a chance to understand what truly happened during that period and provide understanding as to why Cambodians killed Cambodians. (Cambodia NGO #3 and #4)

Such sentiments were apparent, but not expressed as frequently, in interviews concerning the Tribunal. One reason may well be that, in relation to the former Yugoslavia, fewer participants from civil society organisations took part. One NGO participant from Bosnia did believe that "truth" was precisely what victims wanted (Former Yugoslavia NGO #2). A Tribunal Outreach officer thought that truth and a historical record were fundamental expectations that people held (Tribunal Outreach #2): "[there] is an expectation that the ICTY trials would establish 'the truth'—the facts about crimes committed and who was responsible for them—eventually leading to a widespread acknowledgment of the crimes." And another Outreach officer felt that her motivation to work with the Tribunal was the result of its capacity to establish the truth and provide a historical record of the wars (Tribunal Outreach #3). For many respondents then, the utility of answers for the former Yugoslavia was still considered significant.

Several interviewees felt that the courts had managed—to an extent—to answer fundamental societal questions regarding the conflicts. At the Tribunal, a member of the registry believed this expectation had been met (to a degree):

> [W]hat we have definitely been able to achieve is the cases that were brought here and that were tried … there have been findings of fact and so to the extent that these cases covered the conflict, the facts have been established. (Tribunal Registry #1)

A Tribunal Judge agreed with this assessment: "Do we create a history? We do. We certainly do create a history. Whether it is the full history or the correct history I am less certain about. But obviously we do create a legacy or a history" (Tribunal Judge #2). This establishing of facts was one that would "prevent manipulation, with figures, with you know facts, truth about who did what" (Former Yugoslavia NGO #3). Although the Chambers had only completed one trial at the time when fieldwork was conducted a similar expectation was also held:

> [I]t has already helped verifying the facts in the Duch case and now we have the closing orders and so a lot of the facts have been confirmed and data as well. There has been more research and more studies that have

> been done by the tribunal, so it really helps. It has helped verifying the facts to a greater extent. (Cambodia NGO #8)

As such a profound expectation of transitional justice, the question remains whether isolated transitional justice courts are well equipped to satisfy such expectations.

The second type of answers for which there were expectations were in response to individual questions. For example, one NGO participant from Bosnia relayed how this was felt quite strongly by the association of victims he represented: "[W]e cannot exclude the need for justice. Of course, the truth comes first. We all want to know exactly what happened, how they were executed" (Former Yugoslavia NGO #2). In our interview, he relayed this story:

> [O]ne woman … was summoned by the Court in The Hague a couple of years ago to testify against the Serb general in a genocide case, a Srebrenica genocide case. She asked the judge to address the indictee, who was there and she cried, and asked this Serb general. She said she would actually forgive him everything if only he told her where her son was at that moment. 'Please, General, tell me where my son is. I will forgive you everything that you did.' That is what she said. I think that is how most mothers whose sons have been taken away and executed feel. (Former Yugoslavia NGO #2)

Another NGO respondent agreed that answers to individual questions were of deep significance to victims and a valid expectation:

> [T]he individuals need to know. There is like an individual right to truth, and here we can speak of families of the missing. They have an individual right to know, but then there is also a societal right to know. (Former Yugoslavia NGO #1)

This was also an expectation in Cambodia:

> [W]hen people hear that millions of dollars are being pumped into this court then they would naturally, I would think that they would naturally

> say, because of all those millions of dollars, maybe this court can foster reconciliation and maybe it can answer my questions about what happened to my family. (Cambodia NGO #14)

Disappointment was clear in one response regarding victims and the Tribunal: "The main sentence was 'I want to know whether he suffered a lot before he died.' This is what most of us were hoping to find out but we actually never found out" (Former Yugoslavia NGO #2). It may be difficult for people to reconcile the cost of institutions like the Tribunal and the Chambers with their inability to provide answers to pressing questions that they need answered in order to move forward in the transitional justice process. Of course, it will never be possible to answer everyone's individual questions after mass atrocities. In fact, what these interviews indicate is that isolated transitional justice mechanisms—such as the Tribunal and Chambers—will answer very few at all. As a consequence, satisfaction of these expectations will only be achieved for a fraction of those who desire it.

The last area where expectations regarding answers were observed was a desire to provide one's own answers. This was considered a very strong motivation for involvement in transitional justice activities arranged by civil society groups in Cambodia:

> [T]hey want to contribute to the truth of the Khmer Rouge regime, where they can share their stories and experiences together with other people in the community and also to share the story again with their children, with the younger generation. (Cambodia NGO #6)

This expectation was observed in both Cambodia and the former Yugoslavia. Interviewees often related how witnesses would frequently wish to tell the court of their loss and suffering during conflict: "[A] lot of the witnesses would just like to tell a much wider story about how it had an impact on their life now" (Tribunal Media #1). This was considered difficult for the courts and many witnesses needed to be redirected to include in their testimony only the information that was directly relevant to proceedings (Tribunal Registry #1). However, those who could provide testimony about their experiences often found it rewarding:

> Many of these witnesses would actually thank the court for having had the opportunity to, number one, tell their story and to contribute to what they can see is a kind of reconciliation, of finding truth. (Tribunal Registry #1)

This may have been, as a Cambodian NGO worker put it, "because victims want recognition, want people to recognise their suffering" (Cambodia NGO #1). One judicial official explained how trials would only provide such satisfaction to a very limited number of individuals:

> On the concrete level, we are providing happiness to a very limited amount of victims but for those victims who actually do get heard and do become recognised it is extremely important and that spills off I suppose to some extent even to those who did not make it, didn't make it all the way into the indictment. Because I think that I've seen this time and again, for the witnesses who come to testify in our courtroom who are also victims, for them to tell the international community about the suffering that they had to go through is extremely important. The best relief you can give a victim is to acknowledge their suffering and have it published and recognised so that they don't sit back in isolation, and know that the world have been told of their suffering. And that is probably the only thing that we can really do for the victims, to provide some closure to their traumas. (Tribunal Judge #2)

This desire for acknowledgment may attach to several entities. The above passages indicate that the acknowledgment of an official institution such as a court is important. It can also extend to acknowledgment by the perpetrators themselves. One interviewee recounted how a woman, when asked what justice meant to her, responded by saying that "justice for me is that I want the perpetrators to acknowledge what he did to my father. This is my justice" (Cambodia NGO #4). The desire for acknowledgment—as evidenced by these quotations—was considered widespread. Given the ratio of victims to victims who have an opportunity to testify, it is questionable how well the Tribunal or Chambers could ever satisfy this need. Similarly, one can question how much "spill-over" of acknowledgement occurs from victims who are directly acknowledged in proceedings to those victims who do not get to participate.

A profound expectation of acknowledgment also existed for the type of crime and, hence, the type of victimisation. Most significantly, this manifested as severe dissatisfaction when courts did not declare crimes as genocide. One respondent claimed to be furious about the loose usage of the label *genocide*, coupled with the importance that donors and media placed on the concept, that led to this expectation:

> [Genocide] has become a political currency almost. To the extent that the victims have been kind of included into that wager of what is genocide, and what happened to me is not bad enough because it is not called genocide and therefore I wasn't afforded true justice. It is very dangerous. But it was created and it was created mainly among the Bosnian Muslim population and it was created clearly and mainly because of the politicians and the religious segments … So the term is completely de-legalised, it is cheapened, it is politicised and it has had a complete opposite effect and a very negative effect on the society there. Especially in terms of expectations—especially for victims—and that is what makes me angry the most: that they did this. (Tribunal Media #1)

Another respondent believed that managing expectations for genocide convictions was a necessary but unfortunate task:

> I think that the misuse of genocide is one of the big issues that we face in this area [managing expectations]. I mean, we have seen it over and over. And the Krajisnik case is a good example where we charged I think 28 counts and we got convictions on 27 if my memory is correct and had convictions, from crimes against humanity, for extermination, and for very serious crimes and we didn't succeed in proving genocide … It was seen as a kind of failure by the victims and others because genocide is the crime of crimes… So, I think it is a really serious issue … and the idea that there is some kind of hierarchy [of crimes] I think we really have to resist. But in a way we have kind of lost some of that battle and it ends up with bad results. (International NGO #1)

This was an expectation where a clear management strategy was necessary. Media and public figures were seen to fuel expectations for genocide convictions while also painting anything less than a genocide conviction as an insult to victims. In these circumstances, transitional justice institutions have a considerable task in realigning expectations about acknowledgment through convictions. As respondents pointed out, other crimes against humanity should not be seen as a lower level of offending than genocide (Tribunal Media #1; International NGO #1).

Forward Looking Expectations

A final category of expectations is labelled in this study as forward looking: expectations concerned with creating a better future for affected communities. Within this category were several expectations that exhibited strong interconnections. Although not an exhaustive list, these expectations emphasised reconciliation, prevention, and education. For many respondents, the Tribunal was expected to play a role in reconciliation, though the opinions on the extent of that role differed. In Cambodia, after some initial scepticism, the community "think that now the [Chambers] is very important—one of the important factors in order to achieve reconciliation" (Cambodia NGO #1). Reconciliation was also stated to be "one of the court goals" (Cambodia NGO #14), and a purpose of the Chambers (Cambodia NGO #1). One respondent believed the Chambers contributed to reconciliation by allowing for victim and offender interaction:

> The court is one of the reconciliation mechanisms because the perpetrators and victims have an opportunity to explore information from each other, to find out the truth of what happened. So it also plays a role for the reconciliation. (Cambodia NGO #20)

How effectively the Chambers can facilitate perpetrators and victims exploring information together is questionable. Other mechanisms may provide for reconciliation in this manner more successfully. Speaking about the contribution of the Chambers to reconciliation, a court official felt that justice was a necessary component:

> Reconciliation and healing and accountability, I think they go hand-in-hand. I think it is difficult to have healing and reconciliation unless you have some kind of justice mechanism. I think it is here, even here in a Buddhist country, where you have a very clear philosophy about karma. I think it is still necessary for people to see that accountability is present. Otherwise, if no-one is being held accountable, I think it is difficult, even in a Buddhist society, to heal and reconcile. (Chambers Media #1)

These statements suggest that courts play a role in reconciling communities, but that it is not something the courts are likely to achieve in isolation.

Reconciliation was a goal frequently attached to the Tribunal. When speaking about trials at the Tribunal, one defence lawyer thought:

> The point of all these trials is to actually, to bring, to draw a line behind the war so we can move on. And in case the guilt is being made collective, that can just create resentment, cause future resentment between people. (BWCC Defence #1)

Individualising guilt through trials was contended by many—in interviews, the surrounding literature, and in the content analysis—to promote reconciliation. A former prosecutor at the Tribunal certainly believed that "you can actually bring about reconciliation, and probably more effectively by having a judicial process. That's why we have it and that's why it works" (Tribunal Prosecutor #1). However, after considering this assertion, he wondered "whether [a trial] brings about a process of separation. So, the disintegration of the former Yugoslavia is a good example of that" (Tribunal Prosecutor #1). A valid criticism of trials in transitional justice could certainly be that they are not focused on fostering reconciliation in any direct way.

Prevention and deterrence of future violence and conflict were also raised as expectations of the Tribunal and Chambers. This was not an overwhelming expectation in interviews, but was mentioned frequently. In Cambodia it was remarked by several respondents that the Chambers would "prevent these crimes from happening in Cambodia again." Another, who worked with a multitude of communities across

Cambodia in connection with transitional justice and the Chambers claimed that trials of Khmer Rouge leaders acted as a deterrent:

> From my experience from the countryside with the villagers and the students, they said they can learn from the trial as a lesson for other people, and not only for Cambodians, but also the world as well. To learn that if you commit crimes and do bad things you will be punished. (Cambodia NGO #11)

This expectation was also discussed in interviews regarding the Tribunal. One interviewee, describing their time in the witness support unit at the Tribunal, noted a category of witnesses whose motivation for testifying was to promote deterrence:

> [They would tell me] they are testifying in the hope that if they do this now, maybe it will have a preventative effect: maybe no other woman will have to go through their experience; maybe no other parents will lose a child. So there is real hope for the future. (Chambers Victims Support #1)

Some respondents extended this perceived deterrent effect beyond local conflicts to a global audience. One prosecutor regarded trials at the Tribunal as having a global deterrent effect: "[Trials have] a tremendous impact on people who think that they can do anything in the course of an armed conflict and to be free to ignore the consequences from doing so" (Tribunal Prosecutor #1). These respondents elaborated that this effect could be discerned in conflicts in Africa, where atrocities could have been far worse without the deterrent effect of international criminal trials (Tribunal Prosecutor #1; Tribunal Defence #1). This position was maintained by others: "trials have a significant role that helps prevent future conflicts. For one, responsible people in positions of power know that they might be tried" (BWCC Defence #1). However, other respondents expressed scepticism regarding the work of tribunals and their contribution to deterrence. One judicial official remarked: "I have no major expectation that war crimes will not be committed any further because of what we are doing" (Tribunal Judge #3). This remark was made with seeming exasperation that hinted at the sort of oversized expectations his work had been saddled with at the Tribunal. Of course, it would seem nonsensical to expect otherwise. Yet this should not detract from the relevant question of whether a reduction in the commission of war crimes can reasonably be expected as a deterrent effect of international criminal trials.

The final forward looking expectation was about education. Some interviewees expected the court to perform an educative role. This linked closely with expectations regarding truth, historical records, and the search for answers. This expectation is evident in passages quoted above, particularly when phrased as an expectation to "learn from" the courts (Cambodia NGO #11). One respondent believed that the Tribunal had been established to perform an educative function (International NGO #1). A prosecutor working in Bosnia felt that the burden to educate about the conflict had fallen on the court: "Normally education [schools and universities] is what teaches history, but this just can't happen in Bosnia: it has to be the court" (BWCC Prosecutor #1). This may well be a feature resulting from the specific context of the former Yugoslavia, and Bosnia in particular, where three competing histories exist, taught from separate textbooks, to classes segregated along the ethnic lines that were fought over during conflict (Clark 2010; Cole 2007).

Many felt that the courts had performed an educative role within society. In Cambodia it was suggested that as a result of the Duch trial "a lot more people are familiar now with S-21 [the infamous prison also known as Tuol Sleng] than what they were before" (Chambers Media #1). Similarly, at the Tribunal it was considered that trials had performed an educative role:

> There was an educative aspect to it and the Tribunal went some way—I think a long way, frankly—to educating the population, the local population, certainly went a long way to educating the European population. (Tribunal Prosecutor #1)

This educative role was also seen to have a potential impact upon continuing hostilities in the former Yugoslavia. Another prosecutor who had worked at the Tribunal before working at the Chambers believed trials had taught salient lessons about errors that had led to war:

> They have created an important, objective historical record [that] has assisted in … young people recognising that blatant nationalism and that type of thing is not really a great goal for a society. (Chambers Prosecutor #1)

It was also felt that the trials had spurred on further education efforts (Chambers Media #1), and a significant number of interviewees in Cambodia believed that it had created a space for discussion on what had previously been a taboo subject (Chambers Outreach #2; Cambodia NGO #3; Cambodia NGO#4; Chambers Prosecutor #1; Chambers Prosecutor #2; Chambers Prosecutor #3; Cambodian NGO #19; Cambodia NGO #10). At least one respondent, however, was strongly opposed to the court being expected to perform any educative function, saying that it would not be within the court's expertise: "When the court wants to become an education institution or forum, I think that you lose the principle of being a court" (Cambodia NGO #5).

Limitations of Courts and Trials

The most prevalent expectations discussed in interviews related to truth, reconciliation, prosecutions, punishment, justice (though this was conceived of in multiple ways), and education. What is immediately evident is that only two of these—prosecutions and punishment—are most readily associated with the work of courts. While these reflect a traditional retributive approach to justice that courts may be well-placed to deliver, other expectations relate to forms of justice (such as restorative models of justice) that courts are poorly equipped to provide. As research was conducted in respect to single (official) institution efforts—the Tribunal and Chambers—they were often seen as the focus for all transitional justice hopes in those communities.

Participants recognised that it would be unrealistic to expect courts to completely satisfy broader expectations. This is by no means surprising, given the complex social, personal, political, and emotional contexts that transitional trials are conducted in. An outreach officer with the Tribunal put it succinctly: "It's a difficult thing to expect that a judicial sentence which comes from a judicial process will work towards satisfying the communities for their suffering" (Tribunal Outreach #1). A victims' association representative (a survivor of one of the greater atrocities from the wars in the former Yugoslavia) also conceded the following:

> There have been so many frustrations. Of course, even if they had arrested all of them [war criminals] in the first twelve months after the war we would still have been frustrated just by the very fact that this happened to us, that our loved ones were killed in such a horrible way. (Former Yugoslavia NGO #2)

Given that these conflicts usually touch all members of society, it is no stretch to extend the impossibility of satisfying all expectations to a much broader cross-section of post-conflict communities. This does not, of course, excuse failing to try to satisfy as many needs of post-conflict communities as can be accommodated. Rather, it serves to put into perspective the size of troubled waters upon which transitional justice must sail.

Finding answers—otherwise referred to as finding the truth, establishing the facts, or setting the historical record—was one expectation where the courts' limitations were frequently discussed. One reason for this limitation was that the nature of proceedings did not permit a proper inquiry into facts that were outside the boundaries of whether the accused was guilty (Tribunal Registry #1; Chambers Prosecutor #1; Tribunal Defence #2). One registry official explained it this way:

> The judges here they don't go out on a fact-finding mission. They have a limited power to call witnesses and admit documents. But generally speaking, we have a very party-driven process. So the judge would only look at the evidence presented by the prosecution and the defence. Or let's start even one step further … the formulation of the indictment and the inclusion of people and places, it is not arbitrary, but it is a decision

> that has to, of course, pick. You cannot cover entire conflicts, you have to choose … the parties have to decide on what evidence to present … you can't present everything because otherwise you will never finish a trial. (Tribunal Registry #1)

That there was a limited capacity to call for witnesses and evidence was echoed by other participants, with one reminding us "It is not a truth commission where each and every victim can come in and state what happened to them" (Chambers Prosecutor #1). (As an aside, it is prudent to point out that truth commissions do not manage to hear from every victim of mass atrocity either.) Such reasoning led to a second explanation for why courts and trials were ineffective at finding the truth: with an emphasis on efficient and expeditious trials, only limited and narrow indictments were likely to be presented (Tribunal Judge #2; Tribunal Registry #1). A registry official provided one example:

> You see it in the Milutinovic judgment … they dropped charges relating to three of the crime sites because they found that it was representative of the indictment as a whole and they wanted to make sure that they used their time efficiently. So the victims of those crime sites that were not included in the trial, how do they feel about that? I would imagine, unless a national court then goes and tries the perpetrators, that victims probably feel very unhappy. (Tribunal Registry #1)

This issue was also spoken about at some length by judicial officials, who appeared to believe it was unfortunate, yet necessary, to limit trials in a way that might disappoint community members, particularly victims. One judicial official explained it this way:

> [If] two other farms have fallen out [of an indictment], the survivors from those two farms, let's say it is a girl and a little boy, and they saw their parents being killed, their mother raped—terrible, terrible things. And they now sit back and say, 'But I saw it happen, but I am no longer there. What happens to me? Who is going to recognise my pain, my suffering?' Nobody, because he fell out of the ICTY's indictment and who knows whether he will be covered later on in another trial, a domestic trial. It is unlikely. So he can just sit back and say, 'Fuck'. And that causes

> frustration and unhappiness and understandably so. That is a feature of international criminal trials. I guess it will always be like that: that you can't cover it all. (Tribunal Judge #2)

Similar limitations were considered to apply to the Chambers. It was also remarked that the restriction of conducting prosecutions against only the most senior leaders was likely to have a comparable limiting effect (Tribunal Judge #2). While the effects of limited trials on an expectation of truth or fact-finding are clear, it is also evident that it may affect the capacity of trials to satisfy other expectations as well. The need to provide one's own answers to the transitional justice process is important for both individual and societal healing. The space for this to take place is of course restricted when official transitional justice mechanisms are limited to courts alone.

Interviewees also believed that courts and trials were particularly limited in their abilities to promote reconciliation. This was often considered an expectation that the courts were not well-suited to meet, with one interviewee describing such attempts as "a nightmare" (Cambodia NGO #5). As with expectations about the truth, it was similarly considered that the rules within which trials operate served to restrict a court's contribution to reconciliation (Tribunal Registry #1). While either the Tribunal's or the Chambers' contribution to reconciliation was questioned, a number of participants felt that the court played some role but that this role was limited by several factors. A defence lawyer at the Tribunal said:

> [We do not] know how much that institution [the Tribunal] actually promotes reconciliation. I'm sure it does to some limited extent and God knows that the people there are well-motivated … and I think for the most part everyone else working there really wants to see that system work reasonably well but the system itself was not well thought through. (Tribunal Defence #2)

Another interviewee provided an insight that the Chambers was performing reconciliation at a macro rather than a micro level:

> [The Chambers is] more focused on national forms of reconciliation and in some ways it is going to help people come to terms with the past and say, 'Now okay, now that the issue is done we can move on and we can continue to develop our country', but a lot of people are going to need something beyond that. (Cambodia NGO #3)

And while it was felt that both the Tribunal and Chambers had some limited role in contributing to reconciliation, it was suggested that "the court more so has generated a space for it [reconciliation]" (Cambodia NGO #3). Respondents, however, often felt that other efforts were necessary to achieve reconciliation.

As was also explained by a judicial officer from the Tribunal, many limitations of international criminal trials are also limitations of domestic trials:

> Everyone is talking, 'War crimes should never be committed again and we have to prosecute them.' Now if you would say the same in a domestic context for murders, 'murders shouldn't happen again, we should prosecute those who commit murders.' Well, I am not aware of many states being successful in—by prosecuting—in preventing murders. (Tribunal Judge #3)

It is important to bear in mind that in many respects, international criminal trials share significant features with domestic criminal trials. It will come as no surprise that international trials— premised as they are on their domestic counterparts—share many of the same shortcomings. While the above quotation speaks directly to the deterrent capacity of trials, this also extends to other expectations identified in this chapter. Many of these would be considered as unlikely outcomes when applied to domestic trials and there is no compelling reason to assume that they will be any more likely simply because the trial is conducted in The Hague. What the quotation above may best exemplify is a form of overreaction to the expectation overload. This respondent sought to highlight how the rhetoric in transitional justice was often about a complete end to atrocities and a complete end to impunity. This was to be contrasted with the more modest expectations held in national jurisdictions. Unfortunately, expectation overload may contribute to a form of nihilism that obfuscates the appropriate discussion of what are the reasonable deterrent contributions such trials might make.

Another limitation was that a lack of awareness or interest in proceedings would restrict whatever positive contributions courts and trials may make towards the many expectations held of them. This concern was primarily voiced in regard to the Tribunal. Officials at the Tribunal stated that "people are tired of hearing about war crimes," (BWCC Defence #1) and that "people do not watch anymore and don't care very much" (Tribunal Judge #1). An outreach officer saw this as an entrenched problem:

> It's not even about acceptance of the judgment [as to whether the Tribunal had an impact]. People haven't even heard about certain cases, or people don't believe they happened. So immediately there is really no room to even discuss the judgment itself. (Tribunal Outreach #3)

In such an environment, it is perhaps unfair to expect a court to make much headway towards satisfying many expectations. However, another outreach officer of the Tribunal believed people were, and are, engaged with its work:

> What the Tribunal is doing I think it still is being followed in the region. Maybe not as in-depth as it should be in terms of the correct facts or the correct information, but I think people are still following it. (Tribunal Outreach #2)

The problem of correct information or facts regarding the work of tribunals is important. It is easy to speculate that incorrect information or facts may have a detrimental impact on expectations. This was seen at the first instance sentencing of Duch at the Chambers, when media reports did not fully explain the considerations that were taken into sentencing. This incorrect information led to perhaps more dissatisfaction with the sentence than would otherwise have occurred.

During interviews, respondents enunciated many shortcomings and limitations of trials. These inevitably influenced what expectations courts could reasonably be expected to contribute towards. Many saw the narrow focus of trials as anathema to a full historical record of the truth. For these reasons, the Tribunal's or Chambers' contributions to establishing a historical record were considered suspect by many. Additionally, some saw the Tribunal and Chambers as performing a deterrent role locally and globally, but views on this point were by no means unanimous. In particular, the Tribunal and Chambers were not considered to be particularly adequate in meeting the needs and expectations of victims. While this may have been foreseen for the Tribunal, it came as a surprise in respect to the Chambers, where victims could participate as civil parties. As respondents noted, however, given the limited number of victims who can participate (even at the Chambers) in prosecutions, these institutions are not necessarily successful vehicles for addressing victim needs. Respondents also felt that certain expectations were wrong. One lawyer in the former Yugoslavia believed "that people in the region of the former Yugoslavia have a wrong perception of the ICTY that led to wrong expectations. People do not understand [the] concept of trial[s]" (BWCC Defence #1). This concern was echoed by another participant:

> Personal expectations are always also heavily influenced by media reports and statements of high government officials. This, coupled with a lack of general knowledge about the mandate and the work of the institutions, can create high and somewhat misinformed expectations, but this is inevitable. (Tribunal Outreach #3)

It is perhaps telling that both of the above interviewees believed that inappropriate expectations were a result of misinformed—or ill-informed—perceptions of the court. In these quotations, the idea of "managing expectations" can be observed: if perceptions are wrong, if there is a lack of knowledge, if expectations are misinformed, then the implication is that they would benefit from being corrected or informed. Efforts at correcting and informing are a manifestation of the "management" of expectations about transitional justice courts.

Conclusion

What this chapter makes clear is there is a vast number of expectations that are held of transitional justice trials. Many expectations discussed by respondents were recognised as deeply held, widespread and pervasive. The expectation problem was raised most commonly in response to questions regarding the extra-judicial roles that trials might play in transitional justice. Those outside the court (NGO staff, for example) were often sceptical of the contribution that courts could make towards the desired transitional justice goals of communities. When respondents elaborated upon why the court was so limited, this was frequently attributed to the need for efficiency in international courts and trials, the legal rules that constrain trials, and the proper role for courts and trials. Most respondents recognised that the expectations frequently held by members of affected communities were often broader transitional justice goals and not of narrower trial goals. Thus, many interviews revolved around the perceived disconnects between what was expected of transitional justice trials and courts and what these trials and courts could *actually* provide.

This begs the question: for transitional justice to be successful/legitimate, must it also address those expectations that are deep, widespread and pervasive, even if they are not institutionally appropriate? The answer is yes. Therefore, we ought to consider not only whether we have *institution appropriate* expectations, but also whether we have the *appropriate institution* to satisfy expectations. With this in mind, it is important to promote greater understanding about the capacity of courts and trials but also to exhibit greater honesty about the limitations that courts and trials have in the broader goals of transitional justice. In fact, it may be necessary to manage expectations so that prosecutions are not burdened by all the hopes held for transitional societies. One respondent had recognised this: it is important to manage expectations so that community members do not believe trials are the sole vehicle for providing all their needs for justice in transition (Tribunal Defence #6).

References

Clark, JN 2010, 'Education in Bosnia-Hercegovina: The case for root and branch reform', *Journal of Human Rights*, vol. 9, no. 3, pp. 344–362.

Cole, EA 2007, 'Transitional justice and the reform of history education', *International Journal of Transitional Justice*, vol. 1, no. 1, pp. 115–137.

4

Managing Expectations of the Tribunal and Chambers

As we saw in the previous chapter, expectations were broad and many did not align with the usual goals of criminal trials. This, of course, led to an expectation dilemma. This chapter examines how respondents viewed this dilemma and understood its solution. Across The Hague, the former Yugoslavia, and Cambodia many interviewees commented on the need to "manage expectations" as the surest way of avoiding disappointment. No fewer than eight interviewees specifically referred to "managing expectations" of the trials (Cambodia NGO #14; Cambodian NGO #19; Tribunal Media #1; Chambers Outreach #1; Tribunal Defence #6; Cambodia NGO #5; Tribunal Outreach #2; International NGO #1). A few informants were uncomfortable with the language of "managing expectations" as a presumptuous assumption of power over ordinary people by those who would assume to manage expectations. However, a far greater number talked about and advocated activities aimed at doing just that. By way of example, the late establishment of Outreach at the Tribunal was considered to have hampered the capacity to manage expectations:

R. Nickson and A. Neikirk, *Managing Transitional Justice*,
Palgrave Studies in Compromise after Conflict,
https://doi.org/10.1007/978-3-319-77782-5_4

> [Had Outreach been established sooner] we would have managed to manage the expectations ... of the victims and other people who felt or expected that the Tribunal would have just finished the whole job. (Tribunal Media #1)

An NGO worker in Cambodia believed managing expectations was necessary to avoid disappointment: "[I]t could get dangerous because then you have people who are disappointed when their expectations aren't managed enough" (Cambodia NGO #14). Managing expectations was also seen as a tool for encouraging a broader conception of transitional justice: "[E]xpectations do need to be managed so that there is not a belief that tribunals like the ICTY are the most important mechanism for creating peace and security after conflict" (Tribunal Defence #6). Recognition that courts and tribunals should not be invested with every hope and goal for transitional justice is important. In particular, interviewees believed that expectation management was the primary mechanism for ensuring expectations aligned with likely outcomes. This chapter focuses further on how participants viewed expectations, the key factors influencing expectations of trials (and transitional justice) along with distinctions and similarities between the Tribunal and Chambers. In both of these contexts, the role of the local media is significant (the role of the international media is discussed in the following chapter).

Appropriate and Inappropriate Expectations

Participants' statements regarding an expectation problem could be arranged into three broad categories. The first was that there were simply too many expectations, overburdening the court with tasks and functions. The second was that expectations were too high, exceeding the contribution that the court might reasonably make to any given goal. Third, some expectations were regarded as inappropriate: they were ill-suited to criminal courts and trials. These categories were not mutually exclusive, as the same or similar expectations were considered by different interviewees to fall within several of the categories. For some they were also overlapping: what was too high was also inappropriate, or something could be both inappropriate and an unnecessary burden on the court. Many, if not most, participants believed that much of what people wanted from transitional justice was unlikely to be provided by criminal trials.

The problem of there being too many expectations of criminal trials and courts was expressed about both the Tribunal and the Chambers. This was directly stated by 28 interview participants, who expressed concern that expectations were out of step with what the Tribunal or Chambers could provide: "I think a lot of people are expecting a court to do too many other things, than actually conducting criminal trials" (Chambers Media #1) and "I think there are too many expectations, as for like changing or improving the rule of law, there are too many" (Chambers Prosecutor #2). One interviewee, talking about transitional justice generally from her experience at the Tribunal felt as follows:

> These courts, are they are supposed to try people charged with war crimes, contribute to the creation of an accurate historical record, contribute to peace and reconciliation in the region? I mean, how much are we going to ask these courts to do? (Tribunal Defence #2)

Often respondents believed that too many expectations had been attached to transitional justice courts. This was sometimes characterised as dumping inappropriate responsibilities on them:

> [I]f you say 'We are setting up a tribunal to find out who did this and to convict those who are guilty' that's one thing. But then to dump all of these other responsibilities is another. Because people then have expectations that that is what is going to happen. (Tribunal Defence #2)

Many respondents commented that expectations were inflated. For example: "I am always a bit concerned about expectations that go far too high" (Tribunal Judge #3) and "[T]he expectations [of the Tribunal] were extremely high" (Tribunal Outreach #4). This caused problems for the courts, as an Outreach officer explained, "Those expectations were too high and there was nobody to correct and to explain the mandate and the role and then people were disappointed and frustrated and then it is difficult to correct that" (Tribunal Outreach #6). This led one respondent to surmise that people's expectations did not correlate with what courts could provide and "people expected too much of the ICTY" (BWCC Prosecutor #1). At least five interviewees used the word "unrealistic" in reference to expectations (Chambers Prosecutor #1; International NGO #1; Tribunal Judge #3; Tribunal Outreach #2; and Tribunal Outreach #1). Respondents did not believe that only local communities held unrealistic expectations of transitional justice trials. One judge divulged his concern that unrealistic expectations were also held by the international community (Tribunal Judge #3). This was considered to raise difficulties for transitional justice institutions: "[U]nrealistic or inappropriate expectations [were] a problem for the ICTY" (Tribunal Outreach #1). As an extension, another outreach officer felt that:

> in [the] case of the ICTY many people have certainly had unrealistic expectations—in particular the earlier years after its creation—which inevitably led to sometimes profound disappointment almost 20 years on. (Tribunal Outreach #2)

It is troubling to think that unrealistic expectations may have engendered profound disappointment for so long. This is more troubling considering how widespread the problem of unrealistic expectations, and too high expectations, was believed to exist by participants.

One reason for the existence of high expectations was that international courts were seen as powerful actors in the transitional arena:

> The temptation is that you get this international criminal court and prosecutor that's a bit of a magic wand who can … hold the individuals accountable but [also] have this huge sea change and it is just not going to happen; it's important but the effect is limited and a lot of other things need to happen. (International NGO #1)

This same interviewee, who had worked at the Tribunal and was now at an NGO, went on to say:

> So I think we have, even in our ordinary lives, outsize expectations of courts and if you create an international criminal court … despite all the experience to the contrary … people somehow believe that there is some kind of super power, when actually in the case of these courts these powers are pretty limited. (International NGO #1)

Other interviewees felt the same. One participant from Cambodia explained that it was partly the result of such courts being one of the few functioning public institutions in many post-conflict societies, and one of the few (if not only) institutions invested heavily with international funds (Chambers Victim Support #1). Another respondent believed that the build-up to establishing transitional justice courts contributed to this perception (Chambers Prosecutor #1).

Another concern was that the motivations for establishing transitional justice courts, and consequently the expectations attached to them, may be different between local and international communities. A staff member at the Chambers thought that "it seems like the international communities may have different motivations than the Cambodian society might have of these trials" (Chambers Media #1). Similarly, a participant working for an NGO involved in monitoring the Chambers commented, "The expectations of the Cambodian public may be very different to the international community" (Chambers NGO #9). It is less than ideal that transitional justice institutions should be created with such disconnects between donors and local communities. This may be partly due to local needs and context: "[T]hose expectations are really country specific, depending on what people have been through and what their current situation is now" (Chambers Prosecutor #1). This suggests the need for further dialogue, so that transitional justice efforts might better reflect local expectations.

After initial interviews had been completed, follow-up questions were posed to participants, asking directly what they considered to be appropriate and inappropriate expectations (terms used by the interviewees themselves). The most common expectation that respondents perceived as inappropriate was whether courts would contribute to reconciliation.

This was declared to be "the most unrealistic expectation" (along with truth) by a respondent who worked as defence counsel at the Tribunal (Tribunal Defence #3). One respondent felt it was inappropriate to expect "that tribunals such as the ICTY will fully resolve inter-ethnic problems which are still a legacy of the war" (Tribunal Defence #6). And another stated it was inappropriate to expect trials "to contribute to reconciliation and lasting peace" (Tribunal Outreach #1). Two NGO workers in a joint response saw a link between limited prosecutions and the extent that trials could contribute to reconciliation (Cambodian NGO #3 and 4). An expectation that tribunals would produce truth was a second—and almost equal—inappropriate expectation according to respondents. One lawyer from the former Yugoslavia felt quite strongly that this was an inappropriate, but common expectation:

> Expectations are more focused on some weird concept of establishing the truth of the war, and it is pretty much impossible, especially considering the war in BiH that ended without a winner. (BWCC Defence #1)

One other expectation that was seen as unrealistic was that it would be inappropriate to expect such trials to be "free from political agendas, as even the donor money needed to run such an expensive trial is based on the various agendas of other countries" (Cambodia NGO #3 and 4).

Interestingly, truth was considered by other respondents to be an appropriate expectation. In respect to the Chambers, it was felt that "it is appropriate to expect that international tribunals should shed some understanding of various conflicts" (Cambodia NGO #3 and 4). The same expectation about the Tribunal was considered appropriate by one follow-up respondent: "Appropriate expectations would be … that the international tribunals will in the end provide a historical record regarding the events which took place during the conflict" (Tribunal Defence #6). The same respondent also believed fair trials to be an appropriate expectation. Others had a far more restricted view of what constituted appropriate expectations. One defence lawyer limited appropriate expectations to narrow functions of the court: "The only appropriate expectation is to determine the guilt or the innocence of the accused as charged by the prosecutor" (Tribunal Defence #3). Another defence lawyer reduced the appropriate functions and expectations further:

> The most appropriate expectations are that they will hold accountable those highest ranking officials suspected of the most serious violations of international humanitarian law, and that they not try to address every crime nor write the history of the conflict. (Tribunal Defence #4)

While these last two statements may represent a more realistic set of expectations for trials, they fail to recognise the wider significance of these trials to societies in transition.

Respondent Views on Expectation Management

During interviews, many participants provided their insights about how expectations could, or should, be managed. When asked directly about how expectations should be managed, an overwhelming majority cited outreach or similar public information campaigns. For example, one Outreach officer declared that "Outreach is fundamental in getting the court's message out and managing expectations about what it can or cannot do" (Tribunal Outreach #2). The purpose of outreach was considered multi-dimensional: it would translate actual judgments from legalese into an intelligible form for a wider audience, while "getting the message across: what the actual judgment means" (Tribunal Prosecutor #2). It was noted that this had to be done:

> actively and in a way which catches the attention of the public. The courts, tribunals, have a big problem in communicating because what strikes, what catches the attention of the public are colourful items. The more extreme the better. It doesn't even matter whether it is very intelligent or not, but if it is loud and brightly coloured then it catches the interest. Courts, by their very nature, must be moderate. (Tribunal Judge #1)

Not only was outreach required to be attention-grabbing, it also had to be contextually relevant to the location, culture and conflict of the recipient community. Outreach efforts had to be tailored to their audience:

> [The] most important thing about outreach: that you actually have to create it in accordance with the realistic needs of the country that you are dealing with … it has to approach many different people at the same time … [it is] very important to define a programme for each of the different segments of the society. And each one of them has to be defined differently, taking into account different needs and expectations of the people. (Tribunal Media #1)

The second most common response on how to manage expectations was that care should be taken to avoid raising them in the first place:

> Care must be taken by those who are involved in creating policies of such tribunals to avoid raising unrealistic expectations among the people affected of what a tribunal alone can achieve, both in terms of its legal and extra-legal mandate. (Tribunal Outreach #2)

This was considered to be particularly the case in terms of the mandate and was viewed as problematic for the Tribunal:

> It was a mistake to spell out the contribution to reconciliation and peace as part of the mandate of the Tribunal. I believe these two possible results should have been discreetly desired as by-outcomes of the Tribunal's work but not as defined goals. (Tribunal Outreach #1)

As a solution, it was suggested that "[m]ore precise definition of their [tribunals' and courts'] mandates is necessary from the beginning" (Cambodia NGO #9).

Managing expectations was predominantly conceived as a remedial measure and this remedy was largely considered the sole purview of outreach efforts. The following section will look differently at the challenge of expectations—how participants felt that endeavours outside the court were required to adequately address expectations. This in turn will lead to later discussion on how expectations might be incorporated into the structures and frameworks of transitional justice more effectively and how expectations can be shaped and informed through dialogic efforts before institutions are established, as well as during their operation. It is important to see both measures collectively.

One perceived impediment to the effective work of Outreach was a conservative attitude of many judicial staff towards promoting a court's work. This was not universal—several felt judicial officers were quite supportive—but it was nevertheless a feature of the work of Outreach. Hostility by some judicial staff towards Outreach was evidenced from its very inception at the Tribunal: "a couple of the judges said that this Outreach thing was just kind of a female, soft, touchy-feely thing" (International NGO #1). Reluctant and dismissive attitudes towards Outreach were partly seen to be a result of courts traditionally being conservative institutions (Tribunal Outreach #6). It was noted that "judges in national systems never do any outreach" (International NGO #1), and so it was perhaps unsurprising that an international judiciary staffed largely with national judicial officers would be reluctant to engage in outreach (Tribunal Media #1). This was also an issue at the Chambers:

> Some chambers [within the Extraordinary Chambers] are more reluctant to provide information because they feel that judgments should speak for themselves. Others are very proactive in collaborating with public affairs and giving advance notice and information about key decisions that may need additional explanation in the media, so it varies from chamber to chamber. (Chambers Media #1)

A practical effect of this attitude was that when corrections to media articles were thought necessary by the media and Outreach offices at the Tribunal, they were not always approved by chambers (Tribunal Media #1).

The challenges to effective outreach were not limited to attitudes within the court. Funding and resources were an immense problem for the work of Outreach and were mentioned by every Outreach officer interviewed at either court. The Chambers and Tribunal were impeded in their efforts to manage expectations, or to better inform them, by limited funding and staffing for Outreach and sometimes by a judicial reluctance to perform public information work. Both the Chambers and Tribunal suffered from insufficient funding, while interviews revealed that Tribunal Outreach was significantly understaffed in key regions and positions for extended periods. The lack of funding required Outreach officers for both institutions to collaborate with regional NGOs to spread their message. Outreach and NGO cooperation in Cambodia had become sophisticated and quite successful. Regular meetings were staged between both groups which allowed them to coordinate their efforts and permitted the sharing of information and answering of questions more readily.

Funding shortfalls were even more problematic given the perceived importance of Outreach activities, by all participants in this research. At the Tribunal, the work of Outreach was sustained by external funding and not by part of the court's budget. Many respondents saw this as problematic in ensuring that Outreach could perform the important work it had been created to do. Indeed, the external funding that Outreach received was only sufficient to cover wages, leaving no funding to undertake any outreach activities. This served to severely limit what Outreach was able to do in the former Yugoslavia: "[If Outreach] want to engage in any meaningful activity we have to actually find money elsewhere, and given the situation in the world you can imagine it's not the easiest of tasks" (Tribunal Outreach #1). And although it was suggested that the "bosses" had "woke[n] up and said, 'We have got to do a better job'" (Tribunal Outreach #6), the future activities that Outreach officers described as part of the Tribunal's upcoming legacy projects did not have funding allocated to them at the time of interviews. This challenge had also been experienced at the Chambers:

> One of the obvious challenges ... was the lack of resources given to public information activities. When you have to go out and get ad hoc funding for the first editions of these newsletters. We had to get ad hoc funding for basic information about the court. That is obviously not the ideal way of running. This has been remedied later on by more allocations. (Chambers Media #1)

This lack of funding was also a problem for civil society groups, on whom the Chambers relied heavily to carry a significant portion of the outreach work in Cambodia. Not only does this situation limit the activities that Outreach can perform directly, but also indirectly, by requiring staff to spend time campaigning for funds rather than conducting outreach. That staff might be required to campaign for funds was a further concern. While Outreach was said to be understaffed when all positions were filled, there were significant periods when field offices in the former Yugoslavia had important Outreach positions completely vacant. This was viewed to be an increased problem for Tribunal Outreach, as the court was located some distance from the affected region.

A further problem for outreach, which was fortunately not replicated in experiences at the Chambers, was the gap between the establishment of the Tribunal and the establishment of the Outreach office. Experience from the Tribunal demonstrates the disadvantages of not conducting a robust outreach programme from the beginning. Of the four Outreach offices where interviews were conducted, staff at three explicitly stated that this had been a significant challenge. As a Tribunal Media Officer explained:

> [It] left a permanent mark, and it left a permanent obstacle for the Tribunal because if you look at the years of the functioning of the Tribunal, or of any institution, especially the one that is kind of established through the will of the international community and not because people in that region came out and said they wanted it, you need to spend, you know, the first days of your life are the most important to go out and hammer in your message and tell people what you are here to do and why it is wrong that certain things are being done there and how they can be addressed. And had that been done … we would have had … a small counter voice to the politicians who filled in the gap with their propaganda … [and] also managed to manage the expectations. (Tribunal Media #1)

It may be that this difficulty is experienced with future courts. At the Chambers and other courts established after the Tribunal, the importance of outreach has been recognised from the outset. This recognition, however, has not always translated into appropriate or sufficient funding (see, for example, Clark 2009; Hussain 2005).

An important way that the work of Outreach could be improved and enhanced was considered to be through collaboration with NGOs and civil society organisations. Participants deemed this a necessity. In Cambodia, it was felt that NGOs' and the Chambers' outreach complemented one another, permitting greater scope for public information activities. One reason was a high degree of coordination between the Court's work and the work of NGOs. This was achieved through regular meetings that permitted an exchange of information and ideas between the various actors. In addition, it was easier for Outreach and NGOs to avoid replicating efforts in one location and to ensure the widest spread of outreach activities.

Thinking Outside the Court

As explained previously, the Tribunal and Chambers were selected because they represented single official transitional justice institutions for their respective conflicts (though the Tribunal would later be supplemented by the work of regional courts). It was hoped to study transitional justice trials in isolation from other official mechanisms. In reflecting upon this isolation, many participants felt that it was a limitation on the transitional justice process. What was preferable, if the positive effects of transitional justice were to be enhanced, were broader efforts and deeper engagement with affected communities.

Courts and trials alone could not adequately address all the expectations that were held of the transitional justice process. This did not mean that they had no role, but were part of a bigger tapestry of transitional justice efforts:

> Criminal trials or prosecutions are necessary but not sufficient because it's essential that all of those who are most responsible for the most serious crimes are accountable, but you need to go further than that. And outreach programs I think in a sense complement that, as do truth

> commissions and commissions of inquiry, and reparations programs and so forth. So, it is part of, it has to be part of, a bigger strategy for peace and peacebuilding. (International NGO#1)

Similarly a Tribunal registry official commented:

> [Trials are] only part of the puzzle and I think you need other measures. You need national trials. You might even need something like a truth and reconciliation commission. You need, in Germany what we did, we opened the archives … So it is very important not to just focus on the criminal trial, but also in my view to try and find other measures to bring the truth to light. (Tribunal Registry #1)

As one participant who had worked at both the Tribunal and Chambers explained, transitional justice responses should be "almost as complex … as the events were complex … one intervention I think is never enough" (Chambers Victim Support #1).

In particular, criminal trials were considered poor vehicles for addressing the needs of victims after conflict. Given the levels of victimisation during most conflicts that lead to transitional justice, this represents a sizable proportion of affected communities. A judicial officer at the Tribunal questioned the contribution trials made to meeting victims' needs:

> The question is to what extent criminal proceedings are the best way to meet the needs of victims. To some extent they can meet some of the needs and in many respects it cannot. And therefore you have to find other mechanisms as well to support and to meet the needs of victims … I know one thing for sure: that most of what victims need has to be provided also by others outside of the courtroom. (Tribunal Judge #3)

As will become clear from the following chapter that analyses print media coverage of the Tribunal and Chambers, an invocation of victims as the purpose for such trials was not uncommon. But when trials do not adequately provide victims and victim communities with what they need, such invocations seem hollow and self-serving. An Outreach officer believed victims, or members of victim communities, often found trials disappointing:

> You wait for so long for someone to be arrested. And then there are four years of the trial and excellent, and then the judgment comes in: 35 years. And you're empty. And no court can fill in that emptiness because for these people it has to have more approaches … to soften their suffering. (Tribunal Outreach #1)

The necessity of more than one response in transitional justice was clear in the feedback of many participants.

The most common mechanism that interviewees referred to beyond courts was the truth commission model. The work of truth commissions was considered by some participants to be compatible with trials:

> You should have a combination of truth commissions and trials. Because, you know, in trials we just cannot and should not tell the whole story. Because trials are about convicting the person who is on trial. And although it is difficult because the victims often want to tell the whole story, but it [the trial] can't. (BWCC Defence #1)

Although there may be clear advantages for adopting both trials and truth commissions, it is necessary to recognise that truth commissions are not capable of responding to *all* the residual problems that trials have left untouched. As Stanley (2002, p. 2) has observed:

> In states where the judiciary, the security services and military, the media and the economic powers have each contributed to and are complicit in the efficient workings of totalitarianism, it is perhaps naïve to expect that stories of state brutality alone will negotiate structural and social change.

Unfortunately, efforts for a truth commission that worked in conjunction with the Tribunal had been unsuccessful. Several explanations were provided by participants for this failure. One problem for a truth commission in the former Yugoslavia was considered to be the difficulty of establishing such an institution by agreement between six nations—some of whom had not had close relations since gaining independence (Tribunal Registry #1). A further explanation was that while the Tribunal was established during the wars of the 1990s, it would have made little sense—or been incredibly difficult, if not impossible—to establish a truth commission while conflict was raging in the former Yugoslavia (Tribunal Judge #3). Considering that conflict continued until the end of the decade—and according to some participants is continued in the political arena—there was a considerable delay from when the Tribunal was created to the point when conditions would have been more appropriate to establish a commission. One respondent felt the former Yugoslavia was not ready for a truth commission (BWCC Prosecutor #3). The political context—the prevalence of ethnic nationalism and the structure of the Bosnia's rotating Presidency (for a full explanation of the rotating Presidency see Sebastian 2010)—was also relevant to having a truth commission in the former Yugoslavia and were seen to hamper efforts in that direction (Tribunal Outreach #2).

It was also thought that victims had been opposed to a truth commission as they had assumed that it would include amnesties (Tribunal Outreach #2). The position of one victim's association was neither to advocate for a truth commission nor oppose one provided it was compatible with trials (Former Yugoslavia NGO #2). This remark was surprising considering the importance that this respondent, and the group he represented, placed on the desire for answers to questions arising from the conflict. What was also evident in other remarks by the same respondent was that he and the victims he acted as spokesperson for were clearly dissatisfied with the prosecutorial response. In this way, a dialogue that counsels affected communities about the limitations of trials—or any other transitional justice mechanism—may be an important feature of improved transitional justice responses. For stakeholders to dismiss the benefits of one mechanism, while holding unrealistically high expectations for another, is likely to lead to dissatisfaction with the process overall. What might have been preferable for this group was to understand that they would not get all the retributive justice they hoped for, but that other mechanisms may fill some of the gaps that exist in what courts could provide.

This sentiment was echoed by a prosecutor, who said he was "not in favour of truth commissions—in the Balkans you have to punish" (BWCC Prosecutor #1). However, upon further elaboration that same prosecutor explained that he was only "against a truth commission that offers amnesties." In fact, he believed "it would be great if there were a separate truth commission that could put all the pieces together." This further demonstrates the need for processes in which local voices are given the capacity to influence them. If these attitudes represent the majority of opinion, then transitional justice should be implemented in a way that recognises this. Interviewees highlighted that steps toward implementing a truth commission were under way in the former Yugoslavia and that these steps were the united efforts of civil society groups from across the region (Tribunal Outreach #2; Former Yugoslavia NGO #3, Tribunal Outreach #6; Tribunal Outreach #5). In Cambodia, civil society had taken on this role from the beginning, and various groups had conducted their own truth work when Government support for a complementary truth commission was not forthcoming. It is important to recognise that immediate support for a truth commission may be low but can grow over time.

Not only was it considered that transitional justice should operate more broadly, but that it also needed to be more inclusive and penetrate deeper into affected communities. It was thought that trials should provide for greater involvement of community members, particularly survivors, to "let them open their opinion, to really engage directly in the trial" (Cambodia NGO #11). One way that trials were seen to be able to do this was through victim participation. This was a much stronger feature at the Chambers, where victims could act as civil parties to proceedings, than at the Tribunal, where victims were limited to acting solely as witnesses. The scope for victims to participate in proceedings at the Chambers was seen to make them preferable to proceedings of the Tribunal:

> [In] the Yugoslavia case, I think without the participation of the victims, I think it is less meaningful. Because people do not participate actively: it is just only an affair of the judges and the prosecutor and the lawyer. It is not an affair of the victims themselves. And this process [the Chambers]

> I think is more meaningful because the victim is considered by the process as one party to the process. Justice is not an affair of the court, is not an affair of the judges; it is also an affair of the victims too. (Cambodia NGO #18)

And while greater victim participation was seen as one avenue, participation was also seen to require broader engagement with a wider variety of people from affected communities:

> The court should have more people, more survivors, to get more interaction, to engage, directly engage face-to-face in the court while they have the trial hearing so people can give their opinion, you know, of what is their question. And if they can talk, they can talk directly, can see the trial, they can express their feelings, express what they are wondering. Like I collect a lot of questions from youth and from the villagers and we combine all the questions and have a legal associate and a legal expert to answer these questions as well. And if they get the answer, then they could be satisfied on some level. (Cambodia NGO #11)

It is important not to restrict our concepts of court-community engagement to the trial proceedings themselves, as there are many other forums where court representatives and community members can come together to enhance the contributions that trial proceedings can make to transitional justice. Such activities may include the "Bridging the Gap" series of conferences conducted by the Tribunal. These conferences brought court staff, including prosecutors and judges, to local communities and facilitated a dialogue between groups. The conferences were universally considered successful and valuable by those who spoke of them (Tribunal Prosecutor #2; Chambers Prosecutor #1; Tribunal Outreach #1; Tribunal Media #1; Tribunal Judge #1; Tribunal Judge #2).

Non-judicial forms of justice that permitted deeper engagement with affected communities were also considered beneficial. In Cambodia, many of these non-judicial forms of justice related to concepts of memory. Activities conducted by many civil society NGOs in Cambodia sought to empower community members through the use of memory about the Khmer Rouge period. One interviewee explained how he would tell participants in such programmes that they would be contributing to future generations' understanding of Cambodian history, and how their memories and experiences would be preserved for posterity (Cambodia NGO #8). This was seen to effectively motivate greater participation. Memory was considered by an interviewee from a prominent Cambodian NGO to be an important form of justice in itself (Cambodian NGO #1). For another respondent, memory was intertwined with justice:

> The way that we see justice is more than just legal justice of the court. We believe that that formal justice is obviously very important, but at the same time, our main thing is non-judicial forms of justice: truth telling. We really believe that by having—by helping—villagers talk about what happened to them in the community format they are basically getting their memories acknowledged and reaffirmed—that this actually happened to them; they actually did suffer. Because after not being able to talk about their experiences for decades, and having young children doubting what happened to them, because the education system doesn't teach about it, they need their memories reaffirmed. They need to say, 'This happened to me and I need someone to believe this happened to me.' And in that way, it is a form of justice. (Cambodia NGO #3)

Memory work features prominently at several of the NGOs whose staff participated in this research. These activities represent just one other way to promote deeper engagement in transitional justice by affected communities. Ultimately, respondents saw the work and contribution of trials at the Tribunal and Chambers as limited. They also overwhelmingly believed that where the Tribunal had failed to inform expectations and opinions, the media had succeeded.

Perceived Role of the Local Media

The role of local media and their potential impact on expectations was a concern to respondents discussing the Tribunal. Studies that have looked at the impact and perceptions of the Tribunal have emphasised the importance of the media. The fact that the media has frequently been controlled by the same political elites involved in the conflicts has been cited as an obstacle to the Tribunal in communicating the "truth" of the wars to affected communities (Akhavan 1998). As Hodzic (2010, pp. 114–115) observes, an imperfect picture of the Tribunal was conveyed to the public: "The information generated by such elites and by the media that operate under their influence did not provide a complete or accurate picture of the trials or the facts established by them." Several studies have analysed the representation of the Tribunal in local and Western media. Unfortunately, similar studies for the Chambers could not be located.

In relation to the Tribunal, the media in the former Yugoslavia were considered by many interviewees, and all of those who worked in outreach, to play a significant—and largely negative—role. This impacted not only on the perception of the Tribunal in the region, but by extension the views of how far it had gone in meeting the expectations held of it. This was not raised by participants in respect to Cambodia, with one notable exception. One tribunal monitor in Cambodia felt that the information provided by the media was biased in favour of the Chambers and did not raise any of the legitimate criticisms or concerns about the court (Government interference, for instance) (Cambodia NGO #19). This monitor speculated that recent studies by the University of California, Berkeley into the perception of the Chambers by Cambodians were incomplete because they did not account for the quality of information that Cambodians had been provided about the Chambers (those studies are Pham et al. 2009, 2011). This participant felt that the court carefully stage-managed its public events—such as radio talk-shows—to avoid any negative publicity or press. This extended to the information that they provided to the media. Hostility by the media, however, appeared to be a prevalent feature for the Tribunal that was not replicated in interviews regarding the Chambers.

Every Tribunal Outreach office, with the exception of Pristina, was interviewed. At most offices, more than one staff member was interviewed (bearing in mind that regional offices are only at full-staffing if they have two employees and some were not fully staffed at the time of fieldwork). Every Outreach officer raised serious concerns about the media portrayal of the Tribunal, the lack of correct information, and bias. One Outreach officer characterised the media coverage as unproductive and in need of attention (Tribunal Media #1). It was felt the Tribunal was unable to make the kinds of contributions that had been expected of it because the landscape "is really contaminated by the poison that is spewed by the media and the politicians" (Tribunal Media #1). Many shared the view, expressed by one Outreach officer, that "the media depiction of the Tribunal is mostly negative" (Tribunal Outreach #1). It was also observed by many participants that the media were predominantly concerned with maintaining the hero status of prominent identities from the war, most of whom were indicted or convicted war criminals. But observing the negative role of the media in the former Yugoslavia was not limited to Outreach officials. A prominent human rights activist in Belgrade said of the media:

> [They] are not a factor of change, they are a factor of status quo, and they have been instrumentalised since the beginning of war, creating the atmosphere by confusing people with their interpretation and all that and now they are not willing to engage in true dialogue. (Former Yugoslavia NGO #3)

It is no great step to question the impact that the Tribunal could make when an important vehicle for disseminating its work was unlikely to relay positive messages.

The concern that negative media could have a profound impact on the Tribunal's work was heightened because the media was seen to provide the majority of people in the former Yugoslavia with their information of the court. One interviewee referred to research conducted in the former Yugoslavia that "shows that the media is where people turn to find out about the tribunal" (Tribunal Outreach #1). Reinforcing this, a defence lawyer from Bosnia and Herzegovina agreed:

> [The] media don't seem to realise the role they have and the influence they have. Because most people don't follow trials, they don't read judgments as such. The general public just reads the media or watches TV. And that is very problematic. (BWCC Defence #1)

It was not uncommon for participants to speculate that people were unlikely to read judgments for themselves. Hodzic points out that the discourse in Bosnia and Herzegovina regarding the Tribunal has been predominantly shaped by the media (Hodzic 2010). Nettlefield (2010) demonstrated that of her study's participants, 88% received their information about the Tribunal from television news, and more than 70% also received it from the print media. Yet the influence of the media was not just a result of accessibility, but also trust. As one Outreach officer explained:

> People form their opinion without having the facts. When they form their opinion about the Tribunal it is formed on the basis of what they read or hear in the media. When it is the question of which person in the media, who do you trust the most, who carries the force of the news from the Tribunal? Do you trust the Tribunal, do you trust the politicians, do you trust the journalists? They trust the politicians and the media. (Tribunal Media #1)

The reliance of community members on the media was troubling when it was recognised that much of the media were biased:

> Bearing in mind the media can be quite biased and one-sided, especially when it comes to the Tribunal and the events of the past. So people in the region tend to rely on the media a lot more than looking for information themselves on the internet or finding out what really happened. So their knowledge is pretty much based on what they read in the papers or what they hear in the news. So it is very one-sided. (Tribunal Outreach #3)

This had led to some severe distortions. The coverage of the Milosevic trial in Serbia was provided as a rather telling example of biased media spin. Here the media transformed an unfamiliar adversarial system into the style of TV talk show debates for a Serb audience. Milosevic was presented as having triumphed in these debates:

> This anti-Hague sentiment is very strong because it is suggested through media. There was never really a true reporting on what Tribunal does: it always ended up in some sort of anti-Serb sentences, never providing

> context. Milosevic's trial was transmitted on a daily basis, but it was shot as if he was in a TV talk show winning all this … Nobody understood this Anglo-Saxon approach. Nobody explained. So apparently the image of Milosevic is apparently that he was the winner in these talk shows, and that the narrative that he engaged with in the trial, apparently is what is now official or unofficial truth about the war. (Former Yugoslavia NGO #3)

If these portrayals were widely accepted in Serbia and the Serb regions of Bosnia it is difficult to imagine how the Tribunal will have had much impact in moving those communities towards reconciliation or an acknowledgment of the crimes. Such portrayals when viewed by other communities (such as victims) may engender even greater dissatisfaction.

Studies of reporting in the former Yugoslavia supports the perception of participants that the media had a troubling post-conflict role. For example, a study of the Dobrovoljacka case—concerning the Bosnian army's attack on a column of Yugoslav National Army soldiers withdrawing from Sarajevo—found that reports were split along ethnic lines (Erjavec 2011). The background to the case was portrayed very differently between newspapers considered to have either a Serb or Bosnian Muslim audience (Erjavec 2011). The study demonstrated significant points of departure between the various representations of the events. Sarajevo daily newspapers presented a narrative that "leads readers to the conclusion that the attack was a legitimate defense of B&H and President Izetbegovic" (Erjavec 2011, p. 70). Serb media, however, was found to have portrayed the event as a massacre:

> [This] created a breaking point which caused the war in B&H. Such a viewpoint leads readers to conclude that the event in question was a crime and that the Bosniaks started a war in which Serbs only defended themselves. (Erjavec 2011, p. 70)

The research found that the newspapers were attempting to fashion history according to ethnic affiliations and "attempting to ideologically and politically reconstruct history" (Erjavec 2011, p. 70). Similar issues were found between Croat and Serb coverage of trials relating to Vukovar. Croatian media coverage of the Vukovar trials was observed to extol the example of Vukovar as a site of patriotic defence of the homeland, while pillorying the Serbs on trial as deserving the worst of punishments (Markovic and Subasic 2011). Croatian media referred to defendants only by their ethnic identification as Serbs and not as affiliated with the Yugoslav army (Markovic and Subasic 2011). Serbian coverage, however, portrayed the trials as evidence that the Tribunal was a politicised and anti-Serb court (Markovic and Subasic 2011).

Similar patterns were found in other studies. The coverage of Karadzic's arrest was reported differently among media outlets depending on their audience (Dzihana and Hodzic 2011). Sarajevo media portrayed Karadzic as a war criminal, while newspapers from Banja Luka (capital of the Republika Srspka) were far less likely to make that association (Dzihana and Hodzic 2011). This led the researchers to conclude that "B&H media still nurture patriotic practices in reporting on issues related to war crimes" (Dzihana and Hodzic 2011, p. 235). Another study that analysed coverage of Karadzic's arrest in Serbia found that the Serbian media were equally as reluctant to associate Karadzic with war crimes. Instead, they "invoked a nostalgia for the prospect of the creation of Greater Serbia" (Erjavec and Volcic 2009a, p. 76). Serbian newspaper coverage of the death of Milosevic was not very different: nationalism reverberated in the coverage, portraying Milosevic as "a legendary leader," (Erjavec and Volcic 2009b, p. 125) and contributing to the view that Serbia is the "victim" (Erjavec and Volcic 2009b, p. 142). Yet coverage of other high profile trials in Serbia was seen to:

> [transmit] the ideas of ethnic prejudice, xenophobia, intolerance and expansionism, which prompted the conflict, and which pose a serious risk to reconciliation efforts in the region. (Zdravkovic-Zonta 2011, p. 173)

Research found that defendants in war crimes cases were frequently presented as heroes and patriots (Zdravkovic-Zonta 2011, p. 168). The various studies found that coverage usually sought to redeem leaders and was rarely critical of them. It should be noted that these studies largely looked at Serb media coverage of trials with Serb defendants. Similar patterns of reporting were anecdotally mentioned by participants in the current research in respect to other ethnic groups. Coverage of Karadzic attempted to promote the image of a hero who had fought so that Serbs could live together (Erjavec and Volcic 2009a). Coverage of Milosevic was very similar: "Milosevic was represented primarily as a defender of the Serbian nation, a victim of The Hague Court, a mythical leader, a family member, and the embodiment of the Serbian nation" (Erjavec and Volcic 2009b, p. 143). These themes were echoed in coverage regarding Biljana Plavsic (Zikic 2011).

There was a consensus that popular media outlets in the region were predominantly biased against the work of the Tribunal. It was observed by respondents that the media did not report on cases when their audience would be considered part of the victims' community but would report when their audience was part of the alleged offenders' community. Coupled with a perceived tabloid reporting style, this was seen to contribute to hostility towards the Tribunal. The effect of this may often have been negative expectations: that the Tribunal would decide matters with bias, or would do nothing to help. This bias was frequently the manifestation of nationalist agendas, along the same lines that separated the various warring sides in the 1990s. This was a constant feature of reporting, at least in Serbia, where "every week there is at least one article about Seselj and then there is a lot of articles about Mladic, obviously favourable" (Tribunal Outreach #3). This bias was also seen in the Croatian media, who were said to only invite experts who would be critical of the Tribunal to speak on television (Tribunal Outreach #5). While fieldwork was being conducted, the Gotovina case was a prominent topic in relation to the Tribunal. In Croatia, the Gotovina defence team was considered quite astute in providing the right information to a receptive media (Tribunal Outreach #6). Coverage that was favourable to Gotovina and critical of the Tribunal was seen to have generated "a massive nationwide hysteria, largely fuelled by the media" (BWCC Defence #1).

A further troubling feature of alleged media distortion was in relation to the coverage of victims. It was seen that the media was unwilling or reluctant to cover trials where their own ethnic group had been victims. This gave space for politicians to later claim to a receptive audience that the Tribunal had done nothing for them, but had only punished them. This was a significant obstacle in the work of Outreach:

> In Belgrade they cover trials where Serbs are on trial. They don't cover the trials where Croats are on trial for the Serb victims. And therefore the politicians will come out and say this Tribunal never did anything for Serb victims. You know, their words fall on fertile ground. (Tribunal Media #1)

That obstacle was not limited to the work of Outreach in Serbia. The same problem was seen to exist in Croatia:

> The problem is also the media does not report on the cases where the Croats were victims, unless, again, there is something spectacular in that case ... But they do not follow the trials; they are not interested. Even though those guys are indicted for Croat victims as well, there are no stories about it. There are no stories about the witnesses who testified about it and that actually those trials against people who are charged with crimes that were fully or partially committed against victims in Croatia. They just don't care. All the media reporting is focused on Croatian indictees, not on Croatian victims. (Tribunal Outreach #5)

This surprising feature of the media in the former Yugoslavia was revealed in interviews. It also poses profound problems for the Tribunal in communicating its work. Such biased, victim-unresponsive reporting also serves to limit whatever contributions a tribunal might make to some of the broader expectations held about them. Expectations for answers, education, acknowledgment and reconciliation are likely to be affected. If people are not provided with information on the breadth of prosecutions and their outcomes, the perception of how well tribunals and trials have met their expectations on these issues is likely to be diminished.

Not only bias was seen as a problem: lack of interest in covering trials and a failure to report accurately were also problems:

> The media is not just biased. They are not interested in war crimes cases at all. Either the reporting is very poor or else it is scarce or, you know, when you have local war crimes trials, you will have like three lines about it, and not regularly. When the ICTY trials are concerned only the sensational issues get to the front pages. (Tribunal Outreach #5)

The media in the former Yugoslavia's quality of information about the Tribunal was considered to be rather lacklustre. This was also observed in Cambodia in one of the few interviews that raised media issues about the Chambers (Cambodia NGO #9). There had been fewer opportunities for the press in Cambodia to conduct the same sorts of distortions, given that only one trial had been completed and another just begun. Yet the accuracy of media information provided about the Duch sentence was considered quite poor, with articles more inflammatory than informative (Cambodia NGO #9).

The problems with the media in the former Yugoslavia were partly explained, according to many respondents, by the nature of the media industry in the region. One reason was that the media tended more towards tabloid than investigatory journalism: "Media reporting is very tabloid like and if anyone tried to do a proper analysis it turns out into an extremist view" (BWCC Defence #1). It was also explained that the media was shifting towards tabloid style and content:

> One of the problems is that the media in the former Yugoslavia is going through transition from basically providing information to providing sensationalism. Because everyone is interested in who shags, but not many people are interested in really what's the explanation behind the judgment from The Hague Tribunal. So if they engage in reporting on the Tribunal at all it will be huge title, 'Tribunal Demonises Serbs Again'—I am just giving an example—and then there will be two lines and a big picture of someone and that's more or less it. Analytical journalism is almost extinct in the former Yugoslavia. (Tribunal Outreach #1)

This was also linked to the editorial policy of major media outlets, where Tribunal stories and war crimes issues were not considered popular topics (Tribunal Outreach #5). Additionally, rather lax standards in the media of the former Yugoslavia were observed by several respondents (Tribunal Outreach #2; Tribunal Outreach #5; Tribunal Outreach #6; BWCC Defence #1). It was also postulated that new-found press freedoms in post-Tito Yugoslavian states were employed to a large extent by nationalists (Tribunal Media #1).

While it appeared from interviews that little could be done to change attitudes within the media, encouraging greater engagement of journalists and editors with the Tribunal had been partly beneficial. Verfuss (2004) has noted that given the financial constraints on the media in the former Yugoslavia, many media outlets have been unable to provide correspondents for significant periods at the Tribunal and on many occasions there are no journalists present from the former Yugoslavia. In addition to the cost barriers for journalists, visa regimes in The Netherlands were an obstacle to reporters covering trials first-hand (Verfuss 2004). Outreach efforts at media engagement were considered successful:

> [The Tribunal invited] this group of journalists from Serbia last year and they had a session with the prosecutor … These people left completely, you know, 'Ah but he is such a nice guy.' But of course he is a nice guy. What did you think that he was, a bloody Nazi? … I remember this one woman saying, 'Now you see, you should [have brought us to] tour, to see 10 years ago, because from this day on (she was a manager at the regional TV station) from this stage on there will be different coverage of the tribunal on my station'. (Tribunal Outreach #1)

Media visits such as the one described above were a common Outreach activity for the Tribunal. While not all visitors will be as positively influenced by the experience as others, the above passage does suggest that there is great value in encouraging and facilitating these interactions. Close cooperation between transitional justice mechanisms and the media should be a primary consideration when planning such efforts. It has previously been remarked that costs associated with the distance of proceedings from the region had hampered the media's efforts to provide coverage (Klarin 2009). For this reason, there also need to be resources for journalists to report on and work with transitional justice mechanisms first-hand. This is of increased significance for institutions like the Tribunal that are conducted some distance away in third countries.

Conclusion

In the views of many respondents, the attachment of a raft of expectations to criminal trials did not reflect the reality of what they can provide, or of their function. There was no consensus among respondents, however, about what were appropriate or inappropriate expectations. Respondents often perceived reconciliation as an inappropriate expectation, while the "truth", or a historical record, was variously considered appropriate and inappropriate depending on who was asked. It was observed in relation to the work of the Chambers that the provision of a reparations programme raised expectations about what would be provided. When these expectations were not met, it was necessary to manage the expectations and anger that civil party victims felt. Expectations that a community's victimisation will be recognised as genocide are troubling. Respondents noted that convictions that fell short of finding genocide could disappoint victim communities. Responding to this expectation may be difficult, given the weight that donors, the media, politicians, and others place on genocide in their public statements. The circumstances of many crimes during conflict may lead to profound expectations for convictions as well. As one participant observed, many local community members questioned the need for lengthy and expensive trials when evidence of crimes could be found all over Cambodia (Chambers Media #1). Two respondents saw expectations for trials free from political agendas as problematic (Cambodia NGO #3 and 4). This response appeared to be the result of personal experience from working with the Chambers. It is, however, an expectation that must be addressed.

Tribunal respondents provided a disturbing insight that local media rarely report on cases where their own community is a victim. Instead, it was noted that media in the Balkans almost exclusively reported on cases where a member of their community stood accused of war crimes. It is not difficult to conceive that media reports exhibiting this bias may severely skew perceptions of transitional justice institutions. Importantly, it may serve to reinforce a narrative of oppression and victimisation: "We continue to be persecuted by a biased court that fails to recognise that we were victims of atrocities." In many ways, this may play into constructions of recent history that reflect local folklore regarding national identity, such as the idea that "Serbs always win the war and lose the peace", a sentiment that Korac (1993) notes was used to mobilise support for nationalist agendas leading up to and during the wars in the former Yugoslavia. It is important to recognize that all stakeholders (both local and international) have expectations of transitional justice, though some stakeholders have more authority to decide which goals are appropriate and which require management (Nickson 2017, p. 197). The following chapter delves into media coverage of the Tribunal from an international perspective to provide yet another lens for examining the complex relationship between news media, expectations, and transitional justice.

References

Akhavan, P 1998, 'Justice in The Hague, peace in the former Yugoslavia? A commentary on the United Nations war crimes tribunal', *Human Rights Quarterly*, vol. 20, no. 4, pp. 737–816.

Clark, JN 2009, 'International war crimes tribunals and the challenge of outreach', *International Criminal Law Review*, vol. 9, no. 1, pp. 99–116.

Dzihana, A and Hodzic, S 2011, 'The Karadzic case: The analysis of media reporting about Radovan Karadzic's arrest and trial' in Dzihana, A and Volcic, Z (eds), *Media and national ideologies: Analysis of reporting on war crime trials in the former Yugoslavia*, Media Centar Sarajevo, Sarajevo, Bosnia and Herzegovina.

Erjavec, K 2011, 'The case of Dobrovoljacka: An analysis of the Serbian and Bosnian-Herzegovinian daily press' in Dzihana, A and Volcic, Z (eds), *Media and national ideologies: Analysis of reporting on war crime trials in the former Yugoslavia*, Media Centar Sarajevo, Sarajevo, Bosnia and Herzegovina.

Erjavec, K and Volcic, Z 2009a, 'Journalistic (re)production of history: Televized coverage of Radovan Karadzic's arrest in Serbia', *Solsko Polje*, vol. 20, no. 5/6, pp. 75–99.

Erjavec, K and Volcic, Z 2009b, 'Rehabilitating Milosevic: Posthumous coverage of the Milosevic regime in Serbian newspapers', *Social Semiotics*, vol. 19, no. 2, pp. 125–147.

Hodzic, R 2010, 'Living the legacy of mass atrocities: Victims' perspectives on war crimes trials', *Journal of International Criminal Justice*, vol. 8, no. 1, pp. 113–136.

Hussain, V 2005, 'Sustaining judicial rescues: The role of outreach and capacity-building efforts in war crimes tribunals', *Virginia Journal of International Law*, vol. 45, no. 2, pp. 547–561.

Klarin, M 2009, 'The impact of the ICTY trials on public opinion in the former Yugoslavia', *Journal of International Criminal Justice*, vol. 7, no. 1, pp. 89–96.

Korac, M 1993, 'Serbian nationalism: Nationalism of my own people', *Feminist Review*, vol. 45 (Autumn), pp. 108–112.

Markovic, P and Subasic, K 2011, 'The case of Vukovar: A comparative analysis of reports on trials for war crimes committed in Vukovar in 1991 in The Hague and Belgrade' in Dzhiana, A and Volcic, Z (eds), *Media and national ideologies: Analysis of reporting on war crime trials in the former Yugoslavia*, Media Centar Sarajevo, Sarajevo, Bosnia and Herzegovina.

Nettlefield, LJ 2010, 'From the battlefield to the barracks: The ICTY and the armed forces of Bosnia and Herzegovina', *International Journal of Transitional Justice*, vol. 4, no. 1, pp. 87–109.

Nickson, R 2017, 'Unmet expectations and the legitimacy of transitional justice institutions' in Karstedt, S and Brants, C (eds), *Engagement, contestation and legitimacy*, Hart Publishing, Portland, Oregon.

Pham, P, Vinck, P, Balthazard, M, Hean, S and Stover, E 2009, *So we will never forget: A population based survey on attitudes about social reconstruction and The Extraordinary Chambers in the Courts of Cambodia*, Human Rights Center, University of California, Berkeley, California.

Pham, PN, Vinck, P, Balthazard, M, Strasser, J and Om, C 2011. 'Victim participation and the trial of Duch at the Extraordinary Chambers in the Courts of Cambodia', *Journal of Human Rights Practice*, vol. 3, no. 3, pp. 264–287.

Sebastian, S 2010, 'Statebuilding in divided societies: The reform of dayton in Bosnia and Herzegovina', *Journal of Intervention and Statebuilding*, vol. 4, no. 3, pp. 324–344.

Stanley, E 2002, 'What next? The aftermath of organised truth telling', *Race and Class*, vol. 44, no. 1, pp. 1–15.

Verfuss, T 2004, 'Trying poor countries crimes in a rich city: The problems of the press from the former Yugoslavia', *Journal of International Criminal Justice*, vol. 2, no. 2, pp. 509–515.

Zdravkovic-Zonta, H 2011, 'The case of scorpions: Media, nationalism and war crimes', in Dzhiana, A and Volcic, Z (eds), *Media and national ideologies: Analysis of reporting on war crime trials in the former Yugoslavia*, Media Centar Sarajevo, Sarajevo, Bosnia and Herzegovina.

Zikic, B 2011, 'The Biljana Plavsic case: Nationalist and gender narratives in the service of media (non)reporting on the Plavsic case in Serbia and Bosnia and Herzegovina (The Republika Srspka)', in Dzhiana, A and Volcic, Z (eds), *Media and national ideologies: Analysis of reporting on war crime trials in the former Yugoslavia*, Media Centar Sarajevo, Sarajevo, Bosnia and Herzegovina.

5

The Media and Expectations of the Tribunal and Chambers

> Pol Pot is a criminal, a criminal against humanity. But I have to say that we have to provide a fair trial. (Mydans (1997a) quoting Prince Ranariddh)[1]

At the arrest of Milosevic, the *NY Times* quoted the Tribunal spokesman as claiming the following:

> [The Tribunal] is now closer to fulfilling the mission for which it was set up, that is, to deal with the commanders and the architects of the policies that wrought so much havoc and caused so much misery to the people of the Balkans. (Simons with Gall 2001)

These quotes, from the *NY Times*, highlight significant expectations expressed in the international media: trials are central to bringing justice to affected communities and prosecuting senior leaders are key to that mission. Much of the coverage of the Tribunal and the Chambers

[1]All *NY Times* articles were accessed via the newspaper's online archives. This allowed for the most comprehensive search of all published articles. However, page numbers were not available for articles accessed this way and so are not included here in the references.

R. Nickson and A. Neikirk, *Managing Transitional Justice*,
Palgrave Studies in Compromise after Conflict,
https://doi.org/10.1007/978-3-319-77782-5_5

in the *NY Times* reflects expectations of guilt and convictions. The implications of this coverage for expectations may be quite pronounced and likely to contribute to retributive attitudes, rather than temper them. Trials that afford due process cannot be assured of convicting defendants. The earlier chapter highlighted that participants thought local media coverage may distort expectations regarding trials and potential justice outcomes. However, local communities and local media are not the only parties that invest trials with expectations. International media coverage, such as that found in the *NY Times*, also create, reflect, and at times, distort expectations.

Although some articles displayed an awareness of the limitations of tribunals in satisfying expectations of them, such articles were uncommon and were overwhelmed by articles that were more likely to affirm, encourage, and generate expectations regarding the Tribunal and the Chambers. Expectations may be distorted by professional rules that dictate the sorts of stories that will be reported, as well as the manner of their presentation. Coverage of the trials, like the reporting of crime more broadly, mirrored several professional rules that reflected the value of events as news: immediacy; dramatization; personalisation; simplification; negativity and titillation; conventionalism; and novelty (Chibnall 1977). Unfortunately, what appears to be the most important expectation from a media perspective is the expectation of a good story.

This chapter discusses the results of a content analysis of *NY Times* articles covering the Tribunal (472 articles) and Chambers (193 articles) between 1993 and 2011. Not every expectation that appeared will be discussed in this chapter. Rather, the focus is on media expectations that feature prominently in the articles. These media expectations, though they did not remain static, reflected specific themes such as: normalizing courts as the central means to end impunity and that the identity of defendants, along with number of prosecutions, were integral to justice being served. These key expectations were particularly evident when examining the arrest and trials of Slobodan Milosevic and Pol Pot. Reporting was not always positive and at times very negative. Regardless of the compliments or criticisms, coverage seemed to affirm the importance of trials as the ideal means to achieving justice.

Covering the Tribunal and Chambers

Participants expressed severe reservations regarding the objectivity of the various local media outlets and the impact reporting had on transitional justice expectations. This was very pronounced regarding the former Yugoslavia but less a concern in Cambodia. This impression is supported by studies examining media coverage of the Tribunal in the former Yugoslavia—a significant amount of nationalism and ethnic bias exists. Media reports were often written and published through a lens of ethnic identification, while serving to reinforce nationalism and nationalist ideas. The role of the media has been seen as crucial in both the creation and representation of national/ethnic identities (Volcic and Dzihana 2011, p. 8). Volcic and Dzihana (2011) assert that political elites, seeking to maintain their hold on power through resorting to nationalism, have enlisted the media to this end.

There have been several studies focused on media in the former Yugoslavia, but there have also been studies of Western media coverage and potential bias during the conflict. In a study of photographs appearing in *Newsweek, Time*, and *US News & World Report*, Nikolaev (2009) detected a bias against Serbs and in favour of Kosovo Albanians. His study showed that Serbs were invariably shown in military uniforms, with photos always attributing civilian casualties to Serbs. At the same time, representations of Albanians showed them mostly as civilians and victims but never as perpetrators of crimes. Nikolaev (2009) concluded that the publications exhibited bias in their reporting of the war in Kosovo. Brdar and Vukovic found that Western media demonised Serbia (frequently drawing similarities between Serbs and Nazis) (Brdar and Vukovic 2006). Brdar and Vukovic (2006) argue that the purpose of such coverage was to legitimise intervention in the conflict. That many journalists sought to influence Western responses to the wars in the former Yugoslavia has been labelled as "journalism of attachment", where reporters see themselves as participants and seek to "take part in the public debate about the conflict" (Ruigrok 2005, p. 2). Ruigrok (2005) notes that as journalists sought to compel the international community to intervene they often invoked Holocaust frameworks, comparing Serbs with Nazis and ineffectual Western leaders with Neville Chamberlain. Many of the observations of Western media coverage of the Tribunal tend to suggest that coverage will be superficial: a preference for pithy quotes; a focus on stories about people, not trials; a focus on sensationalism; writing about arrests as if they were political thrillers and the guilt of the accused a foregone conclusion; and the observation that there is no audience for reports regarding functional and operations details (Simons 2009).

Negativity and drama were evident frames for discussing the establishment of the Chambers and the Tribunal's position in peace negotiations. As can be seen in Fig. 5.1, periods of negotiation for peace in the former Yugoslavia presented the court with unique obstacles. Although it may seem obvious that codes such as "complicating peace negotiations" and "subject to realpolitik" would occur between 1995 and 1999, the important point is that they appear at all. In 1995, there were 29 articles about the Tribunal. Thirteen of those articles (44.8%) raised the concern that the Tribunal might complicate peace negotiations. In 1999, there were 36 articles that discussed the Tribunal; six of these raised the concern that the Tribunal might complicate efforts at peace in Kosovo. Although, at 16.6%, this represents a lower number, it is less dramatic after considering that there was more to write about the Tribunal in 1999: a significantly higher number of trials as well as the

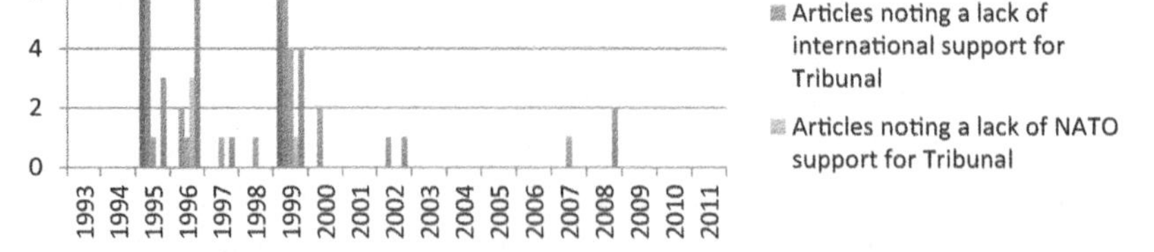

Fig. 5.1 Negative coverage of the Tribunal and peaks during periods of peace negotiations

indictment of Milosevic generated a great deal of coverage. Additionally, 10 articles in 1995 and 6 articles in 1999 discussed the impact of realpolitik on the Tribunal.

Such criticisms—that the Tribunal might complicate peace or is inferior to the more important considerations of realpolitik—may act to severely undermine courts, especially their legitimacy and integrity. They may also diminish positive expectations of the court while fuelling negative expectations and perceptions. The negative influence of the court on peace in the former Yugoslavia was trumpeted in various articles during 1995. For instance, one article made this chilling prediction:

> The price of making negotiations impossible by issuing arrest warrants for one side can be terrifyingly high. Without peace talks, the ever-deeper Western involvement can bring Europe to where it stood 81 years ago this week—at the cusp of a world war. (Rosenthal 1995)

Such claims were common regarding the Tribunal's issuance of arrest warrants for Karadzic and Mladic in 1995 (Cohen 1995a, b; Simons 1995) and again with respect to the arrest warrant for Milosevic in 1999 (Erlanger 1999).

At these times, it was also frequently reported that, for those in the former Yugoslavia working towards peace or providing aid, the issue of such arrest warrants by the Tribunal was almost inconsequential. The spokesman for the UNHCR was reported to have said that "it would be of no practical interest to him if the Bosnian Serb leaders were indicted as war criminals" (Cohen 1995b). There were also articles that pointed out that leading negotiators intended to deal with indicted war criminals despite the existence of warrants for their arrest (for example, Lewis 1995). Similarly, coverage was rife with speculation that any peace negotiations might offer amnesty to indicted leaders, or at least do nothing to guarantee their arrest or surrender (Lewis 1995; Engelberg 1995; Bonner 1999a, c; Frankel 1999; Erlanger 2000). It is possible, and indeed likely, that coverage such as this not only undermines confidence in the court but may also encourage negative expectations of the court. It is clear that this coverage reflects a perceived need for drama and negativity in media reports. The drama is heightened by the threats to the function of the Tribunal and the conflict between ending the wars and securing justice and accountability. In the process, the coverage paints a negative picture of justice at the mercy of *realpolitik*.

In a similar manner, coverage during the negotiations surrounding the establishment of the courts and trials may have served to undermine perceptions of the Chambers, of Cambodian involvement in proceedings, and driven a wedge between civil society groups and other court advocates. While negative coverage during the negotiation phase was not quantitatively high, it was expressed forcefully on multiple occasions. For instance, the head of the Cambodian Bar Association is quoted by the *NY Times* as stating: "A Khmer Rouge trial in Cambodia cannot be completely impartial, because there is too much corruption" (Mydans 1999d). Even Cambodia's political leaders were reported to have questioned Cambodia's capacity to undertake trials fairly: "The nation's leaders have acknowledged that their justice system cannot provide a fair, unpoliticised trial of Pol Pot" (Editorial 1998). In the following year, the *NY Times* provided another explanation for why Cambodia would be unable to try the leader of the Khmer Rouge: "still traumatized by his [Pol Pot's] brutal rule, [Cambodia] is too fragile and too frightened by its past to be able to consider putting him on trial" (Mydans 1998c). Far more common, however, was an observation that the Cambodian system was too flawed to be involved in trials of the Khmer Rouge. One article described how only 20 of 135 judges had college degrees (Mydans 1999d), while others provided unglamorous pictures of the Cambodian legal system: "Cambodia's legal system is primitive and riven with graft and political influence" (Mydans 1999b). Another article supported this:

> Most foreign analysts argue that the Cambodian court system is not capable of carrying out fair trials of this magnitude. The international lawyers recommended an international court because of the primitive and politically dependent nature of the Cambodian legal system. (Mydans 1999c)

Similarly negative coverage took place once trials began. Out of 49 articles in that period, 18 (36.7%) discussed politicisation of the Chambers and 12 (24.5%) discussed corruption or allegations of corruption at the

Chambers. It is important to recognise that some of this coverage may not have been presented in the media in Cambodia. One interviewee, questioning the validity of a survey of perceptions of the Chambers amongst Cambodians, suspected that results were skewed because local media persisted in providing only a rosy picture of the Chambers (Cambodia NGO #19). Coverage such as this may have an impact on the international donor community, however. Although this coverage was founded in real concerns about local capacity and the influence of corruption, it did focus on these aspects without a similar level of coverage on positive or promising aspects.

Potential problems regarding the Chambers were flagged early in *NY Times* coverage. During the period of negotiation, many concerns about the suitability and capacity of the Cambodian judicial system, the ability of any court situated within Cambodia to avoid political pressure, and various other issues were raised. In the phase that covers the trials, issues such as corruption, internal disagreement and politicisation became dominant themes. During this period, negative coverage tended to overshadow the positive aspects of the Chambers (that included the completion of one trial and the sentencing of its defendant, as well as the commencement of a second trial). Considerable negative coverage, particularly about corruption, occurs in 2009 (Mydans 2009a, b, c; Editorial 2009; Becker 2009):

> The latest revelations about alleged misconduct and corruption at the Khmer Rouge tribunal have startled even its most jaded critics. Indeed, the nature of this dirty laundry suggests that the UN-backed tribunal is so deeply flawed that its very existence needs to be reevaluated. (Editorial 2009)

In 2009, six out of 21 articles discussed problems with corruption at the Chambers. In other criticisms, it is claimed that the Chambers "stands on the brink of ignominious failure due to political interference from the Cambodian government and the indifference of the international community" (Goldston 2011). With such overwhelming negative coverage of the court at a critical juncture in its operations, it is not difficult to imagine the detrimental impact that may result in attitudes towards and perceptions of the court, let alone expectations concerning what the court should or may achieve.

What is evident is that coverage of both the Chambers and the Tribunal focused, or at least paid a great deal of attention to, negative aspects of the courts. At the Tribunal, early coverage tended to highlight problems and failures and the possibility that the court would make peace more difficult to attain. One passage from a 1995 article captures this attitude quite well:

> [T]he United Nations tribunal on the former Yugoslavia in The Hague has succeeded in bringing only one defendant to trial; a Balkan peace is still far from guaranteed, and the principal figures under indictment, the Bosnian Serb leaders Radovan Karadzic and Ratko Mladic, are apparently safe from arrest in their Balkan redoubts. (Cowell 1995)

In the following year the *NY Times* informed its readers that the Tribunal was "facing fundamental problems that could undermine its ability to bring suspects to justice" (Perlez 1996). Other articles highlighted different critiques of the court, for instance by repeating internal criticisms from Tribunal staff that many judges were unqualified to preside over trials at the Tribunal (Simons 2002). It is not difficult to see how expectations of the Tribunal and Chambers can become distorted by coverage that seeks to apply media values—such as negativity and titillation (Chibnall 1977)—that do not necessarily conform with the work of transitional justice institutions. Coverage that is framed in this way may provide a good story, but it is less likely to provide information relevant to understanding institutions that seek to provide justice for communities in transitional societies.

Crimes and Punishment

Although there may be limitless ways to raise expectations through media coverage, some features were particularly prominent. The first was an almost mantra-like chant of particular details of crimes or the quantity of crimes and victims. In this regard, details of crimes were a more regular topic in coverage of the Tribunal than they were at the Chambers. Details of crimes were provided in 58 articles about the Tribunal, or approximately one in every six articles. Much of this coverage was graphic. At the Chambers, 13 articles (6.7%) described the details of crimes of the Khmer Rouge. Additionally, the number of crimes or victims, while common for coverage of both courts, was more frequently asserted for the Chambers. While the quantum of crimes or victims was given in 72 articles (18.5%) covering the Tribunal, 109 articles (56.5%) provided figures of the number of victims or crimes to be dealt with by the Chambers. Secondly, articles often contained assertions of guilt about individuals involved in the conflicts. Finally, there were also common claims in articles that evidence had been discovered, or existed, that proved that certain crimes had taken place or that certain people were responsible. This was reported in 20 articles (10.3%) for the Chambers.

The regular mention of the number of crimes or victims, and the details of crimes, represents a subtle way in which expectations may be generated and affirmed. In particular, expectations regarding punishment and severity of sentence may be affected. Figures 5.2 and 5.3 demonstrate that for both courts, presentation of details and quantities of crimes occurred frequently.

In coverage of the Tribunal, figures relating to the number of crimes alleged to have taken place or the amount of victims usually refer to

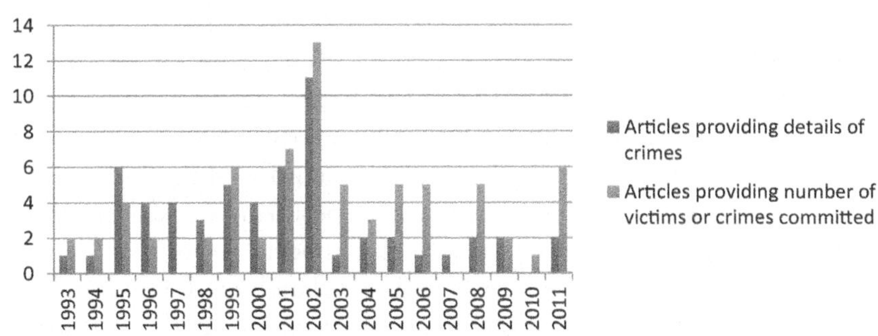

Fig. 5.2 Frequency of *NY Times* articles discussing details and number of crimes—International Criminal Tribunal for the Former Yugoslavia

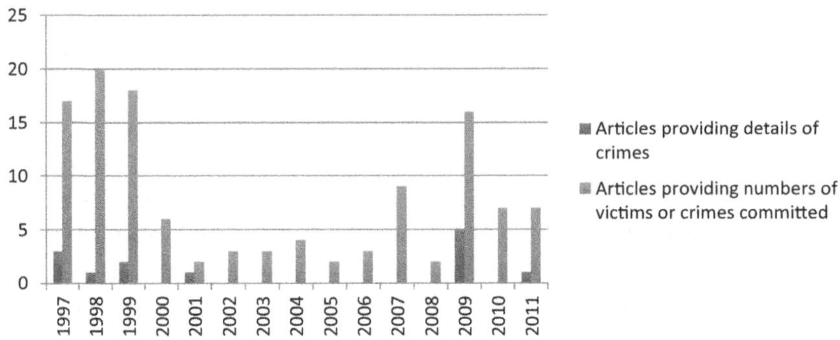

Fig. 5.3 Frequency of *NY Times* articles discussing details and number of crimes—Extraordinary Chambers in the Courts of Cambodia

the events surrounding Srebrenica. This focus is to be expected, as the massacres that followed the fall of Srebrenica were perhaps one of the most widely covered and well-documented crimes of any war. Following closely in terms of coverage are the crimes that took place in prison camps and the notorious "rape camps". What are very common in coverage of the Tribunal are the graphic details of crimes that are presented in print. This conforms to Chibnall's study that demonstrates how media coverage of crime is selected based partly on negativity and titillation: the more severe the crime or violence, the more likely it is to be reported (Chibnall 1977). When the *NY Times* provides details of crimes committed in the wars in the former Yugoslavia, it is commonly of a sexual nature. For instance, the allegation is described multiple times that Dusko Tadic, an early defendant at the tribunal, "forced one Muslim prisoner to silence Mr. Harambasic's screams by covering his mouth while another bit off one of his testicles—a mutilation that led to the prisoner's death" (Cohen 1995c). Similarly, a later article regarding the same defendant recounts the prosecutor's allegations that he forced male prisoners in Omarska Camp to perform oral sex acts on one another (Simons 1996a). Further coverage repeats Tribunal documents that "men and women [were] mutilated and slaughtered, children killed before their mother's eyes, a grandfather forced to eat the liver of his own grandson" (Sciolino 1995). Other examples of the graphic details of crimes published in the *NY Times* include an elderly man having a patriotic badge of the Muslim Party for Democratic Action nailed to his forehead (resulting in death) (Hedges 1996); the placing of a victim's head inside a bucket and then beating the bucket until the victim died (Cowell 1997); and inmates in one camp being forced to drink the blood from another inmate's slit throat (Gay 2011). Unfortunately, dramatization and titillation that deliver on the expectation of a good story commit a disservice to many other expectations. Negativity and titillation, for example, are likely to hinder efforts at reconciliation. By frequently focusing on the very worst atrocities in detail, the space for discussing positive steps forward can be restricted. Even if positive steps were covered, it is possible that negativity and titillation will be more persuasive in shaping attitudes. Titillation may also impede efforts at survivor dignity. This is a pronounced risk when the focus of pervasive media coverage repeatedly discusses victims only in the context of suffering the worst forms of victimisation. Such reports about victims rarely seek to reinvest survivors with humanity and dignity.

Coverage of the Chambers focused less on the details of crimes but relied heavily on reiterating the number of victims of the Khmer Rouge regime. Indeed, over half of all the articles concerning trials in Cambodia provide the number of victims or crimes. These numbers, expressed as either the total number of deaths or sometimes as a proportion of the entire Cambodian population, are frequently conflated. That is, direct deaths through executions and massacres are not separated from deaths caused by overwork from forced labour, malnutrition, and famine. This conflation may create misunderstandings for readers who are unfamiliar with events in Cambodia during the Khmer Rouge regime. Because many of these articles are about Comrade Duch, they may also influence perceptions that he is responsible for a broader range of crimes and victims than the victims who died at Tuol Sleng Prison where he was commandant. Associating scores of victims to individual defendants in media coverage may prove to be problematic if the audience assumes a causal connection when one does not exist. Here, media reports are seeking to simplify complex events and actors into the categories "good" and "evil". Such simple paradigms inadequately represent the context of mass atrocities. In multi-party conflicts like those in the former Yugoslavia, it may serve to entrench interpretations that do not recognise the widespread nature of offending on all sides. For institutions trying low-level defendants, it may certainly serve to encourage a belief that the individual was responsible for harming a greater number of victims than actually occurred. Of course, in trials of senior leaders, this may be less problematic, though in some cases it may also be misleading.

The effect of such coverage on expectations may be quite pronounced. The widespread nature of crimes and their heinousness may well serve to raise expectations that arrests and trials will be swift and far-reaching. It is also likely that the expectations of trials will not be limited to a few senior leaders but to those who conducted themselves with the viciousness described in the articles. The reality of criminal trials, however, as evidenced by the Tribunal and the Chambers, shows that very few perpetrators will ever be held accountable, and often not those who directly committed murder, torture or rape. This disparity is only infrequently addressed in articles in the *NY Times*—in only three articles for the Tribunal and in no articles for the Chambers. Three broad reasons are provided when this disparity is addressed. The first is perhaps the most pertinent, which is that the number of crimes that may be provable to a legal standard may fall well below the actual number of crimes that were committed. Second, a few articles address the limited capacity of the courts and their subsequent incapacity to manage anything more than a limited number of trials (O'Connor 1996; Wren 1999). Related to this is the restricted jurisdiction of the courts and a resultant inability to address what may be quite terrible crimes that occur outside the ambit of the court. Lastly, in at least one article, the disparity between the estimated number of victims of mass killings and what is shown to be the verifiable number of victims for these alleged crimes is discussed (Erlanger and Wren 1999). The fact that only three articles across coverage for both courts (nearly 700 articles in total) addressed this disparity should be cause for alarm. The media is an influential source of information regarding transitional justice institutions. Consequently, it is likely that many will be uninformed as to why this disparity occurs. If the media are unlikely to address this problem—and this research suggests that they are—then it will be up to others to convey this information. Finally, reiterating the number and details of crimes within a retributive framework can serve to reinforce the primacy of legal responses and retributive justice, above other responses or forms of justice, in transitional justice efforts. This may be counterproductive in satisfying many expectations.

A similar issue is a presumption of guilt in *NY Times* articles. In coverage of the Tribunal, the guilt of particular individuals is readily assumed. By way of example, one article titled 'The Monster in the Dock' describes Slobodan Milosevic as "the author of three horrible wars of ethnic cleansing in the heart of Europe, and now a sulky, self-pitying defendant" (Keller 2002). Often, in a manner that no doubt adds weight to the claim, assertions of guilt are made by other high-profile public figures, who are then quoted corresponding to Chibnall's (1977) conclusion that news articles frequently utilise quotes from authorities to provide 'structured access'. Richard Holbrooke, a figure familiar to many who were aware of the US peace brokering that led to the Dayton agreement, was quoted as saying at the arrest of Radovan Karadzic in 2008:

> Of the three most evil men of the Balkans, Milosevic, Karadzic and Mladic, I thought Karadzic was the worst. The reason was that Karadzic was a real racist believer. Karadzic really enjoyed ordering the killing of Muslims, whereas Milosevic was an opportunist. (Bilefsky and Simons 2008)

The implicit assertion of the guilt of indictees in such a statement is not difficult to observe. Not only is the assertion of guilt implicit, it is attributed to a leading authority and participant of the diplomatic resolution to the Balkan wars and expressed in a way that casts the subjects as demonstrably evil. This is by no means a singular event in the media coverage, which is littered with references to the evident guilt of high-profile individuals, often in very provocative terms. For instance, Senator Biden (later Vice-President Biden) stated that Milosevic is "… one of the most dangerous and maniacal European leaders since Hitler" (Simons with Gall 2001). Comparisons and analogies with Nazis and Nazi Germany are not uncommon in the coverage, and there can be little dispute that this represents a very powerful image.

Similar coverage occurred in relation to the Chambers, particularly in respect to Pol Pot, whose guilt was freely asserted in almost every article that discussed him. In various articles, Pol Pot is asserted to be: a criminal (Mydans 1997a); a mass murderer (Opinion 1997); a demon (Mydans 1997b); a mass killer (Mydans 1997c); someone who oversaw a murderous rule (Opinion 1998); someone who turned Cambodia into a slaughterhouse (Mydans 1998d); and "one of the most horrible monsters ever created by humanity" (Shenon 1998a, quoting King Norodom Sihanouk). In addition, in no fewer than eight articles appearing in 1997 and 1998 Pol Pot is declared to be "responsible" for the deaths of a million or more Cambodians (Mydans 1997b, c; 1998a, b, e; Becker 1997; Shenon and Schmitt 1998; Shenon 1998a). In at least four further articles it is claimed that Pol Pot "caused" the deaths or "committed" the murder of more than a million people (Mydans 1998d, e, f; McFadden 1998; Editorial 1998). In addition to these statements made by the authors of the various articles, there are statements made about Pol Pot's guilt by influential Cambodian figures, such as Prince Ranariddh (Mydans 1997a) and King Norodom Sihanouk (Shenon 1998a). The articles in which these statements appear represent the greater proportion of coverage that dealt with Pol Pot throughout the period of study. The discussion here does not seek to dispute Pol Pot's responsibility for the crimes of the Khmer Rouge regime. Rather, it highlights a concern that assertions of guilt in the media are not treated with the circumspection accorded Western domestic defendants and may not be confirmed at trial. This would likely exacerbate problems regarding expectations, especially of prosecutions and convictions.

To further compound the assertions of guilt that arise in connection with individuals, coverage often refers to the Tribunal and Chambers as trying those who are responsible for crimes. Indicative of this theme is an article regarding positive steps in the negotiations to establish the Chambers: "to set up a special court to try those most responsible for mass killing" ('Deal Reached on Trials for Khmer Rouge' 2003). Not those *alleged* to be so. Similarly, courts are referred to as "trying war criminals". Implicit in both ways of representing the work of courts is an assumption that those being tried *are* responsible and *are* war criminals.

Big Fish, Small Fry

From an international media perspective, Marlise Simons of the *New York Times* has observed several problems in covering international criminal trials in The Hague. Simons states that while interest in arrests are high, that interest quickly wanes (Simons 2009). The coverage of the Tribunal and Chambers was event-driven and generally increased when there was a high-profile arrest or death, a verdict, or during the initial discussions of establishing courts. Unfortunately, this often meant that trials were not consistently followed. For example, a preference for drama meant that arrests were often given greater coverage than convictions. The case of Croatian General Ante Gotovina is telling. The first verdict against Gotovina occurred in the same year but received less attention than the arrest of Mladic. Twelve articles appeared for the year of Mladic's arrest (2011). In that year 10 articles focused on the arrest of Mladic, with the arrest mentioned in one other. Mladic's arrest was obviously considered more newsworthy than the conviction of Gotovina (noting that the acquittal of Gotovina fell outside the temporal scope of this content analysis). Also, in terms of overall coverage, more articles (58) appear about the Tribunal in the year of Milosevic's arrest than any other. In observations regarding the Chambers, coverage in the year of Duch's arrest (21 articles) is more than double the coverage in the year Duch was convicted (10 articles).

There is often a heightened sense of drama, action and even political intrigue involved with arrests of indictees. Images of NATO arrest operations and shootouts, as well as standoffs—such as the one that ended with Milosevic's arrest—are exciting fare for news publications. In contrast, courts lack equivalent drama. As a result, coverage of court proceedings tends to focus on the more dramatic aspects or moments of trials, which does not always reflect well upon the court. At the beginning of the trial of Comrade Duch at the Chambers, one article painted the proceedings as near farcical, focusing primarily on the behaviour of defence counsel who, it is said, "erupted at the judges" ('Lawyer Scolds Cambodia Tribunal Judges' 2008). Otherwise, coverage tends to focus on graphic aspects of testimony and the detail of crimes.

There is another reason that coverage of arrests may be favoured over coverage of convictions. It is that the arrest of an accused is likely to upset only one side (if it upsets anyone), whereas a verdict or sentence may potentially upset all sides. There are numerous occasions in the coverage of both courts that demonstrate this point. Dissatisfaction with the Tribunal's first sentence for genocide tainted what was otherwise a momentous occasion:

> Some lawyers and human rights workers who follow the court said they were shocked at what they called a short sentence. 'So genocide is worth only one extra year … I'm appalled'. (Simons 2001a, Quoting Avrid McDonald, a lawyer at the Asser Institute for International Law in The Hague, who compared the Krstic sentence (46 years) to the Blaskic sentence (45 years)).

Likewise, the sentence of Biljana Plavsic was not well-received and appeared to disappoint the expectations of victims and human rights groups who labelled it lenient (Simons 2003). Such sentiments were echoed after the first sentence against Comrade Duch was announced. The *NY Times* quoted two significant victim-witnesses (Chum Mey and Bou Meng who have the status of minor celebrities for surviving the notorious Tuol Sleng prison complex and subsequently testifying) who both expressed outrage at the perceived brevity of the sentence (Mydans 2010). It is also open to speculation that the psychological impact of arrest and capture is more pronounced than the denunciation that follows the end of international judicial proceedings.

That arrests receive high levels of coverage may mean a variety of things for international criminal tribunals. Arrests will provide important opportunities for communicating the work of courts and emphasising their role in post-conflict societies. In this way, they can be important platforms for greater moves towards satisfying important expectations of courts. They also represent, however, expectation pitfalls for courts, especially when arrests are not conducted. The experience of the Tribunal and the impunity of indictees in the face of international authorities demonstrates this: following the Daytona Peace Accords but before the arrest of Milosevic, eight out of 51 articles discussed NATO's inability to arrest indictees (over 15% of all articles for the period). The discussion of impunity in the same period was slightly higher, with nine articles. This was an important phase during transitional justice when it was necessary to consolidate the negotiated peace achieved at Dayton. Negative coverage in this period, particularly about the incapacity to secure defendants, may have had a telling impact on perceptions of the Tribunal in the former Yugoslavia. It is similarly problematic when subsequent proceedings fail to fulfil the expectations that the arrests generated or encouraged.

The need to personalise and simplify stories in media reports was often expressed through a focus on high-profile accused. Similarly, the need to simplify stories into good and evil paradigms meant that high-profile accused were largely portrayed as guilty. The relationship between media reporting and expectations is particularly evident when discussing "big fish". This term refers to those identified as senior leaders (politically or militarily) and perhaps high-profile individuals who may not have held a senior rank but are widely considered more responsible than others for crimes. "Small fry" should be taken to refer to rank and file soldiers, who are usually those that directly carried out crimes. In respect to the Tribunal, not only did coverage focus on individual accused, but it frequently criticised the Tribunal for prosecutions of lower-level defendants, or small fry. This further served to emphasise the importance of big fish in media coverage.

Figure 5.4 displays the coverage of both criticisms of the Tribunal for dealing with small fry, alongside positive coverage of the court for trying the big fish of the wars in the Balkans. In coverage of the Tribunal, 12 articles appear that are critical of the Tribunal for dealing with small fry. All these articles appear between 1993 and 1999: the criticism is absent from 2000 onwards. Fourteen articles discussing a focus on big fish appear, with all but three of those articles published after 1999. Thirty-six articles (9.3%) dealt with this issue, indicating that it was a matter of significance. The pattern in this graph displays a clear shift, beginning in 1999 from criticism of the Tribunal for dealing with small fry before this point, to positive commentary of the Tribunal for dealing with big fish after this point. In this respect, the pattern is similar

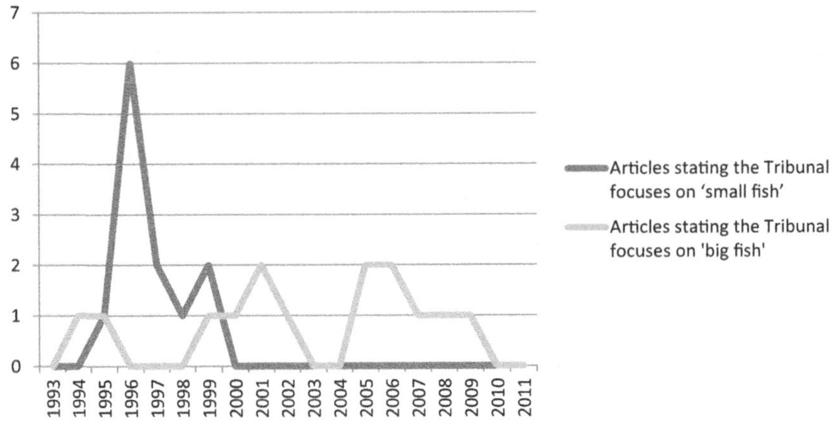

Fig. 5.4 Critical and favourable coverage of the Tribunal's work in prosecuting high-profile war criminals

to the one observed in Figure 5.8 that displayed results relating to the coverage of impunity. As with the coverage of impunity (discussed later in this chapter), it is clear that early negative coverage later shifted to exclusively positive coverage. No negative coverage on this issue appears from 2000 onwards. Although the overall numbers are relatively small, the pattern is distinct. This issue was not dealt with in a comparable way in coverage of the Chambers. It was clear from the negotiations to establish the Chambers that only high-level leaders would be prosecuted. Because of this, no lower-level accused have been tried at the Chambers and so no articles are critical of prosecutions of small fry. Although nine articles about the Chambers refer to prosecutions as of the big fish, these are dealt with in a different and more factual manner than the articles that either criticise or praise the Tribunal.

Expectations that the Tribunal would try the most senior leaders were repeatedly encouraged. Not only does the full title of the court affirm this expectation (*The International Tribunal for the Prosecution of Persons Responsible for Serious Violations of International Humanitarian Law Committed in the Territory of the Former Yugoslavia since 1991*), but coverage by the *NY Times* may have a similar effect. An article stated that the Tribunal was created to "prosecute people at the highest level"

(Cohen 2001). In earlier coverage the Prosecutor, we are told, has claimed that all future indictments would be of senior officials ('U.N. Prosecutor Plans Bigger Push in Balkans' 1999). Indeed, in some of the earliest coverage of the operations of the Tribunal, it is claimed that trials of small fry will be conducted to lay the foundations for cases against the bigger fish (Lewis 1995). However, these lower-level indictments and trials left the Tribunal open to a great deal of negative, and often scathing, criticism early in its life. This also led to a media perception that the court was not meeting the expectations that had been held of it. At the trial of Dusko Tadic (a small fry), the following was pointed out:

> His appearance thus reflects coincidence—a fortuitous arrest—rather than any contention that Mr Tadic bears preeminent responsibility for the Serbian military campaign that ousted about 700,000 Bosnian Muslims from their homes in 1992. (Cohen 1995c)

Over a year later, readers are reminded that "Mr. Tadic is but a small fry in a war where others bear greater responsibility" (Simons 1996b). Yet these rather mild observations about the seniority of the Tribunal's first defendant to face trial pale in comparison to the critique that would follow:

> At Nuremberg, famous men, personifications of their century's evil who had sent forth their legions to murder millions of civilians, were in the dock. Now it is a Bosnian Serb café owner who says somebody else did the killing and torturing of Croat and Muslim prisoners with which he is charged. Hermann Goring never pleaded mistaken identity ... Laws improvised by victors to bring down leaders of losing armies and nations are being directed at a man who at worst is a garden-variety thug and sadist. All the costumes and the ceremonies are dignifying someone who would look more at home in police court. (Goodman 1996)

In coverage of other courts and transitional justice endeavours, the prosecution of small fry by the Tribunal is sometimes reported as a mistake that other tribunals wish to avoid (Parker 2004). The importance of big

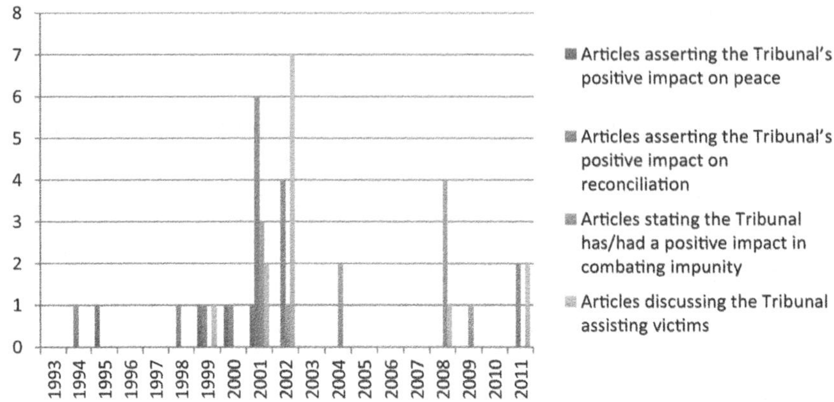

Fig. 5.5 *NY Times* and statements of the positive contributions made by the Tribunal

fish is not limited to expectations that they will be held to account. It appears from the coverage of the Tribunal that shifts to arresting and trying the big fish of the Balkan wars had the greatest impact in promoting the legitimacy of the Tribunal within the coverage itself. At the same time, arrests and trials of the big fish appear to have the effect of raising more positive media expectations in general, and are considered the best opportunities to meet those expectations.

As is clear from Fig. 5.5, it is in the years that correspond to Milosevic, Karadzic and Mladic events that significant increases in the various positive codes appear. By way of example, the increase in media expectations that victims will be assisted by Tribunal proceedings is higher for the year of Milosevic's arrest (two in 2001) and his trial (seven in 2002). A similar increase may be observed in the same year for the assertion and expectation that trials will assist in reconciliation between the people and states of the former Yugoslavia. The historical and legal significance of the Tribunal is noted most frequently during the trial of Milosevic at 21 and 12 articles respectively. Similarly, more than a quarter of all articles that regard the Tribunal as having made progress appear in the Milosevic trial phase: 20 appearances out of a total of 73. A quarter of all positive impunity articles (asserting that the Tribunal is combating impunity) appear in this phase, as do over 45% of all articles asserting that the Tribunal will make positive contributions to the historical record of the wars in the former Yugoslavia. Finally, almost one quarter of all articles asserting that the Tribunal is bringing people to justice occur in this phase. That is only outnumbered by four more articles in the years after the trial of Milosevic, when three other high-profile defendants were "brought to justice": Radovan Karadzic, Ratko Mladic, and Goran Hadzic. This is of course a double-edged sword, as the higher that expectations are raised, the more difficult it may be to bridge the expectation gap and therefore easier to disappoint those expectations.

Upon closer examination, the correlation between big fish and certain expectations of the court becomes more abundant. For instance, following the arrest of Milosevic, it is claimed that "[t]he trial could help calm the desire for revenge on the part of Mr. Milosevic's victims, which would further the cause of Balkan reconciliation" (Editorial 2001). It is also stated that "the transfer of Mr. Milosevic is a crucial and necessary step towards the reconciliation of Serbia with the rest of the world, let alone with the rest of the region" (Erlanger 2001). Further, it is claimed that "Mr. Milosevic's trial would go a long way toward healing the divisions in Serbia, as well as rehabilitating the name of Serbs in the eyes of the world" (Fisher 2001). Such connection between big fish and expectations of the courts' role in reconciliation are evident at other arrests as well. The arrest of Ratko Mladic is feted as providing "an unprecedented opportunity for reconciliation among the fractious countries of the Balkans" (Castle 2011). One author in the *NY Times* voiced their expectation in this way: "We hope the arrest will also facilitate reconciliation among Bosnia's ethnic factions" (Editorial 2011). Noticeably, the expectation that courts can assist victims finds greater voice at the arrests of bigger fish, particularly Milosevic (Crosette 2001), Karadzic (Bilefsky and Simons 2008), and Mladic (Castle 2011).

The attachment of so many expectations to a few individuals is not necessarily desirable. As became clear during the trial of Milosevic, the initial high expectations that the promise of his trial generated were often—if not completely—disappointed by the conduct of the proceedings and the whimper with which they concluded. In Fig. 5.6 we can see that many articles during the trial of Milosevic focused on

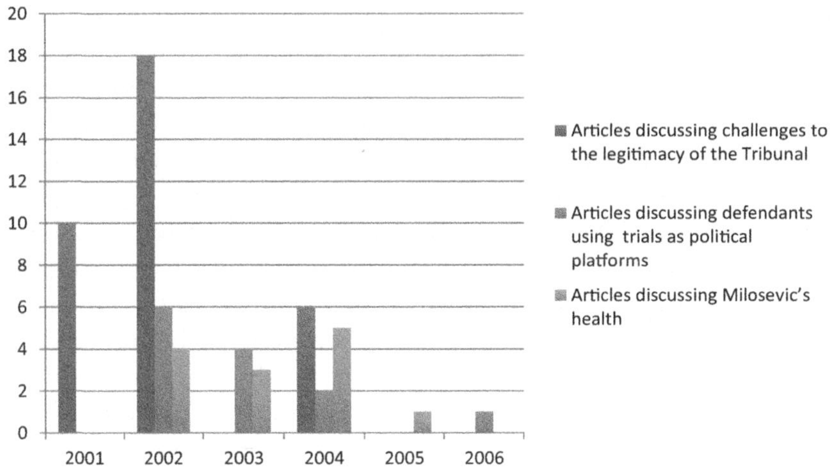

Fig. 5.6 Dominant negative themes in *NY Times* coverage during the Milosevic trial

negative features and events. For example, out of 131 articles published during this period, 11 were critical of the length of proceedings and 13 discussed the use of the trial as a political platform by Milosevic. The media portrayal of the Milosevic trial presented it more as a farcical drama than significant legal proceedings. Particular attention was given throughout to the many ways in which Milosevic challenged the legitimacy of the court. With 24 articles having discussed Milosevic's challenges to the legitimacy of the Tribunal, this was by far the highest count for any issue during this phase (excluding references to the number and details of crimes). Frequent commentary also focused on the state of Milosevic's health (13 articles or one in every 10 during this period). Although arguably an important aspect surrounding the trials, it may not have warranted the prominence over other aspects of the proceedings that it frequently received. The poor perception of the Milosevic trial is perhaps best expressed in the following passage regarding then chief prosecutor Del Ponte's courtroom behaviour:

> The posture of his [Milosevic's] opponent is also telling. Mrs. Del Ponte reacts visibly when her most famous suspect has the floor, sometimes rolling her eyes, at times leaning back in her chair, showing contempt with

> her laughter. Her reactions have drawn comments from some conservative European lawyers, not used to courtroom antics who have called her gestures inappropriate for this tribunal. (Simons 2001b)

It is not difficult to imagine how this might impact upon expectations of the Tribunal's sobriety and value. This represents a considerable fall from the high expectations expressed at the commencement of the Milosevic trial: "[Milosevic's] trial is a triumph of the civilized world, which has created a court capable of condemning the most heinous crimes with appropriate gravity and fairness" (Opinion 2002). The same article that lauds the prosecution of Milosevic as a crowning achievement of civilisation goes on to claim that the Tribunal will be judged largely on its performance in trying Milosevic (Opinion 2002)—given later developments, one can only hope that this was not so.

Another complication of expectations resting predominantly with the arrest and trial of specific individuals is that those individuals may never be available for trial, or that the trials might never conclude. When this has occurred at both the Chambers and the Tribunal, it has widely been expressed as a lost opportunity, an injustice, and a lack of accountability. Following the death of Pol Pot in 1998, Youk Chhang (the director of the Documentation Center for Cambodia) is quoted as saying "We are sad because we have lost a criminal we cannot punish" (Mydans 1998d). A similar statement is attributed to Dith Pran, the survivor of the Khmer Rouge regime whose story became the basis for the Oscar-winning film *The Killing Fields* (McFadden 1998). A third article in the days following the news of Pol Pot's death calls the lack of a trial for Pol Pot "a tragedy" (Shenon 1998b). However, perhaps the most profound expression of a lost opportunity in any of the coverage is a statement made by Diane Orentlicher in the *NY Times*:

> But by not having a trial and not punishing Pol Pot and the Khmer Rouge over the past two decades we have, in effect, told the Cambodians that what happened wasn't a crime … If there was no punishment, there was no crime. (Becker 1998)

In the same manner, the death of Milosevic was rued as a lost opportunity: "a successful prosecution of Mr. Milosevic would have gone a long way toward enhancing the authority of international tribunals" (Editorial 2006a). Of course, such lamentations were not reserved exclusively for Pol Pot and Milosevic; they also found expression after the death of figures such as Ta Mok ('Ta Mok, Khmer Rouge Head Facing Genocide Trial, Dies' 2006). Considering the age, health and the potential length of trials, further "lost opportunities" may arise in future trials at other courts charged with transitional justice. Indeed, one defendant passed away and another was deemed unfit to stand trial (before also dying), halving the number of defendants in Case 002 at the Chambers before a conclusion to the trial was reached. Similarly, in 1999 the death of Pol Pot is treated as a lost opportunity, much in the same way that the death of Slobodan Milosevic would also be treated some years later. What appears to follow is diminished enthusiasm after the death of such a significant figure.

The importance that media attach to big fish is not necessarily in the interests of transitional justice. It was evident in coverage following the death of Milosevic and Pol Pot that their passing was considered a "lost opportunity" that no other trial could replace. Considering that in many instances it will not be possible to try (or convict) the big fish, it may be damaging to transitional justice if such endeavours are seen as the key activity of transitional justice. Transitional justice must find ways to employ mechanisms that do not require the trial and punishment of big fish and recognise these as making equally valuable contributions. Even for issues such as impunity, there may be alternative mechanisms that will address such expectations. This will be difficult when the officially sanctioned efforts at transitional justice are restricted to trials.

The Scope of Justice

In the rhetoric that surrounds international criminal trials, the claim to be "ending impunity" is voiced frequently. This idea is reflected in the coverage of both courts. Impunity in this context relates to expectations for prosecution, punishment, and sentencing. These expectations may appear in the coverage as either disappointed or affirmed and satisfied by the work of courts. In coverage of the Tribunal, 35 articles discuss impunity. Of those, 11 discuss impunity positively (i.e. the Tribunal is having a positive impact on reducing impunity), while 24 articles discuss impunity negatively (i.e. the Tribunal is having no impact in reducing impunity). This represents almost 9% of all the articles written about the Tribunal—more than two-thirds of that nine per cent is negative. Regarding the Chambers, 30 articles discussed impunity: eight were positive and 22 negative. In total, that equated to more than 15% of all the articles regarding the Chambers—with nearly three times as many negative as positive discussions.

As can be seen from Figs. 5.1 and 5.2 negative coverage of impunity for both courts is much higher in early years than positive coverage of the courts' impact in ending impunity. During these periods, coverage of this issue often highlights the egregious flouting of impunity, particularly when this occurs in front of relevant authorities. One telling example illustrates this:

> Dario Kordic, a Bosnian Croat political leader who has been indicted as a mass murderer by the war crimes tribunal in The Hague, had breakfast this morning at a hotel coffee shop 12 feet away from a table full of European police officers sent to Bosnia to help re-establish the justice system. (O'Connor 1995)

This was by no means the only example of such impunity in the former Yugoslavia covered by the *NY Times*. In the same vein, outrage was expressed when the impunity of Khmer Rouge leaders was on display. On 1 January, 1999, the *NY Times* described how Khieu Samphan and Nuon Chea holidayed at the beach: "Liberated at last from a life of revolution, two Khmer Rouge leaders came to the beach today with their families, their leisure wear and their sunglasses" (Mydans 1999a). The image of aging Khmer Rouge leaders enjoying holiday sunshine is provocatively juxtaposed with the underlying menace of Khmer Rouge crimes and the apparent unlikeliness that they will face any judicial reckoning for those crimes.

Of course, one argument is that early coverage is unlikely to be positive about impunity because no-one has been tried yet. Most discussion, however, centres around the lack of arrests and efforts to hold people accountable. These are matters that can be addressed early in transitional justice. What coverage such as this may do is to reinforce negative expectations regarding the work of transitional justice institutions. For those who are disillusioned or suspicious of local and international efforts—victims of ethnic cleansing in UN-protected safe havens for instance—coverage like this may affirm expectations that nothing will be done for them, or that transitional justice is a high concept with no real impact on or benefits to them.

It may serve practical ends, however. Negative coverage of impunity during the first years of operation at the Tribunal appears to have highlighted the various flaws of the court. Most obviously, it highlighted issues regarding the Tribunal's perceived impotence, as well as the lack of support the Tribunal was receiving from local authorities, the international community, and NATO. For example, from 1993 to 1999, no less than 22 articles raised the impotence of the Tribunal, primarily its inability to effect arrests. During the same period, 15 articles raised NATO's unwillingness to arrest indictees on behalf of the Tribunal. Coverage of impunity, and non-cooperation by states of the former Yugoslavia, can also be seen as part of a campaign for enhanced accountability. Tribunal prosecutors were sometimes able to harness these messages in efforts to shame uncooperative states and organisations into engaging more collaboratively with the Tribunal. In one example, Louise Arbour, Tribunal Prosecutor, appeared at the border of Serbia and Macedonia with a crime scene investigation team and a bevy of media to record the refusal of access to mass graves by Serbian authorities. This image was then broadcast globally. It is possible, then, to see how negative coverage regarding impunity can work to the advantage of transitional justice institutions, particularly in their formative years. Similarly, the shift from negative to positive coverage of the Tribunal and Chambers' impact on impunity demonstrates that these institutions were able to make positive contributions to satisfying an important expectation (at least from the perspective of the *NY Times*).

Coverage shows that transitional justice institutions can be seen to positively address expectations of prosecution. This is evidenced in the shift of coverage on impunity for the Tribunal and Chambers. Figures 5.7 and 5.8 demonstrate a clear shift toward positive coverage of impunity, and the idea that the court has had an impact in ending impunity through its proceedings. The issue of impunity does not simply become silenced or irrelevant, but rather assertions of a lack of influence on impunity are replaced by assertions of a positive influence. With coverage of the Tribunal, this shift occurs in 2001. The shift in favour of positive coverage of impunity at the Tribunal may be

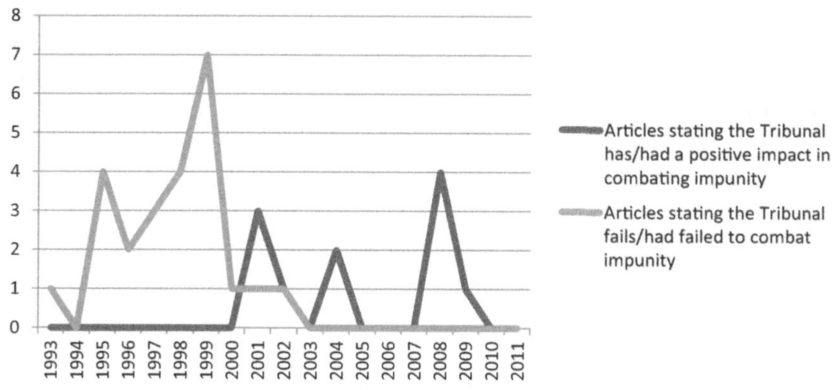

Fig. 5.7 *NY Times* coverage of the Tribunal's impact on impunity

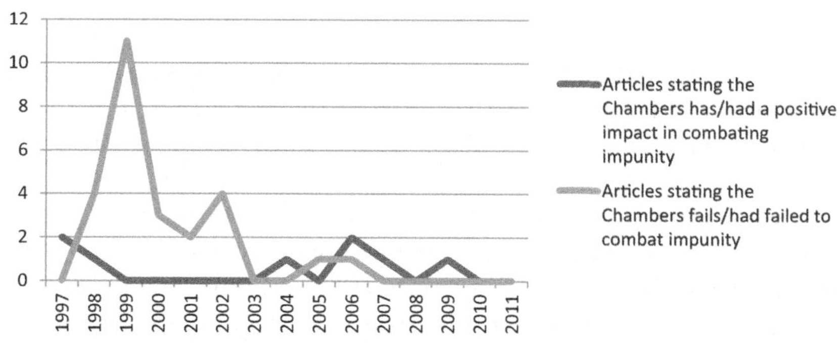

Fig. 5.8 *NY Times* coverage of the Chambers' impact on impunity

attributed to both a higher number of arrests and trials taking place, as well as the arrests of higher-profile accused than the court had previously achieved. It appears, however, that most of this shift is a result of the arrest of high-profile accused and in particular the arrest of one prominent accused: the swing occurs the year that Slobodan Milosevic is arrested.

A closer analysis of the coverage of high-profile arrests and trials supports the conclusion that it is the arrest and trial of high-profile accused—rather than an increased volume of arrests or trials in general—that was responsible for the shift in coverage of impunity at the Tribunal. As can be seen in Fig. 5.7, the highest coverage of positive impunity occurs for the years when Milosevic (2001 with three articles) and Karadzic (2008 with four articles) are arrested. The specific coverage of these events is also telling. At the trial of Milosevic, the following was reported:

> Lawyers, human rights workers and victims of the Yugoslav wars arrived here today on the eve of Slobodan Milosevic's trial, hailing a new era of accountability for war crimes despite anger about other suspects who are still free. (Fisher and Simons 2002)

Similar gravity was attached to the arrest of Ratko Mladic in 2011. The Dutch prime minister stated after the arrest that it "sends a strong message that leaders directly responsible for crimes against humanity will eventually have to account for their deeds" (Castle 2011). It was also stated at the same time that:

> The arrest should be a warning to other butchers that they, too, will be caught and held to account, no matter how long it takes. It is also a reminder that sustained international pressure works. (Editorial 2011)

What these quotations demonstrate—and they are indicative of the coverage surrounding the arrest and trial of high-profile indictees—is that the importance of such trials for combating impunity is considered to be significant. Of course, we might expect that because the impunity of high-profile figures is so glaring, that considerable coverage of an end to that impunity would follow. Yet such reasoning further reinforces the importance of high-profile figures in the coverage of impunity.

In regard to the Chambers, negative coverage of impunity is prevalent early on. As Fig. 5.8 demonstrates, there is initial positive coverage in 1997, when hopes are high after the Cambodian government's request to the UN for help in establishing trials. Although only two articles from 1997 discuss impunity in a positive light, this is equivalent to one quarter of all the positive treatment of impunity throughout the coverage of Chambers in this study. This is quickly overshadowed by the spectre of impunity in the five following years. Negative coverage peaks with 11 articles in 1999 (equivalent to half of all negative coverage), after four articles in 1998, followed by three in 2000, two in 2001 and four in 2002. It is not until after the Chambers is established that the coverage of impunity swings, albeit very slightly, towards favourable coverage of impunity. The counts for impunity coverage of the Chambers do not obviously reflect the same importance attached to high-profile figures as was apparent in coverage of the Tribunal. Rather, coverage reflects in some ways the negotiation for establishing the Chambers: positive coverage when it appears trials will take place; and negative coverage when trials seem unlikely. It is important to note that coverage of impunity in Cambodia almost exclusively relates to particular high-profile identities. The relationship between concepts of impunity and high profile figures is evident in a cursory reading of many of the articles. By way of example, the connection is drawn in relation to a possible trial of Pol Pot:

> [I]f Pol Pot, 69 and reportedly ill, was indeed put on trial, the proceedings would emphasize the long reach of justice, across the 18 years in which he has lurked in the jungles pursuing his war. (Mydans 1997a)

The "long reach of justice" is a phrase that appears frequently in the articles in this study and in support of various expectations. Although this passage deals more overtly with accountability, there are powerful implications for impunity entwined with it. Implicit is the idea that so many years of escaping justice are coming to an end and that this bodes ill for any other war criminal enjoying quiet retirement—resulting in a considerable blow to impunity. Indeed, in one article about the Tribunal, the noted international jurist Theodor Meron is quoted as saying that "without this tribunal, what would have followed is impunity" (Simons 2004).

The coverage of impunity connects with expectations concerning the scope of justice. It articulates an expectation that swift action will be taken in addressing impunity and thereby in conducting prosecutions (and probably securing convictions). Unfortunately, this may not correspond particularly well with the realities of courts and prosecutions. The swiftness that early statements regarding impunity appear to demand may be impossible shortly after the establishment of a court. Ad hoc or hybrid tribunals must address practical issues of staffing and resources first and even determine what criminal code will be applied. Then it becomes necessary to begin investigations and locate suitable detention facilities before any arrests can be made and prosecutions begin. In this manner, coverage of the kind observed in the *NY Times* may contribute to unrealistic expectations: of swifter and farther reaching responses than courts and tribunals can possibly satisfy.

Closely related to expectations regarding impunity is an expectation of the deterrent effect of international criminal trials. Often the extent to which either institution can perform deterrence is overstated. In respect to the Chambers, for instance, it is stated that a trial of Pol Pot "before an international tribunal would … give pause to any fanatic tempted to follow his example" (Opinion 1998). Similarly, the Chambers' Cambodian coordinator goes on the record with the *NY Times* as claiming that one of three goals of the trials of former Khmer Rouge leaders is "to prevent similar atrocities in the future" (Mydans 2006). And as if to highlight the link between the twin expectations of deterrence and ending impunity it is suggested that the "expense [of the Chambers] will be justified if it can … demonstrate to the world that justice, however delayed, awaits those in power who commit heinous crimes against humanity" (Editorial 2006b). These statements appear to be aimed at some form of future global deterrence, rather than any immediate local deterrence of the commission of mass atrocities. This may be contextual rather than intentional: here the conflict has ended and the likelihood of new local atrocities is low.

Ideas of global deterrence are asserted in coverage of the Tribunal as well. For instance, the *NY Times* claims that "[o]ne function of the Tribunal is to serve notice on all mass murderers that they will not escape justice, even if their own people are unable or unwilling to serve it" (Editorial 2004). It is also stated that the Tribunal prosecutors "don't want to create a historical record as much as they want to jail the criminals and deter others from committing similar crimes" (O'Connor 1996). The role of high-profile arrests is invoked to affirm the deterrent effect of the Tribunal. The arrest of Slobodan Milosevic was portrayed as an historic moment: "[I]t will begin to force would-be tyrants to think twice before replicating Milosevic's strategies" (O'Connor 1996, quoting Kenneth Roth, then Executive Director of Human Rights Watch). In much the same way, Ratko Mladic's arrest was deemed a deterrent (Editorial 2011). These are very strong statements in support of the deterrent effect of the Tribunal, yet such expectations of deterrence are not limited to future wars and future war criminals.

Coverage of the Tribunal also claims that the court should have, could have and (in at least one article) did have a local and immediate deterrent effect on potential war criminals. In several articles in 1999, it is made clear that an expected role of the Tribunal was to deter ongoing offences during the war in Kosovo. Early in 1999, James Hooper, the director of the Balkan Action Council and a former US diplomat, is quoted as saying: "If the Tribunal had been aggressive in carrying out its responsibilities in Kosovo, it might have deterred the genocide that is now unfolding there" (Bonner 1999b). The same article claims that the Clinton administration wanted Louise Arbour, Tribunal Chief Prosecutor, to act quickly and issue public indictments in an effort to deter possible crimes in an ongoing conflict (Bonner 1999b). Two months later, the *NY Times* discusses Arbour's strategy of arresting indictees from the war in Bosnia as "a deterrent to Serb troops' committing atrocities in neighboring Kosovo" (Becker 1999). Similar claims about the capacity of court investigations to deter Serb commanders are made again later in the same year (Simons 1999). Perhaps the strongest statement made in support of an expectation of deterrence, however, is reported the year before when "a senior official" is quoted by the *NY Times* as saying that although difficult to prove "it is possible that the prosecutor's several warnings have lessened the crimes" (Simons 1998).

The final statement quoted above is perhaps—though probably unwittingly—the most telling: the recognition that such an effect of international criminal courts is difficult to prove. Anecdotally, it has been noted by others that the worst single crime of the Bosnian war (the massacre following the fall of Srebrenica) took place two years after the Tribunal was established (Barria and Roper 2005; Rodman 2008). Likewise, it seems fruitless to speculate as to how much worse crimes might have been in the war in Kosovo without the deterrent effect of the Tribunal. And yet it is difficult to conceive of the deterrent effect of tribunals being asserted in a more positive manner than occurs on numerous occasions in relation to both the Tribunal and the Chambers in articles published by the *NY Times*.

Conclusion

The portrayal of the Chambers and Tribunal, even when negative, subtly affirms the primacy of legal responses in transitional justice. This is most pronounced when coverage advocates the global impact that such endeavours have in deterring war crimes elsewhere. This expectation appears to be held by local and international stakeholders. Additionally, it serves many international interests and ties in well with international rhetoric from diplomatic and NGO sectors calling for "an end to war crimes" and "an end to impunity". Indeed, coverage of impunity that promotes the role of prosecutions in enhancing accountability and ending impunity may have the same effect. Consequently, the supremacy of a legal and prosecutorial paradigm in transitional justice is supported in such coverage. This may create obstacles in efforts to broaden transitional justice and its capacity to address a greater number of expectations.

Another important insight is that the media are unlikely to convey certain information to their audience regarding transitional justice trials. It is clear that many expectations relate to the number and identity of defendants. It is similarly clear that the great majority of crimes and victims will not be addressed through limited prosecutions in transitional justice trials. Efforts to better communicate the reasons behind this disparity (limited resources, insufficient evidence etc.) ought to be at the forefront of considerations when attempting to manage expectations. This also applies to other information that courts are unlikely to convey adequately. While this may be unsurprising, it is again problematic for transitional justice. Given the importance of media as a source of information about transitional justice trials, coverage that serves to highlight drama at the expense of detail may create an uninformed, or poorly informed, public. Sentencing principles in international law are a glaring example of information not provided in media coverage; this directly links to a wide gap in expectations: outrage at the length of sentences was observed following numerous convictions, such as that of Comrade Duch and Radislav Krstic. *NY Times* coverage also raised some unanticipated expectations. For example, coverage portrayed an expectation that trials would adhere to high standards of international justice as conflicting with an expectation for holding trials in Cambodia. This conflict was reported to take place between the NGO and diplomatic sectors. Whether expectations of fair trial and due process rights must be sacrificed in order to combat impunity is debatable: the construction of the equation as zero-sum may in itself be a contortion.

Importantly for transitional justice, the data indicates that media coverage supports the dominance of legalism in transitional justice. For courts and tribunals this is significant because it highlights how a number of very different expectations will readily be attached to their work. This may be irrespective of their institutional suitability for satisfying such expectations. It further shows the power of the dominant paradigm that has established legal and prosecutorial responses as the most favoured forms of transitional justice. In this way, it shows how such attitudes are entrenched outside of policy and practice circles. If transitional justice truly seeks to respond to as many expectations as possible it will be necessary to re-evaluate this legal and prosecutorial dominance.

References

Barria, LA and Roper, SD 2005, 'How effective are international criminal tribunals? An analysis of the ICTY and the ICTR', *The International Journal of Human Rights*, vol. 9, no. 3, pp. 349–368.

Becker, E 1997, 'Videotape shows Pol Pot facing Khmer Rouge justice', *The New York Times*, July 29.

Becker, E 1998, 'Death of Pol Pot: The diplomacy; Pol Pot's end won't stop U.S. pursuit of his circle', *The New York Times*, April 17.

Becker, E 1999. 'Crisis in the Balkans: The overview; NATO says new bombing is the strongest effort yet', *The New York Times*, May 1.

Becker, E 2009, 'When justice is delayed', *The New York Times*, March 14.

Bilefsky, D and Simons, M 2008, 'Bosnian Serb under arrest in war crimes', *The New York Times*, July 22.

Bonner, R 1999a, 'Conflict in the Balkans: The tribunal; tactics were barrier to top Serb's indictment', *The New York Times*, March 29.

Bonner, R 1999b, 'Crisis in the Balkans: The tribunal; Crimes court not ready to punish Kosovo violence', *The New York Times*, March 31.

Bonner, R 1999c, 'Crisis in the Balkans: The outlook: Despite indictment, politicians and diplomats control Milosevic's future', *The New York Times*, May 28.

Brdar, M and Vukovic, S 2006, 'A semiotic analysis of 'enemy' management: 'Serbs' in the Western media', *International Journal for the Semiotics of Law/ Revuew Internationale de Semiotique Juridique*, vol. 19, no. 4, pp. 435–456.

Castle, S 2011, 'Mladic arrest opens door to Serbia's long-sought European Union membership', *The New York Times*, May 26.

Chibnall, S 1977, *Law and Order News: An Analysis of Crime Reporting in the British Press*, Tavistock Publications, London.

Cohen, R 1995a, 'Tribunal to cite Bosnia Serb chief as war criminal', *The New York Times*, April 24.

Cohen, R 1995b, 'U.N. in Bosnia: Black robes clash with blue hats', *The New York Times*, April 25.

Cohen, R 1995c, 'Bosnian Serb denies all at a war crimes tribunal', *The New York Times*, April 27.

Cohen, R 2001, 'Milosevic to Represent Himself at His Arraignment Today', *The New York Times*, July 3.

Cowell, A 1995, 'Nuremberg journal: War crimes and punishments, then and now', *The New York Times*, November 20.

Cowell, A 1997, 'German court sentences Serb to life for genocide in Bosnia', *The New York Times*, September 27.
Crosette, B 2001, 'Long-range justice raises fears for sovereignty', *The New York Times*, July 1.
'Deal Reached on Trials for Khmer Rouge' 2003, *The New York Times*, March 17.
Editorial 1998, 'Pol Pot escapes justice', *The New York Times*, April 17.
Editorial 2001, 'The prosecution of Mr. Milosevic', *The New York Times*, January 16.
Editorial 2004, 'International justice', *The New York Times*, February 27.
Editorial 2006a, 'The death of Milosevic', *The New York Times*, March 14.
Editorial 2006b, 'The Killing Fields', *The New York Times*, July 6.
Editorial 2009, 'Trial on trial', *The New York Times*, March 11.
Editorial 2011, 'End of the line', *The New York Times*, May 26.
Engelberg, S 1995, 'Panel seeks U.S. pledge on Bosnia war criminals', *The New York Times*, November 3.
Erlanger, S 1999, 'Crisis in the Balkans: Belgrade; Word of indictment stuns Serbs and blights hopes', *The New York Times*, May 27.
Erlanger, S 2000, 'Showdown in Yugoslavia: The overview; Milosevic concedes his defeat; Yugoslavs Celebrate New Era', *The New York Times* (New York), 7 October 2000.
Erlanger, S 2001, 'The handover of Milosevic: News analysis; Milosevic trial; Test on many levels', *The New York Times*, June 29.
Erlanger, S and Wren, CS 1999, 'Early count hints at fewer Kosovo deaths', *The New York Times*, November 11.
Fisher, I 2001, 'Opinion is divided in Serbia over handover of Milosevic', *The New York Times*, June 30.
Fisher, I and Simons, M 2002, 'Milosevic, 'the biggest fish', on eve of war crimes trial', *The New York Times*, February 12.
Frankel, M 1999, 'Our humanity vs. their sovereignty', *The New York Times*, May 2.
Gay, M 2011, 'Dark past in Balkan war intrudes on new life', *The New York Times*, April 3.
Goldston, JA 2011, 'No justice in the Killing Fields', *The New York Times*, April 26.
Goodman, W 1996, 'Television review: Sorting out war crimes and tangles of history', *The New York Times*, May 13.

Hedges, C 1996, 'Balkan war crimes: Bosnia is first to turn in its own', *The New York Times*, May 3.

Keller, B 2002, 'The monster in the dock', *The New York Times*, February 9.

'Lawyer Scolds Cambodia Tribunal Judges' 2008, *The New York Times*, April 24.

Lewis, A 1995, 'Abroad at home: Never again', *The New York Times*, April 3.

Lewis, NA 1995, 'At the Bar: A South African jurist focuses on Bosnia', *The New York Times*, March 31.

McFadden, RD 1998, 'Death of Pol Pot: The Witness; Survivor of Killing Fields is Resolute in Quest for Justice', *The New York Times*, April 17.

Mydans, S 1997a, 'Cambodian rivals say they will bring Pol Pot to justice', *The New York Times*, June 22.

Mydans, S 1997b, 'A stalemate in Cambodia', *The New York Times*, July 2.

Mydans, S 1997c, 'In an interview, Pol Pot declares his conscience is clear', *The New York Times*, October 23.

Mydans, S 1998a, 'Reporter visits Pol Pot still held by Khmer Rouge', *The New York Times*, January 7.

Mydans, S 1998b, 'Khmer Rouge factions battle each other in the jungle', *The New York Times*, March 30.

Mydans, S 1998c, 'For Pol Pot, an endgame', *The New York Times*, April 13.

Mydans, S 1998d, 'Pol Pot is dead, Thai army says; Made Cambodia a "Killing Field"', *The New York Times*, April 16.

Mydans, S 1998e, 'Death of Pol Pot: The analysis; The demons of a despot', *The New York Times*, April 17.

Mydans, S 1998f, 'At cremation of Pol Pot, no tears shed', *The New York Times*, April 19.

Mydans, S 1999a, 'Two Khmer Rouge leaders spend beach holiday in shadow of past', *The New York Times*, January 1.

Mydans, S 1999b, 'Cambodia says it plans trial for jailed Khmer Rouge commander', *The New York Times*, March 8.

Mydans, S 1999c, 'Captured Khmer Rouge leader to face charges in Cambodia', *The New York Times*, March 10.

Mydans, S 1999d, 'Phnom Penh journal: Intrepid lawyer rises for first Khmer Rouge trial', *The New York Times*, May 14.

Mydans, S 2006, 'Former Cambodian leaders to face trial', *The New York Times*, January 23.

Mydans, S 2009a, 'Efforts to limit Khmer Rouge trials decried', *The New York Times*, February 1.

Mydans, S 2009b, 'Trial begins for Khmer Rouge leader', *The New York Times*, February 17.
Mydans, S 2009c, 'Accusations of corruption cast a shadow over the Khmer Rouge trials in Cambodia', *The New York Times*, April 10.
Mydans, S 2010, 'Anger in Cambodia Over Khmer Rouge Sentence', *The New York Times*, July 26.
Nikolaev, AG 2009, 'Images of war: Content analysis of the photo coverage of the war in Kosovo', *Critical Sociology*, vol. 35, no. 1, pp. 105–130.
O'Connor, M 1995, 'At one hotel in Bosnia, hunters and the hunted', *The New York Times*, December 29.
O'Connor, M 1996, 'Grim Reaper; Harvesting evidence in Bosnia's killing fields', *The New York Times*, April 7.
Opinion 1997, 'A trial for Pol Pot', *The New York Times*, June 24.
Opinion 1998, 'Bringing Pol Pot to justice', *The New York Times*, April 10.
Opinion 2002, 'The trial of Slobodan Milosevic', *The New York Times*, February 11.
Parker, T 2004, 'Judgment at Baghdad', *The New York Times*, July 7.
Perlez, J 1996, 'War crimes tribunal on Bosnia is hampered by basic problems', *The New York Times*, January 28.
Rodman, KA 2008, 'Darfur and the limits of legal deterrence', *Human Rights Quarterly*, vol. 30, no. 3, pp. 529–560.
Rosenthal, A 1995, 'On my mind: Arresting the negotiators', *The New York Times*, July 28.
Ruigrok, N 2005, *Journalism of Attachment: Dutch Newspapers During the Bosnian War*, Het Spinhuis, Amsterdam, The Netherlands.
Sciolino, E 1995, 'Bosnian talks snag on fate of two Serbs', *The New York Times*, November 17.
Shenon, P 1998a, 'U.S. seeks China's help in arranging Pol Pot trial', *The New York Times*, April 11.
Shenon, P 1998b, 'U.N. plans joint war crimes tribunal for Khmer Rouge', *The New York Times*, August 12.
Shenon, P and Schmitt, E 1998, 'U.S. is planning a move to seize Pol Pot for trial', *The New York Times*, April 9.
Simons, M 1995, 'Conflict in the Balkans: War crimes; Tribunal indicts Bosnian Serb leader', *The New York Times*, July 26.
Simons, M 1996a, 'Far from former Yugoslavia, first war crimes trial opens', *The New York Times*, May 8.
Simons, M 1996b, 'A war crimes trial starts', *The New York Times*, May 12.

Simons, M 1998, 'U.N. war crimes tribunal steps up its inquiry into Kosovo', *The New York Times*, August 26.
Simons, M 1999, 'Proud but concerned, tribunal prosecutor leaves', *The New York Times*, September 15.
Simons, M 2001a, 'Tribunal in Hague finds Bosnia Serb guilty of genocide', *The New York Times*, August 3.
Simons, M 2001b, 'Milosevic calls tribunal unfair, infantile and "a farce"', *The New York Times*, October 31.
Simons, M 2002, 'An American With Opinions Steps Down Vocally at War Crimes Court', *The New York Times*, January 24.
Simons, M 2003, 'Bosnian ex-leader sentenced to 11 years for her war role', *The New York Times*, February 28.
Simons, M 2004, 'The Saturday Profile: Weaving the threads of law, war and Shakespeare', *The New York Times*, January 3.
Simons, M 2009, 'International criminal tribunals and the media', *Journal of International Criminal Justice*, vol. 7, no. 1, pp. 83–88.
Simons, M with Gall, C 2001, 'The handover of Milosevic: The overview; Milosevic is given to U.N. for trial in war-crime case', *The New York Times*, June 29.
'Ta Mok, Khmer Rouge Head Facing Genocide Trial, Dies' 2006, *The New York Times*, July 21.
'U.N. Prosecutor Plans Bigger Push in Balkans' 1999, *The New York Times*, December 23.
Volcic, Z and Dzihana, A 2011, 'Introduction: Towards peace journalism', in Dzhiana, A and Volcic, Z (eds), *Media and national ideologies: Analysis of reporting on war crime trials in the former Yugoslavia*, Media Centar Sarajevo, Sarajevo, Bosnia and Herzegovina.
Wren, C 1999, 'Judge says Yugoslavia impedes work of war crimes tribunal', *The New York Times*, November 9.

6

A Trying Paradigm

The question for transitional justice is how to respond to as many expectations as possible, as effectively as possible, given the practical constraints such initiatives face. This may well mean greater dialogue in establishing what these expectations are before a transitional justice mechanism is established. A further difficulty is that the context and conditions following mass atrocities may mean that it is impossible to completely satisfy all stakeholders. It is unnecessary to repeat that communities affected by mass atrocity have survived immense personal and collective trauma. What they feel is necessary as individuals and as societies in order to heal is not something outsiders can readily assume or judge. Of course, some expectations may need to be preferred over others for practical considerations. It is worth recalling that one respondent, who is both a victim and a victims' advocate, noted that despite any measures directly following the wars in Bosnia, "We would still have been frustrated just by the very fact that this happened to us, that our

R. Nickson and A. Neikirk, *Managing Transitional Justice*,
Palgrave Studies in Compromise after Conflict,
https://doi.org/10.1007/978-3-319-77782-5_6

loved ones were killed in such a horrible way" (Former Yugoslavia NGO #1). This impossibility should not deter transitional justice actors from their efforts, nor should it deter efforts at enhancing the levels of satisfaction with trials (including such measures as managing expectations).

This chapter weaves the data from interviews and the content analysis together with previous research and academic thought in transitional justice. It draws out the implications of this research, with insights into the expectation problem; issues with specific expectations; how to address the expectations gap; and the limitations of trials. The data from this research indicates that it is preferential to eschew "one size fits all" approaches to the practice of transitional justice: the shortcomings of single institution transitional justice efforts are apparent in the data. These shortcomings limit the expectations that might be addressed, as well as the ways they are addressed.

Satisfying Expectations

While many respondents discussed a need to manage expectations, several recognised the almost impossibility of satisfying all expectations for transitional justice. By way of example, one victim advocate suggested that even if everything had been achieved immediately, victims would still have been unsatisfied by virtue of their circumstances (Former Yugoslavia NGO #2). Others echoed the impossibility of satisfying victims (Tribunal Defence #6; Tribunal Outreach #2). That many expectations went unsatisfied and unfulfilled is a troubling finding. Such outcomes may have profound implications for the transitional justice process. It may hamper efforts at establishing peace (negative and positive) when people feel that their needs have not been addressed. Unsatisfied expectations were not limited to less tangible goals, such as reconciliation. Expectations regarding specific prosecutions were also believed to remain unmet. For example, respondents observed dissatisfaction among local stakeholders with the Tribunal for perceptions it had not dealt with the siege of Vukovar (Tribunal Outreach #5), or prosecuted people for the events in Eastern Bosnia (BWCC Prosecutor #1). Yet content analysis data suggests that courts and trials can—at least partly—play a role in satisfying some expectations. This was most evident with coverage of impunity.

Early coverage was critical of both the Tribunal and Chambers for their inability to counter the perceived impunity of high-profile suspects. Much of that coverage was nothing short of scathing. Yet with the advent of trials at the Chambers, and with increased trials at the Tribunal, coverage by the *NY Times* became more positive. It is evident that a positive impact on impunity is something that courts can be considered to have achieved or are capable of achieving. In this way, it is possible for courts to make progress toward, at least partially, satisfying expectations about impunity. At the same time, it is important that courts actively address impunity in their wider discussions. It may be prudent for courts to establish appropriate expectations by highlighting sensible boundaries for their influence on impunity. This may mean, for instance, an explanation of why certain individuals and not others are being prosecuted.

Such changes from negative to positive coverage—following improvements or advancements in the practice of transitional justice—are evidence of the capacity for trials to satisfy certain expectations. Importantly, media coverage demonstrates relatively speedy recognition for the impact of a court's work on expectations; it is not an impact that can only be measured at some distance in the future. Negative coverage may also be used to the advantage of courts. In relation to early coverage of impunity in Cambodia, it served to highlight the need for a court. In this way, coverage may spur action during periods of negotiation or creation of international criminal tribunals. Similarly, staff at the Tribunal could harness negative coverage, especially regarding impunity and the lack of cooperation from other stakeholders in combating impunity, for positive ends. Because countering impunity is a very real expectation regarding international criminal justice, it is possible for courts to use this issue to mobilise support and shame authorities into assisting. The use of negative coverage must be undertaken with caution, though. It is possible, and even likely, that the image of people believed to have committed atrocities living freely will severely undermine both confidence and support in a court and trials. Not only may it have negative repercussions concerning perception of the court's ability to influence impunity, it may also negatively affect other expectations, particularly those relating to justice and fairness.

Although negative coverage may be used to a court's favour—to compel action, elicit funding and encourage cooperation—it is a dangerous endeavour, as courts risk being undermined and having confidence in them diminished. As expectations in combating impunity appear to manifest early, it is best if courts can make swift advances towards satisfying these expectations. Alternatively, if early advances are not possible, it would be advisable for courts to communicate to local and international audiences their plans for combating impunity. The impact of arrests and trials of high-profile accused is more salient in this regard, and if high-profile accused will not be arrested or tried early in favour of lower-level accused, it is important for the court to explain this. Failure to do so may lead to coverage that reflects poorly on the court, and risks disappointing an expectation that courts may well achieve during their operations.

Negative media coverage is likely to contribute to dissatisfaction with transitional justice overall. The likely ramifications may be a serious impediment to the transitional process. Respondents in interviews clearly felt that dissatisfaction was primarily due to unrealistic expectations (almost half of all respondents directly stated this, with many more referring to expectations as problematic)—coupled with a very negative media (every Outreach officer from the Tribunal remarked on the media's negativity toward the institution). As one respondent claimed, unrealistic expectations from the establishment of the Tribunal continue to result in disappointment (Tribunal Outreach #2). It is troubling to think that unrealistic expectations of transitional justice trials may have engendered profound disappointment that has lasted for decades. Such disappointment can potentially affect many other areas of society, particularly those that relate to goals for transitional justice and transitional societies. For instance, it is plausible to speculate that profound disappointment with the only official transitional justice institution may impede other efforts towards reconciliation or democratisation—both frequent broader aims of transitional justice. In this respect, communication that effectively encourages more institution-appropriate expectations may be significant.

While coverage in the *NY Times* frequently focused on negative aspects of the operations of both the Tribunal and Chambers, it also often served to raise expectations. Coverage that centred on high-profile accused, asserted the guilt of defendants, sought to promote retribution as a response to offending, and retold the number and details of crimes may all serve to raise punitive expectations among affected and international communities. It is also possible that such coverage would increase the perceived desire and need for judicial responses to atrocities. This is even more likely given the preference for judicial responses in the subtext of a great deal of media coverage on the Tribunal and Chambers, coupled with the dominance of legalism in policy and NGO advocacy for transitional justice (McEvoy 2007, 2008; Fletcher and Weinstein 2002). The dominance of legalism is further evidenced by a focus on trials and prosecutions as the preferential response to mass atrocities, a preference observed by Theissen (2004), Drumbl (2002, 2003), and Fletcher and Weinstein (2002). This may have served to fuel expectations for punitive, retributive and judicial responses to atrocities. Negative coverage may also undermine the potentially positive contributions of the available judicial institutions. Consequently, both outcomes are undesirable.

It serves little benefit to focus on retributive, punitive and judicial responses to mass atrocities to the exclusion, or at least the marginalisation, of other responses that may address more adequately some of the many expectations of transitional justice. Further, it is evident from this research (most obviously in the views of respondents) and supported by the research of others, that negative coverage casts a pall over the many positive contributions that trials and prosecutions may make to transitional justice. It stands to reason that negative coverage—as the result of nationalist bias, misinformation, or structural needs of articles—may hamper the efforts of any form of transitional justice in transitional societies. This is not to criticise freedom of the press or transparency for transitional justice institutions. Indeed, both are fundamental for the success of transitional justice. However, the data for this research—and the data from the research of others—reveal a predilection for negative over positive coverage. This is not necessarily a reflection of transitional justice institutions' operations. This is likely to be even more problematic in transitional societies that are still divided between warring factions. Studies of the media from the former Yugoslavia show that in such circumstances, media orient their coverage to suit the attitudes and preconceived interpretations of events along factional lines (Dzihana and Volcic 2011).

Given these complexities and the clear role of the media, there is a need for greater media training in transitional societies (Nettlefield 2010). One respondent spoke directly of the necessity to foster strong relationships with the media. She cited examples of the positive outcomes of media visits to the Tribunal and the direct engagement between staff and journalists that this permitted (Tribunal Media #1).

The Labelling of Expectations

Many respondents asserted that expectations for transitional justice were frequently unrealistic. It is likely that some expectations do not correspond with the realities of what transitional justice can achieve. However, the view that an expectation was unrealistic often appeared to be based primarily on the suitability of the institution. This led respondents to render anything outside the institution's ambit as unsuitable. Mismatched expectations are not always an error of the expectation holder. Frequently, they may be errors in how transitional justice activities have been created. Interviews and the content analysis showed clear support for the supremacy of trials and the dominance of legalism in transitional justice settings. Yet numerous respondents discussed the shortcomings of such a blinkered approach to achieving justice in and for transitional societies.

Many respondents made clear that certain expectations were appropriate while others were partly or wholly inappropriate. There was no overall consensus among respondents about which expectations were appropriate. Similarly, media coverage appeared to have predetermined what were appropriate goals for transitional justice and composed their articles accordingly. In contrast, however, less diversity of expectations was evident in articles. Local needs for transitional justice only appeared to be considered when they called for punishment or yearned for the truth. In this way, the validity of local expectations was reduced to emotional responses of outrage and despair that provided convenient support for coverage: outrage before trials that no one had been convicted and outrage after trials that convictions and sentences were insufficient; despair before trials that the truth is unknown and despair following trials that the truth was withheld.

It is prudent to demonstrate reluctance in labelling expectations as wrong outright. Contextually, it may be sensible to consider certain expectations ill-suited when applied to specific institutions. But it does not follow that those same expectations are inappropriate when considered as part of a broader transitional justice enterprise. Indeed, it would be somewhat arrogant to insist that people affected by conflict have inappropriate expectations for mechanisms intended to assist with their recovery. Certainly, what people feel they need from transitional justice, and what they expect it to provide, may be entirely appropriate within their own conception of what it takes to heal and move forward after conflict. What and whether certain expectations are appropriate for transitional justice courts will be explored further later in this chapter. As will the idea that although certain expectations may be inappropriate to a particular transitional justice mechanism in isolation, they may be wholly appropriate for transitional justice overall. This is a relevant point in favour of broadening transitional justice interventions to include a variety of institutions that may better serve the diversity of expectations. This reflects calls within the transitional justice literature that advocate for a more holistic approach to and practice of transitional justice (Haider 2009; Zoglin 2005; McEvoy 2007). For this reason it is preferable, when possible, that there is engagement with the relevant communities to ascertain what their motivations and expectations regarding transitional justice might be. Ramji-Nogales (2010) has argued that transitional justice ought to design "bespoke" responses, to better address local contexts and understandings of justice. For Ramji-Nogales (2010, p. 3), ascertaining local needs and interests would require research in tandem with transitional justice efforts, the goal of which would be to "reconstruct social norms opposing mass violence." If the failure to meet expectations has resulted in disappointment with transitional justice institutions—as has been suggested—then this seems fundamental to implementing more successful transitional justice activities. It is also relevant that expectations in one transitional location will not necessarily be replicated or applicable in another.

Certain transitional justice mechanisms are better suited to achieving particular transitional justice goals (Aukerman 2002). Consequently, some mechanisms do not address certain goals well. This research suggests that more thought must be given to establishing institutions that are appropriate to meet local needs and expectations of transitional justice. The question cannot simply be, "What are the appropriate expectations for a selected transitional justice mechanism?" We must also ask, "What would be the appropriate mechanism in the particular transitional context?" For that reason, it is necessary to consider what it is hoped transitional justice will achieve in a distinct transitional context and how those goals might best be addressed through relevant mechanisms. This calls for a process of considering the desired outcomes and engaging with stakeholder interests at the very beginning of transitional justice. (Recommendations in this regard are given more detailed content in Chapter 7). As one respondent stated: "Responses to mass atrocities must be almost as complex as the events were complex" (Chambers Victim Support #1). Another respondent insightfully remarked that just as they had to prove crimes were "widespread and systematic", so must transitional justice responses to those crimes be widespread and systematic (although we considered this rather insightful, the respondent did not want the remark attributed to them).

In both interviews and content analysis, there was often a failure to recognise the context of expectations in transitional justice. This was never more evident than when respondents were dismissive of expectations as inappropriate or unrealistic. The needs of different transitional societies will not always be the same. By extension, the goals that communities hold for transitional justice and the outcomes that they hope for will not be identical—or necessarily even similar—between different transitional contexts. Respondents often explained that courts and trials had a specific function with limited capabilities. Such explanations were relied upon to deny or reduce the validity of wider expectations that they had observed. The Tribunal and Chambers operate in isolation from any other official transitional justice mechanism that might alleviate some of this burden by spreading it over multiple institutions. Still, many respondents failed to recognise this context for the attachment of many expectations to the courts.

The *NY Times* coverage of the Chambers and Tribunal fit traditional media criteria for the reporting of crime (Chibnall 1977). Reporting on both institutions was similar in many important respects. Impunity featured heavily in articles for both institutions, and the overall pattern of impunity coverage was similar between the Tribunal and Chambers.

An assumption of guilt—frequently assertions of guilt—appeared in articles for the Tribunal and Chambers. A frequent focus on drama at the expense of information could be observed: for the Tribunal this was readily apparent in the coverage of the Milosevic trial, while in coverage of the Chambers the most glaring example occurred in coverage of the opening of the Duch trial. Other similarities in coverage included the attention given to the number and details of crimes, as well as the focus on high-profile identities from the conflicts with limited attention to other defendants.

Coverage also marginalised the role of victims in a similar way to their marginalisation in the criminal justice process: they were utilised primarily as tools. Victim voice was largely evident only when it served to heighten drama or demonstrate tension in articles. The greatest attention given to victim voice was in the description of their victimisation, especially sexual victimisation. This was followed by expressions of dissatisfaction and despair after sentencing—in many ways this can be portrayed as secondary victimisation by the system. Such coverage conforms to Chibnall's (1977) categories of personalisation, negativity and titillation: it is preferable if stories can be related to some form of personal struggle, and the worse the violence, the better the news story. Significantly, there was little differentiation in the role of victims at the Tribunal or Chambers in *NY Times* coverage.

What are appropriate expectations regarding victims is very specific to the nature of the court. Expectations about victim assistance at the Chambers may reasonably be greater than they were for the Tribunal by virtue of the rules of procedure. While the difference in victims' roles was mentioned in a few articles, the manner in which victim issues was covered exhibited little difference. Dialogue regarding expectations of victims, and about victims, will be fundamental to the success of any tribunal in minimising the expectation gap. Such expectation management, as has been highlighted elsewhere, did occur by both institutions—though how well this was done is open to debate. What might reasonably be expected of the Chambers is likely to differ from reasonable expectations of the Tribunal.

Results from both forms of data highlight, in different ways, the persistence of a "one size fits all" approach. Respondents or the *NY Times* rarely questioned the primacy of legal responses in transitional justice. Indeed, a preference for prosecutions and trials was evident in both data sets. Consequently, respondents often viewed expectations as an unfortunate burden on the work of courts, as well as being incorrectly applied to those institutions. Not all respondents maintained this attitude: all defence lawyers, save one, thought that the value of trials in transitional justice had been overestimated, and that alternative mechanisms might provide greater benefits. In *NY Times* articles, the failure of courts in addressing the (mostly punitive) goals that coverage focused on was rarely framed as a failure of the judicial model. Less than a handful of articles sought to question the suitability of trials and prosecutions to achieve the aims of transitional justice.

The Limitations of Trials

The data from this research suggests that isolated trials—where trials are the only official transitional justice response—are not well suited to addressing the various expectations that people hold for transitional justice. It is true that trials may function well in respect to certain expectations. Countering impunity was an expectation that both the Tribunal and Chambers had some success in satisfying. Additionally, interviews and the content analysis demonstrated support for the role of courts in partly satisfying the search for answers. Yet it appears that the overall burden of expectations outweighs the likely contributions of any single mechanism.

Expectations that evidenced a desire for punishment, retribution and just deserts appeared in the data from interviews and the content analysis. Other research has found that a majority in the former Yugoslavia wish for capital punishment (Ivkovic 2001, p. 255). There is little surprise that such expectations exist: respondents routinely believed that victims desired punishment. Indeed, a spokesperson for a leading victims advocacy group declared that punishment was precisely what they wanted, and the more punishment the better (Former Yugoslavia NGO #2). Interview data demonstrates expectations about the severity of sentences, the number of prosecutions, the identity of defendants, and the likelihood of defendants being convicted. These findings were supported by the content analysis data, where expectations regarding the scope of justice frequently found voice.

Content analysis data indicates that media coverage reports expectations of punishment and retribution. It was clear, for example, that media coverage consistently repeated the number and details of crimes. Repeating the number of victims or crimes, as well as the details of crimes, may alarm, rekindle, stoke, and inflame passions. Of course, an awareness of the details and number of crimes is likely to exist among affected communities already. Expectations of punishment, or at the very least the desire for punishment (as it may be expected that responsible parties will escape justice), will probably already be well established. Yet for both the Tribunal and the Chambers, it is unlikely that such coverage is about raising awareness among local communities—it may be assumed that local communities are aware, if not fully aware, of the gravity and quantity of crimes that have been committed in their midst. In any event, such coverage is more likely to raise expectations for retributive punishment by invoking the suffering of people during the conflict. In certain circumstances, particularly when the details of crimes are singularly outrageous, such coverage may also demonise those believed to be responsible.

In a similar manner, assertions of guilt in coverage may contribute not only to expectations of the likelihood of convictions but also of punishment. Respondents observed an expectation of convictions among local and international communities. An assumption of guilt was usually adopted in the *NY Times* coverage of the accused at both the Tribunal and Chambers. Unfortunately, expectations of guilt and media assertions regarding an individual's guilt do not necessarily correspond to the legal process. This has the potential to create considerable gaps between expectations and reality when it comes to the trial of indictees, and particularly high-profile indictees, at international criminal courts. Although the frequency with which this occurs across the years of coverage for each court is not high, it is important to note that the representation of high-profile accused is almost always coloured by an assumption of guilt. Their guilt is, of course, something that everyone may already "know". Articles in this regard may do nothing more than confirm wider opinion or "knowledge", and it is likely that media coverage alone is not generating the particular expectation (though its appearance in this research confirms the existence of such an expectation). In any event, such coverage may at least exacerbate the problem and this is a significant expectation that courts must deal with.

This phenomenon is not limited to individuals. The content analysis uncovered many instances where events were asserted to have constituted crimes. This is problematic if it generates or contributes to expectations that certain crimes occurred when the existence of a legally defined criminal act or event may not be established. Assertions and expectations regarding particular crimes are most pronounced in the *NY Times* articles in reference to genocide. For instance, the assertion that genocide has occurred has obvious relevance to an expectation that people's suffering will then be recognised by a verdict of genocide. One respondent felt the effect of these expectations acutely in her work at the Tribunal (Tribunal Media #1). She lamented that a great number of victim communities were dissatisfied with the work of the Tribunal, as they often expected their suffering to be recognised as genocide. These expectations were out-of-step with the legal use of genocide. This specific expectation gap serves to demonstrate the disjuncture between media coverage (as well as the statements of officials and NGOs) with the limited capacities of narrowly defined legal concepts and procedures.

Another distinct scope of justice expectation issue was reflected in dissatisfaction with sentencing. Respondents in interviews, along with articles examined for the content analysis, supported the observation that expectations about the length of sentences did not correspond with sentencing practices in international criminal law. Respondents sometimes recognised this as a misunderstanding by community members. For instance, it was considered a misunderstanding in distinguishing between international and national systems, and an indication of a failure in communication. The *NY Times*, however, made very little effort to explain the reasoning behind sentencing. Marlise Simons, a *NY Times* journalist covering international criminal trials, provides an explanation for this disparity. Simons (2009, p. 83) feels that the onus is on transitional justice mechanisms to engage more fully with the media and to better explain sentencing principles to journalists. Yet given patterns and the preference for negativity and drama in media coverage, it is questionable whether such explanations would be included in articles or reports, and one could argue that explanations for sentencing are available to journalists if they read the transcripts. It is clear, though, that expectations regarding sentencing are problematic for transitional justice courts, and this is an area that must be addressed.

Such dissatisfaction also extends to the disparity between the number of crimes or possible defendants and the eventual number of arrests, prosecutions and convictions. This expectation is likely to exist independently of media coverage. Respondents in interviews noted that this particular disparity between expectations and results was a significant source of dissatisfaction with transitional justice for many community members. It is foreseeable that the focus on the number and details of crimes could exacerbate tensions between expectations and likely achievements in regard to the quantum of prosecutions. A focus on high-profile accused and their culpability may in some ways alleviate the burden of such an expectation if it serves to redirect prosecutorial expectations of communities towards the indictment, arrest, trial, and conviction of a limited number of individuals. It is not possible to predict, however, how persuasive such coverage might be. There is also the risk that it may serve to increase the validity of claims by certain individuals that the focus on them is a form of scapegoating.

Better explanations are required to inform stakeholders. Specifically, it is necessary to explain why certain events have not been investigated (for example preliminary investigations suggest events did not breach international law), why certain individuals have or have not been indicted, or why indictments have not progressed to prosecutions. Courts frequently adopt prosecutorial strategies: at the Tribunal and Chambers, the boundaries to any prosecutorial strategies have been limited to "those most responsible" and "senior leaders", two phrases that the Tribunal and Chambers frequently employ when discussing their mandates. These categories have been open to debate within and outside of both institutions. Despite that debate, it is desirable that the prosecutor's office communicate their strategies to stakeholders and communities.

For the Tribunal and Chambers, respondents also noted the lack of satisfaction with both institutions for failing to address the offences of a great number of offenders, as well as direct perpetrators. This is in many ways related to an observed need for acknowledgment among victims. When transitional justice is limited to prosecutions, victims will often need the offender who harmed them to be prosecuted to satisfy their need for acknowledgment. A Tribunal judge explained this quite powerfully:

> Two other farms have fallen out [of an indictment]. The survivors … they now sit back and say, 'But I saw it happen. But I am no longer there. What happens to me? Who is going to recognise my pain, my suffering?' … That causes frustration and unhappiness. (Tribunal Judge #2)

In many ways, the content analysis suggested dissatisfaction with prosecutorial strategies and selections. For instance, early criticism of the Tribunal for not trying higher-profile figures, or for trying such a small number of people, demonstrated disconnects between expectations and the actual work of the Tribunal. It is also possible that coverage, such as that exhibited in the *NY Times*, may increase disappointment of this expectation: coverage of the big fish/small fry dichotomy may increase expectations that senior leaders will be prosecuted. Or it may serve to emphasise big fish trials and fail to recognise the significance of addressing direct offenders and direct offending. Especially in the early stages of transitional justice trials, negative coverage regarding the lack of senior accused in indictments can undermine confidence in the court. This may also undermine perceptions of the court's relevance and value in the community.

These problems were less profound with Chambers than with the Tribunal. It was clear from the establishment of the Chambers that only a few individuals from the Khmer Rouge period would face trial. There have, of course, been disputes over such a relatively small pool of possible defendants, notably in respect to cases 003 and 004 (for a good discussion of this issue see Open Society Justice Initiative 2012). Still, respondents who worked in Cambodia noted dissatisfaction with the limitation of prosecutions to a select few and a desire, if not an expectation, that direct perpetrators should also be prosecuted. So, despite early and relatively clear indications that only a limited number of individuals would be prosecuted, members of the community were still unsatisfied with the prosecutorial strategy. For both institutions, respondents repeatedly cited complaints that not enough people were tried; that one's own suffering had not been addressed through a prosecution; and that symbolic cases had not been conducted. In addition, some respondents speculated that victims might find little personal value in trials that did not address their own victimisation. Each of these unsatisfied expectations relate to common and necessary limitations of trials and the judicial process.

Of course, it will never be possible to address the offending of everyone who committed crimes during conflict. In Cambodia, it would be an impossible burden on the judicial and penal systems to prosecute all the Khmer Rouge. What may help in satisfying some expectations when faced with this impossibility are alternative mechanisms that seek to acknowledge victim suffering, as well as address the culpability of human rights abusers. For this reason, it is important to consider other ways that the needs of individuals and communities might be addressed, perhaps independently of the need for a defendant who may be missing, dead, or shielded from prosecution. In the Cambodian context, a possible alternative mechanism may be some form of culturally appropriate activity such as a Buddhist ceremony that promotes reconciliation between victims and offenders (for a discussion of employing culturally relevant Buddhist practices in response to Khmer Rouge violence, see Marks 1994 and Hancock 2008). Alternative mechanisms are not new to transitional justice, but this research further supports their inclusion in transitional justice efforts to satisfy as many expectations as possible.

The content analysis also demonstrated that with coverage of high-profile accused there was an increased discussion of a wide variety of expectations. This represents a potential additional expectation burden on trials of high-profile accused. This is likely to be the case when many varied expectations are attached to trials of high-profile defendants that prosecutions are ill suited to deliver. While the transitional justice value of prosecuting high-profile defendants is likely to be high, it is important to recognise that many goals and expectations attached to the trial of high-profile defendants may be achieved in other ways. Indeed, many expectations and goals may be addressed more effectively by utilising other transitional justice mechanisms. It is also important to avoid attaching expectations too closely to individuals and their trials. Otherwise, if a trial of that person proves impossible or untenable, the process of transitional justice more broadly will be damaged. It is imperative to have successful transitional justice strategies that are not dependent on prosecuting and punishing a particular individual. The pitfalls of burdening the trials of high-profile accused were amply demonstrated in the content analysis: the death of figures like Milosevic and Pol Pot were lamented as missed opportunities that significantly damaged the chances of success for transitional justice. Such incidences may well be missed opportunities. However, given the likelihood of the passing of older defendants, it is important to avoid attaching all expectations to the successful prosecution of specific individuals. Rather, we need to develop transitional justice responses that can achieve similar goals in the absence of an accused.

Expecting Answers

Both an expectation of and a need for answers to individual and societal questions were evident in the data. Respondents spoke in-depth regarding the desire of communities and individuals to learn the truth and have their questions answered in the wake of mass atrocities. A "right to the truth" in transitional justice was even cited by one respondent (Former Yugoslavia NGO #1). Opinions on the capacity of trials to satisfy these needs and expectations were mixed among respondents. Many saw the various limitations of trials and court processes restricting such mechanisms to making only modest contributions. Others believed that courts had no role in providing historical truths or answers, with some stating that the process was as likely to distort truth as it was to uncover it. Yet there were a portion of respondents who believed quite strongly that transitional justice trials did answer questions, established (some) truth, and provided an historical record. The content analysis served to confirm the ready observation of respondents that these expectations existed. Generally, coverage in the *NY Times* was more favourable overall to the role that courts played in establishing the truth and providing answers to individuals and communities about the conflicts. Again, this reflects what appears to be a preference for trials rather than alternative justice measures.

It was recognised in data from both sources that many individuals held expectations that transitional justice would provide answers specific to them. This was frequently expressed as a desire to know the fate and location of loved ones, why they were selected for atrocities, and why friends or relatives betrayed them. Regrettably, the capacity of trials to effectively respond to these expectations is limited. Many respondents spoke of the disappointment experienced by victims when trials did not address their suffering, failed to provide the answers they sought, and did not allow an opportunity to express their feelings and explain the impact that their victimisation continued to have. As a result, this can be a problematic expectation for transitional justice when the mechanisms in place are limited to answering questions about offenders, not about the conflict or victims. Given that criminal trials are centred around the guilt or innocence of the accused, they are largely directed to answering that question. This leaves less scope in criminal trials to answer larger questions about conflict, individual questions about lost family members, and for victims to contribute their experiences. This can also limit the acknowledgment that victims may receive. Alternative mechanisms—such as the truth commission—may have more success in addressing these expectations. Some respondents, however, claimed that very little support existed for institutions such as truth commissions, or that there was a clear preference for prosecutions. What was evident from responses was that many of these opinions were predicated on misunderstandings of the function and procedures of truth commissions. For example, it appeared to be readily assumed that truth commissions were incompatible with trials, or that truth commissions meant amnesty for offenders.

The experience from both the former Yugoslavia and Cambodia demonstrate that communities and stakeholders often recognise the failure of trials to satisfy the need for answers. In both locations, NGOs have undertaken the task of conducting commissions of inquiry and to establishing truth commissions. Unfortunately, these efforts are hampered by a number of practical issues, such as funding. The fact that support for truth commissions may grow, or that initial misunderstandings and misgivings about truth commissions may later be corrected, support the notion of ongoing truth commissions proposed by Braithwaite and Nickson (2012, p. 443). Considering that this is such a widely held expectation, it is time to recognise the need for further efforts to complement NGO efforts. It is also necessary to admit and seek to address the limitations of a legal paradigm in satisfying these deeply held expectations for answers.

Forward Looking Expectations

An expectation that trials would serve to educate communities was clear from interviews and also arose in the content analysis. How well a court may be able to satisfy an expectation that it will educate about crimes is both difficult to measure and difficult to prepare for. A variety of factors will influence the role that courts may have in educating communities about past conflict. Despite more than 20 years of Tribunal proceedings, many still deny the most basic crimes that have been held to have occurred during the conflict in the former Yugoslavia (no fewer than ten interviewees discussed this problem, for example). The situation in the former Yugoslavia is, however, one coloured by a kaleidoscope of competing histories about the conflict, each constructed and viewed through prisms such as ethnic background. For Cambodia, the situation may not be as complex. While many Khmer Rouge cadres may dispute the dominant narrative regarding the Khmer Rouge regime, there appears much less debate about fundamental events and crimes from the period. How effective the court can be in educating about such crimes and events is unclear. What was suggested in interviews was that the court appears to have created a space for many educative endeavours to flourish—particularly in Cambodia.

Both interview and content analysis data indicate that courts cannot rely on the media to assist in performing an educative role. This is not to malign news media: their own commercial and technical constraints limit the contribution that they may be expected to make. Respondents were very critical of the content and focus of news media in the latter's coverage of the Tribunal (and to a lesser extent the Chambers). While these criticisms of local media were less applicable to *NY Times* coverage in the content analysis—there was little nationalist bias for instance—coverage still tended to eschew mundane but important facts in favour of drama. Overall, coverage was too superficial to contribute meaningfully to education in transitional justice.

That the Tribunal and Chambers have employed other tactics in performing an educative role (often as part of efforts to raise awareness about the courts) must be recognised. Respondents often commented on the benefits of Bridging the Gap conferences that the Tribunal held in local communities for raising awareness and educating people about the function, role, and contributions that it was making. Indeed, these conferences were also venues for managing expectations through direct engagement with community members. At the time of interviews, Tribunal Outreach was about to embark upon an ambitious legacy strategy throughout the former Yugoslavia. Similarly, the Chambers had brought thousands of Cambodians from urban and rural communities to visit their court, observe proceedings, and engage with staff. Yet the greater proportion of respondents felt that outreach efforts for both courts had met with a lack of success. It was clear from interviews that outreach at the Tribunal and the Chambers suffered from funding, staff, and resource shortfalls. And while the Chambers, for example, were considered to have successfully created a space for wider educative efforts, the direct contribution of either institution appeared to be small.

Although respondents and the *NY Times* spoke of the Tribunal and Chambers' roles in satisfying educational expectations, there was less discussion of their role in achieving other expectations for a better future. For example, there was little consensus among respondents on the role of transitional justice trials in contributing to reconciliation or peace. Reconciliation received minimal coverage in the *NY Times*. This was an unexpected result given the wider significance of reconciliation, particularly in the public statements of various international officials and diplomats. New York is the headquarters of the International Center for Transitional Justice—which utterly dominates the reconciliation business—and of the United Nations, so a New York newspaper should be a "most likely case" for reconciliation coverage (Eckstein 1975, pp. 79–138). Given the many setbacks in the path to reconciliation in the former Yugoslavia, it was surprising that reconciliation was not raised more frequently—particularly when considering the media's preference for negativity. Nevertheless, a lack of coverage of such expectations may be to a court's advantage. Minimal encouragement about expected contributions to peace and reconciliation is less likely to raise expectations that the tribunals may be poorly equipped to satisfy. Expectations about the court's role in regard to reconciliation or peace are likely to have existed for both the Chambers and the Tribunal (and probably will for most transitional justice courts) irrespective of coverage by the *NY Times*. Courts will need to explain the limits of the contributions they can make towards meeting these expectations.

These findings further demonstrate the need for activities that surround trials and courts to address these expectations for a better future. To an extent, this already takes place with the work of outreach and justice-oriented NGOs. Data from both the former Yugoslavia and Cambodia, however, evidence a lack of understanding and knowledge regarding the Tribunal and Chambers. As has been noted earlier, previous research has demonstrated that knowledge about both institutions is frequently low, and that levels of satisfaction are similarly low. The need to better inform communities about the role, function and limitations of trials and prosecutions is evident. Yet it is also evident that transitional justice must develop new ways to engage with community members. The assumption that people will access websites and read the outreach summaries is hopeful. In this respect, it may be possible to learn from fields (such as social marketing) that have developed effective frameworks for communicating information of public interest to diverse audiences. It also serves to demonstrate that isolated, single institution transitional justice interventions do not adequately meet the needs and expectations of transitional societies.

Mind the Expectation Gap

Better satisfaction of expectations is not a forlorn hope. Both interview and content analysis data provide insight into how the expectation gap in transitional justice can be reduced. It is clear by now that transitional justice institutions such as the Tribunal and Chambers face significant impediments to successfully communicating with affected communities. Media obstacles include bias and hostility; a narrow news focus; limited overall coverage; constraints in format and content; and the publication of incorrect or misleading information. Local and international media are both affected in various degrees. Outreach faces barriers to effective communication such as inadequate staffing; limited or non-existent funding for activities; community access; as well as negative attitudes from colleagues within courts.

The primary response from informants was that expectations needed to be "managed". This can be considered the traditional approach toward expectations in transitional justice (if one accepts that traditions have had time to form in transitional justice). In any event, it is certainly an approach that conforms well with the legal paradigm and prosecutorial focus that dominate current transitional justice practice and advocacy. It is worth noting that managing expectations is a largely reactive response to the issue. Even if expectations are managed from initial phases in transitional justice, they will largely be directed at informing and shaping expectations to fit institutions. A better approach would be to consider expectations in the design of transitional justice through dialogue and engagement. At the same time, it would be possible and wise to educate and inform about the benefits, limitations and likely contributions of a variety of possible transitional justice mechanisms. In this way, stakeholders will be better informed when developing opinions about the contributions of transitional justice. Consequently, we propose that stakeholders develop shared aims for transitional justice, informed by the expectations that they hold, as well as the context and conditions of their specific transition.

This process could be considered expectation transformation through institutional transformations. In this conception of transitional justice design and practice, expectations are transformed through dialogue and engagement into feasible projects that reflect the preferences and realities of the transitional society. This takes place as transitional justice institutions are themselves transformed into broader, deeper, and longer institutions that can potentially satisfy those transformed expectations. In the next chapter, a normative theory for transitional justice is proposed that advocates for these measures in an effort to promote justice that is in itself transformative.

The collaborative efforts between Outreach and NGOs at the Tribunal and Chambers are an example of how expectations might be managed when engaging with affected communities. Such collaboration needs to be nurtured in transitional justice activities, and the work of Outreach needs to be further supported with greater funds and resources. There are several advantages to such a collaborative approach to outreach. Not only is the effectiveness of outreach work likely to be increased, but that work is also likely to include more voices and have greater penetration into the community. Importantly, it also opens up avenues for greater participation by local stakeholders, from the level of NGOs down to individuals in rural communities. Ideally, this would extend further and facilitate greater dialogue between courts (or other institutions) and affected communities. For instance, regular meetings might not only be used as a way to coordinate activities to ensure they are conducted in all provinces of a particular region, but could be forums where the needs of community members are brought to the attention of authorities. This could encourage more responsiveness in transitional justice, while also be used to inform communities about the limitations of official institutions in addressing their expectations. They may then also seek to collaboratively design other mechanisms, in and outside of official structures that could address further needs of transitional societies. The recognition that such collaboration could provide to community efforts could further serve to empower local populations and may provide enhanced satisfaction with the process overall.

This research most clearly demonstrates that transitional justice must think and go beyond managing expectations. To truly address the expectation gap, it is necessary to rethink how we conduct transitional justice. It is important that the focus on legalism and preference for prosecutions be re-evaluated. Stakeholder goals must be considered at the very beginning of an anticipated transitional justice enterprise. These goals, frequently expressed in the expectations of stakeholders, can be ascertained through engagement, dialogue, and consultation about what it is expected that transitional justice will provide or achieve. When considering those goals, it is important to bear in mind that trials are not always the best vehicle for their achievement. In this way, transitional justice practitioners and advocates need to recognise the multiple forms of accountability and justice that exist globally and seek to incorporate those into practice.

Conclusion

There are pitfalls in a standard approach to transitional justice: particular forms of transitional justice are likely to be well-suited to a limited number of goals and satisfy a limited number of expectations. For this reason, it is important to consider the desired goals when designing a transitional justice endeavour. Transitional justice scholars, advocates, and practitioners need to engage with affected communities to ascertain their needs and expectations. Transitional justice should seek to act plurally and adopt multiple institution responses whenever possible and appropriate. It is to the advantage of affected communities and transitional justice as a field to consider other forms of justice—restorative justice or distributive justice for example—when appropriate.

Identifying these problems is only the first step in improving the function of transitional justice. So far, we have discussed the existence of an expectation problem and analysed its features. That is of little value to those who might benefit from the activities of transitional justice. What is required is to build upon the understanding of transitional justice expectations that this and preceding chapters have provided, and offer practical solutions to improve how transitional justice addresses the varied and legitimate expectations that are held for it. The following chapter takes that leap. It develops those opportunities for addressing expectations and improving transitional justice that have been identified here.

References

Aukerman, MJ 2002, 'Extraordinary evil, ordinary crime: A framework for understanding transitional justice', *Harvard Human Rights Journal*, vol. 15, pp. 39–98.

Braithwaite, J and Nickson, R 2012, 'Timing truth, reconciliation, and justice after war', *Ohio State Journal on Dispute Resolution*, vol. 27, no. 3, pp. 443–446.

Chibnall, S 1977, *Law and order news: An analysis of crime reporting in the British Press*, Tavistock Publications, London.

Drumbl, MA 2002, 'Restorative justice and collective responsibility: Lessons for and from the Rwandan genocide', *Contemporary Justice Review*, vol. 5, no. 1, pp. 5–22.

Drumbl, MA 2003, 'Toward a criminology of international crime', *Ohio State Journal on Dispute Resolution*, vol. 19, no. 1, pp. 263–281.

Dzihana, A and Volcic, Z (eds) 2011, *Media and national ideologies: Analysis of reporting on war crime trials in the former Yugoslavia*, Media Centar Sarajevo, Sarajevo, Bosnia and Herzegovina.

Eckstein, H 1975, 'Case studies and theory in political science' in Greenstein, F and Polsby, N (eds), *Handbook of Political Science*, Vol. 7, Addison-Wesley, Boston.

Fletcher, LE and Weinstein, HM 2002, 'Violence and social repair: Rethinking the contribution of justice to reconciliation', *Human Rights Quarterly*, vol. 24, no. 3, pp. 573–639.

Haider, H 2009, '(Re)Imagining coexistence: Striving for sustainable return, reintegration and reconciliation in Bosnia and Herzegovina', *International Journal of Transitional Justice*, vol. 3, no. 1, pp. 91–113.

Hancock, V 2008, '"No self" at trial: How to reconcile punishing the Khmer Rouge for crimes against humanity with Cambodian Buddhist principles', *Wisconsin International Law Journal*, vol. 26, no. 1, p. 87.

Ivkovic, SK 2001, 'Justice by the International Criminal Tribunal for the Former Yugoslavia', *Stanford Journal of International Law*, vol. 37, no. 2, pp. 255–265.

McEvoy, K 2007, 'Beyond legalism: Towards a thicker understanding of transitional justice', *Journal of Law and Society*, vol. 34, no. 4, pp. 411–440.

McEvoy, K 2008, 'Letting go of legalism: Developing a 'thicker understanding of transitional justice' in McEvoy, K and McGregor, L (eds), *Transitional justice from below: Grassroots activism and the struggle for change*, Hart Publishing, Portland, Oregon.

Marks, SP 1994, 'Forgetting "the policies and practices of the past": Impunity in Cambodia', *Fletcher Forum of World Affairs*, vol. 18, no. 2, pp. 17–44.

Nettlefield, LJ 2010, 'From the battlefield to the barracks: The ICTY and the armed forces of Bosnia and Herzegovina', *International Journal of Transitional Justice*, vol. 4, no. 1, pp. 87–109.

Open Society Justice Initiative 2012, *The future of cases 003/004 at the Extraordinary Chambers in the Courts of Cambodia*, Open Society Justice Initiative, New York.

Ramji-Nogales, J 2010, 'Designing bespoke transitional justice: A pluralist process approach', *Michigan Journal of International Law*, vol. 32, no. 1, pp. 1–72.

Simons, M 2009, 'International criminal tribunals and the media', *Journal of International Criminal Justice*, vol. 7, no. 1, pp. 83–88.

Theissen, G 2004, *Supporting justice, co-existence and reconciliation after armed conflict: Strategies for dealing with the past*, Berghof Research Center for Constructive Conflict Management, Berlin.

Zoglin, K 2005, 'The future of war crimes prosecutions in the former Yugoslavia: Accountability or junk justice?', *Human Rights Quarterly*, vol. 27, no. 1, pp. 41–77.

7

Reducing the Expectation Gap

Transitional justice faces an expectation dilemma. This book has shown that expectations for transitional justice are diverse, that some mechanisms serve some expectations well while others do not, and that some expectations have to be managed. Of course, not every expectation can be met. There will, almost certainly, always be a gap between what transitional justice mechanisms are expected to achieve and what is deliverable. This gap can be minimized. This chapter provides a critical reflection on the expectation problem and presents a response to these dilemmas. Three complementary steps to address the expectation gap are proposed: robust expectation management; development of shared aims; and an enhanced conception of what constitutes transitional justice.

A degree of expectation management is already undertaken in transitional justice. In some ways, the first step is not new. What is proposed here, however, is that we develop better and more effective strategies for expectation management. Previous chapters have outlined the diversity of expectations, noting numerous specific expectations and how they have been expressed. How expectations can be influenced has also been shown, and insights from practitioners have been provided regarding

R. Nickson and A. Neikirk, *Managing Transitional Justice*,
Palgrave Studies in Compromise after Conflict,
https://doi.org/10.1007/978-3-319-77782-5_7

how expectations may be managed. A more robust strategy for managing expectations can be built upon this knowledge from earlier chapters. Managing expectations alone will not, however, resolve the dilemmas. The second step proposes that if we hope to narrow the expectation gap further, it is necessary to consider expectations before establishing a mechanism to respond to mass violence. The proposed method for including expectations in the design of transitional justice is to develop shared aims; these will reflect the expectations of all stakeholders and are developed through a process that engages local communities with experts and donors. Shared aims can then be used in a collaborative process to craft transitional justice responses. The third step proposes a shift in the current practice of transitional justice. It sees the current legalistic and retributive focus of transitional justice as restricting the attainment of many goals. Rather than limit the aims of transitional societies—as many participants proposed by managing expectations—transitional justice and its practitioners must refocus their justice lens in order to realise a richer diversity of aims. This can be achieved by adopting a broader, deeper, and longer understanding of transitional justice.

As an elemental principle, transitional justice should seek to engage with and realise aims. It is true that some aims for transitional justice may not be realised—or even possible. This is especially true when the extent of transitional justice is equated with the conduct of a handful of trials. But transitional justice should be more than that. Transitional justice can be considered a much longer process than is currently conceived. Distinct institutions may only operate for a defined period, but transitional justice activities and efforts should not be time-limited to (relatively) brief interventions. Many aims for transitional justice will take years or decades to (even partially) achieve. These aims should not be suppressed because they may take years to realise. Instead, those aims must be harnessed. In this way, they will provide the support and momentum for working to achieve goals in the long haul of transitional justice.

Finally, this chapter argues that transitional justice needs to be seen as *transformational* justice. *Transition* in transitional justice describes the political circumstances in which these justice efforts take place. While transition does mean change from one state to another, it does not adequately describe the type of justice that should occur. Transformation describes more accurately the type of justice that is sought. The idea of transitioning from violent conflict to a state of peace, from communities committing human rights abuses against each other or themselves to forms of non-violent interaction and co-existence sounds too seamless. It suggests movement from one situation to the next but does not sufficiently convey the complexities of that shift. Most importantly, it does not suggest that underlying causes for violence have been examined and addressed—merely that they are no longer expressed violently. Alternatively, if justice is transformative, those root causes are addressed as part of the transition. Transformation may not always be possible, but it should always be the ideal.

Between Grounded Reality and Lofty Expectations

A number of sources were used in this research—court websites, academic literature, interviews with transitional justice practitioners, news media reports. All expressed expectations for transitional justice. Unfortunately, many of these expectations dwelt at the far side of a chasm, with the likely contributions of transitional justice institutions on the near side. Imagine the space between likely contributions and many expectations as the space for disappointment; the further the gap, the greater the opportunity for disappointment. Our desire then should be to reduce that gap as much as possible. By adopting the three steps outlined in this chapter, it may be possible to decrease the chances of disappointment. Figure 7.1 provides a visual representation of how this might operate.

With each step, the space between lofty expectations and the realities of transitional justice is diminished. This visual representation still leaves a gap from the top of all three steps to the "lofty expectations". This is because it will probably never be possible for transitional justice to satisfy all expectations. Many expectations will not be lofty, and will be addressed well by the first and second steps. Transitional justice, however, may never adequately address some expectations. Rather than bow to these difficulties and limit transitional justice to addressing

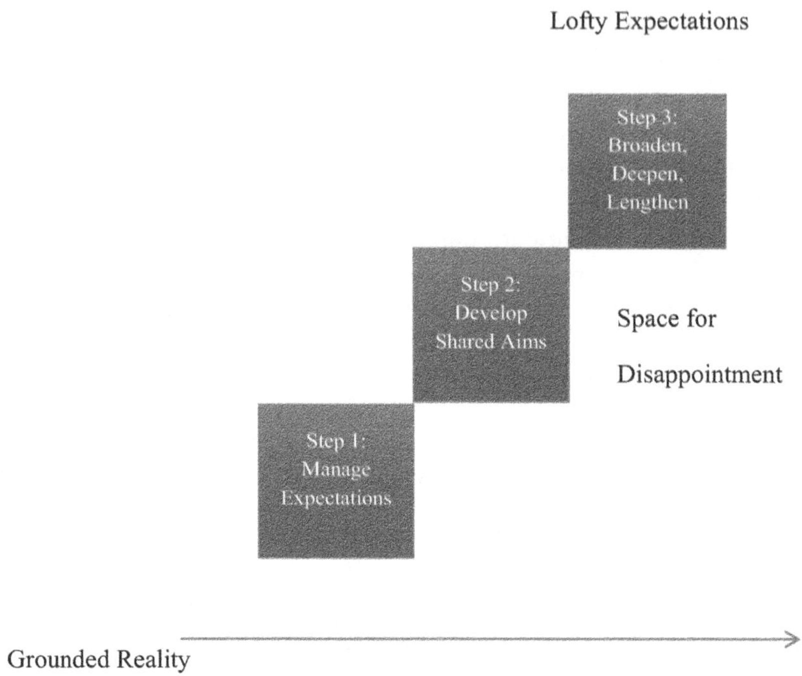

Fig. 7.1 Steps to reduce an expectation gap

smaller expectations that current practice can realise, these three steps promote further attempts at satisfying expectations. As with all steps, they are incremental, so our proposals are suited to incremental adoption. The steps are, however, mutually supportive: to develop sound strategies for expectation management, it is necessary to find out what expectations exist; by engaging with communities to discover expectations, the groundwork for developing shared aims is begun; and by incorporating stakeholders more directly into transitional justice while developing shared aims, we are within reach of broader, deeper, and longer transitional justice.

Developing a Robust Approach to Managing Expectations

Transitional justice must adopt a robust practice of expectation management, based on evidence and the context of the society in transition. Currently, it appears that, like many transitional justice courts, efforts at expectation management are ad hoc. These efforts are predominantly reactive and seek to manage an expectation once it has already been disappointed. Instead, it would be wiser to attempt to ascertain what expectations exist during early stages of transitional justice and develop a pro-active management strategy at the beginning. Research, such as that conducted here, can provide a basis for practitioners in this regard: different expectations that require management have already been identified. Unfortunately, expectations can be raised and then disappointed (and subsequently require management) as a result of the work of transitional justice institutions. This is best exemplified by reparations at the Chambers: a unique reparations programme was offered but poorly understood so that available reparations did not match people's expectations. In this way, it is possible to foresee areas where an expectation gap may exist and take pre-emptive action to avoid the worst of disappointed expectations.

In order to better manage expectations, it will be necessary to identify what they are and develop management strategies in response. Between identification and response, it is useful, however, to conceive of two more tasks: understanding why an expectation gap exists; and assessing which institutional problems mean that the expectation will not be met. Table 7.1 collates 15 expectations evident in interviews. It draws upon respondent insights, data from the content analysis, and knowledge from the literature and previous studies to demonstrate the tasks involved in a robust expectation management strategy.

One of the things this table demonstrates is the need to move beyond single-mechanism responses in transitional justice: one mechanism could not adequately satisfy the expectations in the table and would struggle even more with the plurality of expectations in an actual transitional justice context. This further supports the proposition

Table 7.1 Expectation and institutional transformation

Expectation	Expectation gap	Institutional problem	Possible solution
Arrests and verdicts secure peace and allow refugees to return home safely	Arrests and verdicts inflame anger, and fear of future arrest motivates continued fighting until an amnesty is promised	Weak understanding of local politics by international prosecutors	Research that reveals when verdicts do deliver a sense of closure and safety to refugees and how to prioritise these cases
Convictions must be for the crime of genocide	Genocide is a specific crime that is difficult to prove. Very few convictions at the Tribunal have been for genocide. Specific atrocities may not constitute genocide despite being labelled genocide by politicians, journalists, NGO advocates, and others	The 'G' word sells newspapers and opens donors' wallets	An ICC education campaign that crimes against humanity in the DRC have taken more lives than the genocide in Rwanda
All war criminals responsible for murder should be executed	None executed for the former Yugoslavia or Cambodia	Execution expectations arise from the application of capital punishment for less serious crimes in domestic criminal law or as a reaction to the terrible abuses committed	International human rights campaigning to abolish capital punishment everywhere, supported by an international education campaign on why capital punishment is counterproductive

(continued)

Table 7.1 (continued)

Expectation	Expectation gap	Institutional problem	Possible solution
Big fish must be punished	Big fish know how to keep their hands away from the blood, and set up scapegoats	Prosecutors trained in national performance i ndicator cultures to get easy notches on their gun, do not like to fail on big, hard cases	Rudolf Giuliani prosecution strategies that moved up the food chain on *Wall Street* in the 'greed is good' scandals[a]
The small fish who I saw rape and murder my daughter must be punished	System capacity overload means most small fish are untouched	Media big fish publicity pushes movement to prioritise big fish. Limited funding for courts and prosecutions requires selection between defendants	Restorative justice, truth commission and other alternatives that permit direct victim voice in small fish cases
We should not coo perate with the Tribunal because it is biased against us	Violence may be asymmetrical, with more war crimes committed by one side than another	Media report on cases where their community members are defendants, but not when their community members are victims	Public awareness campaigns to highlight that criminals from all sides will be prosecuted when evidence is available; engagement with the media to ensure that a more balanced portrayal of trials is provided
Reparations orders must provide for education regarding the Chambers' findings about Khmer Rouge crimes	Reparations orders cannot compel news agencies to broadcast or publish Chambers' findings	The Chambers' powers are limited in what they can order other agencies to do. Moral and collective reparations are not adequately explained and poorly understood	Better information on available reparations orders. Collaboration with other groups to see that reparations requests can be facilitated

(continued)

Table 7.1 (continued)

Expectation	Expectation gap	Institutional problem	Possible solution
There are mass graves all over the country: with all this evidence surely defendants will be convicted	The evident nature of crimes does not necessarily translate into evidence capable of securing convictions. Presumption of innocence in trials is difficult to accept	Rhetoric about impunity and accountability serves to raise expectations of convictions; media portrayals frequently assert the guilt of an accused	Outreach efforts to highlight the importance of a presumption of innocence and that convictions must be 'beyond a reasonable doubt'
Sentences for human rights abusers will be commensurate with my suffering as a victim	Criminal sanctions are not capable of adequately reflecting the suffering of victims	Victim needs in the wake of mass violence are complex and not well-considered in the design of transitional justice responses	Engage with victim communities and victim advocacy groups; utilise those insights in the design of transitional justice responses; ensure that when practicable those needs are catered for. Broad-deep-long justice can compensate for the fact that the suffering of punishment is less than the suffering of victimisation with many other dimensions of justice that, over time, are delivered to victims

(continued)

Table 7.1 (continued)

Expectation	Expectation gap	Institutional problem	Possible solution
Trials will tell us why "Khmer killed Khmer"	Trials answer questions of guilt or innocence; why questions may remain unanswered	Trials are limited in what they can examine by jurisdictional and practical constraints	Explore other mechanisms that can examine possible explanations for why "Khmer killed Khmer". Mechanisms may be official transitional justice institutions such as a truth commission. They may also involve collaboration with NGOs, or include local and international universities with the input of historians, investigative journalists, interpretive sermons by religious leaders etc
If we have trials, I will discover what happened to my father and where his remains are	Trial explores wider patterns of violence with the fate of individual victims not addressed	Trials are suited to answering questions about defendants and less suited to answering questions about victims	Encourage alternative proceedings in tandem with trials that provide an opportunity for offenders to reveal the location of loved ones' remains
Because there is a court I will be able to tell my story of victimisation	Very few victims will be able to testify in cases, especially those trying big fish	No other mechanisms provided for victim acknowledgment	Alternative mechanisms run officially or in collaboration with civil society that provide opportunities for victims to tell their stories and have their victimisation acknowledged

(continued)

Table 7.1 (continued)

Expectation	Expectation gap	Institutional problem	Possible solution
The siege of Vukovar is an important crime and must be dealt with in a dedicated trial with senior officials indicted	Trials focus on offenders rather than symbolic crimes, even when offenders have been prosecuted for crimes perceived as symbolic	Ineffective communication and a biased media mean that symbolic aspects of trials are inadequately conveyed to local audiences	Production of documentaries that highlight how significant crimes have been addressed
Trials will educate our younger generations about what happened during conflict	Transitional justice courts provide limited education outlets. Trials may be cumbersome and transcripts inaccessible to a broad audience	Outreach efforts constrained by shortages in funding, resources and personnel. Public education is not a traditional role of courts	Transitional justice courts adapt to include non-traditional role. Transitional societies should seek to include reformation of education to incorporate knowledge from transitional justice trials and other mechanisms

(continued)

Table 7.1 (continued)

Expectation	Expectation gap	Institutional problem	Possible solution
If people are prosecuted it will not be possible to deny the crimes that have taken place here	People continue to deny the occurrence of human rights abuses	Transitional justice courts are unwilling to engage in debates with atrocity deniers. Permission for courts' media officers to respond to egregious statements frequently withheld by senior officials	Engage more directly with local communities. Efforts such as the Tribunal's 'Bridging the Gap' conferences bring prosecutors and judges together with local communities. These events forcefully and directly challenge revisionist or denialist histories

[a]As Braithwaite explains: "That means using comparatively minor crimes like credit card fraud to sit someone down and say you will be going to jail for this credit card fraud and you will suffer the shame of your family knowing the lurid motivation for the fraud unless you provide the evidence of more major fraud against a bigger fish in your organization. Then likewise moving up from that fish to an even bigger fish in the way Giuliani did on *Wall Street* in the 1980s." John Braithwaite, 'Flipping Markets to Virtue with Qui Tam and Restorative Justice' (forthcoming) *Accounting, Organizations and Society*

that transitional justice should be multidimensional: we should think broadly about what constitutes justice in transition and also about what (and how) mechanisms and institutions might provide justice. Limiting transitional justice to one (or perhaps only a few) mechanisms means that a considerable number of expectations may go unaddressed. Instead, a transformational approach to expectation management that casts a wide net in the search for suitable responses is likely to satisfy a greater number of expectations in a greater number of ways. Openness to a variety of responses that might be employed in tandem is a natural complement to a transformational approach to expectation management that seeks to include local, as well as international, voices in designing transitional justice responses.

Not all the possible solutions in the table above are geared toward expectation management: some are more suited to the second and third steps of a more holistic approach to addressing unmet expectations. Yet many expectations can and should be managed. Even when other steps are taken, some degree of management will be necessary. For those expectations that cannot be met (capital punishment, complete prosecutions, a full historical record), management is required so that they better reflect what can be achieved and provided. The table highlights the need for not only identifying an expectation but also understanding the causes of an expectation gap and which institutional problems must be considered when finding solutions. A telling example is an expectation of bias and subsequent non-cooperation with a transitional justice institution. Two things must be understood in responding to this. The first is that trials may appear lopsided if atrocities were predominantly committed by one side in a conflict. The second is that the media are less likely to cover trials where members of their own community are victims but are more likely to cover trials where members of their own community are defendants. This may well cast a biased image of a transitional justice institution. In any response, it will be necessary to take these factors into consideration. In this example, it would be worth communicating that defendants are tried as individuals and not symbolic members of their communities. Akhavan (1998), Fletcher and Weinstein (2002), and Ivkovic (2001) have all discussed the potential benefits of individualising guilt. Communication efforts should point out that human rights abusers from all sides will be prosecuted where evidence is available, and that an artificial balance between warring factions in prosecutions is antithetical to a just criminal justice system. Recognising that the media may not be a productive partner in these efforts is fundamental. It would therefore be sensible to engage with communities via other mediums, especially to highlight how prosecutions have sought redress for the suffering of their own victims.

For expectation management to be more effective it should be considered a necessary adjunct to transitional justice from the outset. In fact, a well-rounded outreach campaign ought to recognise that expectations need to be better informed as part of its function. A gold standard for identifying expectations in transitional justice would be direct consultation with stakeholders. This could be the result of a number of activities, including community forums, NGO advocacy, or a national dialogue. In a later section, the utility of developing shared aims is discussed and the concept of Boards of Transition introduced. These boards could provide one—but an important—venue for identifying the expectations that are held for transitional justice. Of course, a more robust expectation management strategy than currently exists could be accomplished at a lesser standard without Boards of Transition. A simpler, but still effective approach, would entail better identification (based on research such as this and the research of others) followed by a dedicated management strategy. Ramji-Nogales (2010) makes a similar proposal to enhance the legitimacy of transitional justice institutions, arguing for the design of institutions to be informed by research into local preferences for transitional justice. While the kind of research undertaken for this book is a useful resource, it cannot compete with actual consultation through direct engagement with communities in providing an understanding of relevant expectations. This is because the goals and expectations for transitional justice will be contextual and may vary between cases (Ramji-Nogales 2010; Aukerman 2002).

The Limitations of Expectation Management

Managing expectations is an important task in transitional justice. While expectation management can often be an appropriate and necessary response, it is nevertheless problematic. Due to issues of power imbalance, managing someone's expectations is an idea we have been normatively uncomfortable with since it was first mentioned in interviews. Managing expectations was consistently described by respondents in terms of top-down management: *they* have expectations and *we* must manage them. The ordinary meaning among respondents was managing the expectations of those below (often victims) by those above (often prosecutors and tribunals). Of course, the phrase "managing expectations" is not necessarily top-down and unidirectional. It is equally conceivable that expectations could be managed bottom-up. But a bottom-up approach to managing expectations was not how respondents expressed it. It was often a way of shaping or changing the goals of affected communities so that they more closely reflected institutionally relevant goals: the goals that particular institutions were most suited to achieve. There are several problems with managing expectations—as it is currently conceived—that this section seeks to address.

When expectations are considered to require management, it presupposes that some are appropriate, while others are not. This creates a dichotomy of expectations. Often this means expectations must be fashioned to fit a particular manifestation of transitional justice, such as a trial. It was concerning that respondents never asked whether their institution was inappropriate for otherwise legitimate expectations. If these manifestations of transitional justice are imposed or created without the meaningful involvement of affected communities—as they frequently are—the perceived need to manage expectations may be amplified as a result of the greater distance between institution and affected community. Additionally, the expectations held for transitional justice will in many cases reflect fundamental concerns that relate to the quality of life of members of affected communities. For instance, there may be an intention to discover some answers about the fate of a missing loved one to aid in closure; or acknowledgment that one's own victimisation will occur; or an opportunity to have one's story recorded. The realisation of these expectations, at least in part, is likely to make a significant impact upon that person's life. In the context of the Tribunal and Chambers, these are unlikely to be appropriate or institutionally relevant expectations for most members of affected communities. As a result, these expectations will have to be managed. Such an attitude is antithetical to the purpose of transitional justice. If legitimate expectations of affected communities are not addressed, this reduces the scope for transitional justice to make positive contributions in transitional societies. Also, if transitional justice is to be transformative, it must incorporate expectations that seek to address the causes of past violence.

Important personal and societal expectations may well be impossible to manage. Many aims express deep needs for healing, recognition, and transformation. As a result, it may be difficult, or impossible, for people to abandon those aims, even partially. For this reason attempts at managing may be unpersuasive and consequently unsuccessful. Indeed, managing expectations may at times be an unrealistic expectation. In relation to transitional justice in the former Yugoslavia and Cambodia, the creation of institutions without first considering local expectations has meant that many have not been addressed well or at all. This suggests that designing transitional justice responses without considering expectations as possible and appropriate goals for the process can increase the likelihood of dissatisfaction. The view that expectations must be managed is then not only an objectionable way to treat the aims of affected communities but a symptom of transitional justice endeavours that are pre-formed and applied with minimal consideration to local contexts and needs.

Finding Shared Aims

Following from more robust expectation management, the second step is to identify shared aims. Shared aims reflect the goals and desired outcomes of all stakeholders in a transitional justice setting. Developing shared aims requires us to begin by looking at where we want to go. A similar argument is made by Balint (1996, p. 104), who suggests that post-conflict societies should consider "what are the short and long term goals, and what role can law play in the transition, and in the realization of these goals?" That means considering expectations for transitional justice before establishing institutions. Current practice does not appear to do this. Instead we are (quite understandably) captivated by the enormity of the crimes and suffering. As a result we ask: "How do we respond to the terrible crimes that have occurred?" Framed this way, it is hardly surprising that prosecutions and trials, retributivism and legalism, dominate the current practice of transitional justice at an official level. This approach is counterproductive for achieving many of the aims held for transitional justice. We can describe the current process of constructing transitional justice as looking at where we were and seeing what could be done to improve where we are now. With this approach we might say to ourselves: "Our current situation is dire. Can we do something about the crimes of the past to improve it?" What should take place is quite different: we need to look at where we would like to be and think about how we can get there from our current position. This way, the question could be: "We would like to be a society with x attribute(s) [these could be harmony, rule of law etc.], so how can transitional justice help us become that society?"

This is most likely to succeed as an inclusive process: it should involve all stakeholders in the transitional justice landscape. Primarily, it needs to involve affected communities and seek to discover their aims for transitional justice. As Lambourne (2009, p. 28) has observed "decisions about transitional justice are too often made without consulting the population affected." To this end, collaboration ought to begin with the construction of the framework for future transitional justice. One way this might operate in practice involves a pre-process to the transitional justice process itself. A pre-process would give voice to the various aims that stakeholders hold for the transitional justice enterprise. Ideally, this would be a tiered process that begins before any transitional justice institution is selected and established. The first tier would take place as community or interest-group forums, where members determine what it is that they aim to achieve through transitional justice. Groups may be determined by any number of relevant criteria. They may represent geographic locations, such as a particular village. They might also represent a particular class of victim: inmates of a prison camp or victims of gender-based violence. In the former Yugoslavia, the second two groups may be most relevant, whereas the first grouping by village may be considered more relevant in Cambodia. The point is that there are a number of available and appropriate ways that community members might identify collectively in this process. At this stage, official or elite stakeholders would not be excluded. Indeed, they would contribute considerably—though it is preferable if communities are able to enunciate their own aims organically. While this dialogue takes place, elites and community members may also participate in a dialogue through the media and in political spaces. Ideally, this dialogue would be the genesis for ongoing debates about transitional justice and social transformation. It may also provide a peaceful outlet for the resolution of conflicts where conflicts had previously been resolved through violence.

By including in dialogue at these stages a discussion about the strengths and weaknesses of various alternative mechanisms, a more informed decision can be made about which mechanisms to employ. It will also help to enunciate and clarify aims that should be used to inform the decision about which possible mechanisms to adopt. This education and information must be presented carefully. The risk is that the shape of transitional justice could be dictated by the content of educational and informative efforts by elites. The task of educating and informing in this context is similar to managing expectations. It is conceded that in the design of transitional justice it will be necessary for some expectations and aims to be given a reality check. Frequently, it will be the task of transitional justice elites to educate and inform transitional communities in this way. This differs from the expectation management that respondents advocated in that it occurs *before* a transitional justice mechanism has been adopted or institution created. This approach informs expectations so that shared aims are based on outcomes that might reasonably be anticipated. It also permits the "reality check" to operate in all directions. Respondents saw expectation management as uni-directional and top-down. Expectation management does not theoretically have to follow that path, but this research demonstrates that it is invested with this normative construction by transitional justice elites in The Hague, the former Yugoslavia, and Cambodia. Considering this component for formulating shared aims as a process of reciprocally educating and informing among stakeholders is preferable. This shifts the focus from the legitimate parameters of expectations to the likely parameters of institutions. The discussion evolves to one about what contributions an institution might make towards shared aims.

An important feature of educating and informing requires that the rhetoric used to promote transitional justice be toned down. Currently, many claims are made about the positive contributions that transitional justice will make that border on misinformation. It has been observed that the rhetoric of diplomats and international officials frequently overplays the salutary benefits of transitional justice (Nickson and Braithwaite 2014). Although this might be useful to consolidate donor funding, the practice is damaging to perceptions of transitional justice, as well as for affected communities. The rhetoric may well serve to raise or affirm hopes, particularly in relation to specific transitional justice institutions. The need for modesty and to refrain from over-selling is relevant for a number of expectations, such as reconciliation:

> Institutions that seek to assist in this process should be clear that they offer only that—assistance in creating the conditions for future reconciliation—and not a magic bullet that will immediately erase complex and long-standing societal dysfunctions. Raising Expectations beyond this point will serve only to diminish the legitimacy of transitional justice mechanisms, rendering them even less effective. (Ramji-Nogales 2010, p. 63)

This contrasts with informing aims, where any elevation in hopes for achieving aims occurs in reference to information based on knowledge and experience. Currently, many statements in these situations make promises that are then expected to be delivered. These pronouncements are rarely supported by knowledge or experience. This is even more problematic when an institution is not well suited to delivering any significant dividend on those statements. It may also encourage beliefs that such expectations will be realised in significantly shorter timeframes than are likely. The effect of this will possibly be greater dissatisfaction than if the rhetoric had been more measured. This is not to discourage the expression of large or even grand hopes for transitional justice. Grand hopes should be given voice: they reflect our greater hopes for humanity and point the direction that societies in transition will wish to take for the long-term. There needs to be more modesty, however, in what is attributed to limited efforts at transitional justice such as trials.

Efforts at developing shared aims should seek to build collaborative relationships between various transitional justice actors and affected communities. Importantly, it should attempt to provide pathways to securing the goals that official transitional justice institutions may be unlikely to deliver. This process would require transitional justice elites to engage with communities to determine what their aims are, understand what needs they would like addressed, and explain how various mechanisms may operate in relation to those aims. Figure 7.2 provides an abridged sample of the sort of dialogue that this would involve:

The dialogue presented in Fig. 7.2 is overly simplistic. However, it does provide guidance as to the broad-strokes of how such a dialogue would develop. Importantly, dialogues such as this should occur from the very conception of transitional justice initiatives and continue throughout transitional justice endeavours. In some ways, similar work is being conducted by NGOs in parallel with official transitional justice endeavours. The work of Cambodian NGOs, and especially Youth for Peace, exhibits some of the qualities proposed here. The Youth for Peace memory project works with local communities and assists them in designing their own memory projects in response to Khmer Rouge abuses. These efforts fit within the memorialisation suite of transitional justice mechanisms. Such efforts are particularly laudable for facilitating local communities to develop their own unique memorialisation efforts. This approach, however, still provides limited scope for shared aims, as the broader mechanisms—in this case, it is memorialisation—have already been selected by elites. The proposal put forward here goes a step further. Rather than presupposing the type of transitional justice project and facilitating local design of the form, both type and form should be crafted from shared aims.

One potential pitfall for this proposal is an issue of expertise and facilitation. NGOs such as Youth for Peace facilitate projects in areas of their own expertise. If projects within communities do not correspond to NGO expertise, then the quality may (but not necessarily) be diminished. Such problems can be overcome through the networking of transitional justice NGOs locally and globally. In this way NGOs would be able to connect communities and other NGOs where there is a need to respond to a particular aim of a community. This would not prevent NGOs with a particular interest in activities—such as memorialisation—from operating within that community. What needs to be avoided is the imposition of an aim when it is preferable to work towards achieving shared aims. One way this might be achieved is through a transitional justice inventory. Similar to John Paul Lederach's (2010) proposal for a peace inventory, a transitional justice inventory takes stock of the available expertise and current activities for promoting transitional justice. The inventory raises awareness of strengths to be exploited and weaknesses to be addressed in the practice of transitional justice. Lederach has argued, based on practice, that the coordination of efforts is far more successful in peacebuilding if a peace inventory is created. A peace inventory, according to Lederach (2010, p. 100), may be created through research or conferencing, with the latter method "more mutually enriching to the groups involved." It is preferable in transitional justice that a more inclusive and enriching process for creating a transitional justice inventory is adopted as well. In particular, this ought to reinforce the focus on contextual aims when designing transitional justice mechanisms. It also better serves the proposal made here: that transitional justice should seek to identify and achieve shared aims.

It is necessary to recognise that in certain situations it may be impossible to develop shared aims among (formerly) warring factions. Where animosity between groups continues in a way that precludes developing shared aims it may be possible to change hearts without changing minds. This means encouraging groups to recognise their common humanity and to come to the realisation that suffering has occurred on both sides. Collaborative transitional justice efforts that seek to increase empathy can be the most useful in situations of intractable disagreement. One way this could operate in practice is if stakeholders agree on a transitional justice response without agreeing on the reasons for it. This would amount to a "workable agreement" (Eriksen 1994) or an "incompletely theorized agreement"—an agreement that people are willing to accept despite incompatible ethical reasons (Sunstein 1995, 1996).

Community: We would like a trial. The offenders must be punished.

TJ Elite: Okay. Who should be tried?

Community: All the people who committed crimes against us.

TJ Elite: But certainly anyone from both sides should be prosecuted if they committed crimes, including from your community. What would you like trials to do for you as individuals and as a community?

Community: We want our suffering acknowledged, we want the truth of what happened to be known.

TJ Elite: So considering that we might only be able to prosecute a few people how else might you receive acknowledgment?

Community: If they apologised somehow, officially.

TJ Elite: How would this apology need to be delivered to for it to be acceptable?

Community: They would need to show us where our sons lie in the mass graves and help us rebury them properly.

TJ Elite: Would you as a community be willing to do the same?

Community: Yes.

TJ Elite: Now, what things will an apology not give you that are important as individuals and a community?

Such a dialogue could continue, until the most important aims have been discussed, the strengths and weaknesses of various mechanisms for achieving those aims have been fleshed out, and some distinct suggestions for achieving those aims have been proposed.

Fig. 7.2 A shared aims dialogue

While originally conceived in relation to accepting judicial determinations, an incompletely theorized agreement is not limited to the decisions of courts. In the transitional context it could apply to bodies responsible for determining transitional justice responses (such as the Boards of Transition that are discussed in this chapter). An example of this in operation might be where all can agree that a truth commission, a trial, or lustration are needed in the wake of violence, but without agreement among the different sides as to whose culpability has necessitated this. If the subsequent process is transparent and inclusive then this can be fertile ground for the first growth of transitional justice. As Nickson and Braithwaite (2014, p. 449) argue:

> a conscious broadening-deepening-lengthening of the meaning of justice creates a wider contract zone for the discovery of justice outcomes that are widely accepted by folk with opposed rationales for that acceptance. Thereby, transitional justice outcomes that are incompletely theorized can unify the disunited to work together for a better future of peace with justice.

Developing shared aims is an ideal. In many instances there will be scope for a dialogue that crafts shared aims from the expectations of diverse stakeholders. On those occasions when this is not possible an approach that provides shared paths for justice despite disagreement may eventually lead to a shared vision in the long haul of transitional justice.

Broadening, Deepening, and Lengthening Transitional Justice

As this chapter has argued so far, working towards shared aims is a more inclusive approach to transitional justice. Consequently, it seeks to broaden and deepen how transitional justice is undertaken. This leads to the third and final step: that we must conceive transitional justice as broader, deeper, and longer. In order to address more effectively the expectation problem, a broadened, deepened, and lengthened conception of transitional justice should be adopted (Nickson and Braithwaite 2014, p. 445). Broadened transitional justice requires that we provide more opportunities to achieve the shared aims of stakeholders. It eschews limiting transitional justice activities to one response and argues for multiple approaches to justice and dimensions of justice. Deepening transitional justice complements broadening in that it seeks to provide greater engagement of communities with the transitional justice process. It seeks a justice with deep roots in the society. At present, many transitional justice institutions operate within defined, and relatively short, time periods. This may often exclude from transitional justice those who are unready to confront their experiences of conflict within that window, who have not returned from exile, who have been recovering from trauma in a mental hospital, who with the passing of time have reached the point of transcending their former shame at being a rape victim. By lengthening transitional justice, a greater opportunity is provided for all to be involved when they are ready.

A broader conception of transitional justice is a more holistic and multidimensional understanding of what justice can mean and be (Nickson and Braithwaite 2014). Chapter 2 described how legalism had come to dominate the theory and practice of transitional justice. This constrains the positive contributions other understandings of justice can make in transitional societies. In a broadened conception of transitional justice, prosecutorial responses would be problematized to a greater extent and various other responses would be considered in tandem with, or in place of, trials. As atrocities took place during the disintegration of the former Yugoslavia, there were multiple calls for justice and punishment. Yet even with over a hundred prosecutions at the Tribunal (and a number of trials in national jurisdictions), it has not been possible to bring all war criminals to justice. This is not unique to the Yugoslavian experience, as calls for justice and punishment are a common occurrence during, or in the wake of, mass violence (Nickson and Braithwaite 2014). Only a few of these calls can ever be met in transitional justice prosecutions.

If we conceive of transitional justice more broadly, it may be possible to deliver more justice. Nickson and Braithwaite (2014, p. 448) explain, "[t]his response grows from valorizing the idea that international law should have a more international, less narrowly western, character, because it is international." What we ought to include in our vision for transitional justice are alternative forms of justice to the retributive model: forms such as traditional justice; indigenous justice; restorative justice and so on. In this way, it is recognised that justice is holistic and ought to be practised that way. For the world's largest religions, the holism of justice is a constant theme (Nickson and Braithwaite 2014). Zehr (1995) has pointed out that Judaism and Christianity share the Hebrew word *shalom* for holistic peace with justice. Llewellyn and Philpott (2014) state that the word *salam* in Arabic has a similar meaning. *Shalom* and *salam* resonate with the concept of *Ubuntu* (Nickson and Braithwaite 2014). *Ubuntu* is a Zulu, Xhosa and pan-African concept of justice (Nickson and Braithwaite 2014). The holism of an *ubuntu*-informed understanding of justice was outlined in a 2011 hate speech trial in South Africa:

> Ubuntu is recognised as being an important source of law within the context of strained or broken relationships amongst individuals or communities and as an aid for providing remedies which contribute towards more mutually acceptable remedies for the parties in such cases. (*Afri-Forum and Another vs. Malema and others*, no. 20968/2010 S.A. Eq. Ct., [2011] ZAEQC 2 [11–12])

These broaden (Western) justice by incorporating different paths for addressing wrongs. A conception of transitional justice informed by diverse approaches to justice more broadly may well serve to enhance the justice that stakeholders receive. It does this by enabling responses that would otherwise be overlooked or dismissed in an approach to transitional justice that is dominated by legalism.

Broadening our conception of transitional justice can also mean incorporating projects aimed at providing social justice. In the wake of civil wars and other forms of mass violence, critical infrastructure may be destroyed or non-existent. Projects such as building schools can contribute to social justice and may act as important ways to broaden transitional justice. The advantage of these relatively quick projects is that their impact is felt sooner than the impact of a lengthy trial. Prioritising social justice over legal justice in early stages can also work to establish trust in transitional justice efforts by providing tangible benefits in the wake of conflict. This connects to a suggestion made later, where the building of local infrastructure and facilities can form part of restorative efforts between offenders and victims.

Another way to broaden transitional justice would be to consider more actively a focus on harms and needs. Current transitional justice focuses primarily on crimes. This focus is not unique to transitional justice. It is also a dominant feature of most Western conceptions of criminal justice. The adoption of a focus on harms rather than crimes in transitional justice could assist the realisation of a greater number of aims. Many aims relate more to the victim/survivor experience of mass violence and their needs for recovery. Currently, these aims are not well-addressed in official retributive expressions of transitional justice. When we focus on crimes, recovery is rarely considered directly. A crime focus seeks to respond to a wrong, frequently by punishing the wrongdoer. These efforts do hope to provide some redress for those harmed directly by the wrongdoer—yet only for those whose harms are prosecuted. This leaves the victims whose harms have not been prosecuted, or perhaps even investigated, without redress. Simultaneously, a focus on crimes can only ever hope to recognise symbolically the harms suffered by others whose offenders have not had their crimes investigated and prosecuted. This focus has led to a disconnect between the aims of communities and the aims of institutions: the juxtaposition between an aim to try selected individuals to a high legal standard (with any ancillary benefits that may have) with an aim to respond more broadly to the past and ongoing suffering of survivors and victims. The result has been that transitional justice practitioners perceive a need to manage expectations. When the focus is shifted to harms, then recovery can be placed at the centre of transitional justice efforts. This focus places greater emphasis on the wider aims for transitional justice and seeks to discover ways to realise them. The many goals that are ancillary or excluded in a focus on crimes may now be central and included through a focus on harms.

There are several distinct benefits to transitional justice adopting a focus on harms. For societies in transition, the prior human rights abuses were most likely widespread. Hence, offending is similarly widespread. Transitional justice, as it is practiced through trials, has come to accept that the vast majority of offenders will not be prosecuted. This leaves the vast majority of crimes unattended by official efforts. Consequently, the victims of those crimes will not be directly engaged or invested in the transitional justice process. This means that the majority of victims are excluded, which can equate to the majority of a transitional society being excluded. Many of the intended goals of transitional justice can only be realised with the participation and investment of local communities. For this reason, a focus on harms is beneficial, as it can include a far greater number of community members in the transitional justice process. Such a focus could also lead to greater engagement at the negotiation and design phases of transitional justice.

A problematic concept with trials after periods of mass violence is that judging takes place from an entirely different moral order than that which existed during conflict (Aukerman 2002; see also Cockayne 2005, who argues that this confrontation of moral orders is a distinct benefit of transitional justice). Human rights abuses often take place in societies with an absence of law and order and skewed moral frames as a result of conflict. In these conditions, crimes are frequently encouraged, rewarded, supported, and condoned by leaders, military and religious authorities, and even the offenders' communities. Under these circumstances it may be difficult for many to avoid participation in human rights abuses. It may not be uncommon for human rights abusers to face a tough choice between demonstrating solidarity with their own group by participating in abuses, or risk the safety and security of themselves and their family. Judging such conduct when hostilities have abated and a different normative frame is in place may raise questions of legitimacy. A focus on crimes encourages judging from a legal framework. That framework is unlikely to sufficiently account for the moral quandaries some offenders faced during conflict. This in turn may discourage participation by those who are most likely to be in a position to repair harms: offenders, for instance, who know the fate and location of deceased loved ones. A focus on harms does not face this challenge.

A focus on harms redirects attention towards recognising the humanity of those who have suffered.

This is not to dismiss entirely the value of a focus on crimes, a focus designed to designate offensive conduct as abhorrent. The label of crime carries authority and weight: to describe something as a crime is to forcefully declare it outside the boundaries of accepted conduct. The application of the label crime is a powerful form of censure for criminals and provides a degree of acknowledgment for (some) victims. This is as true in transitional justice as it would be in domestic criminal justice. Similarly, a focus on crimes may promote the expressivist function of transitional justice described by Drumbl (2007, p. 12): "the messaging value of punishment to affirm respect for law, reinforce a moral consensus, narrate history and educate the public." While the censure that follows from labelling something as criminal may be severe, the acknowledgment is likely to end at this point. It does not require that we examine the extent of the crime or its ongoing effects. It certainly does not require that we acknowledge the continuing impact of the crime on the victim. It may be a superficial form of acknowledgment for victims when genuine efforts at repair may do more to acknowledge the harms caused by the crime. For these reasons, there is limited scope to the acknowledgment victims receive by labelling the conduct that harmed them as criminal. In contrast, a focus on harms requires a commensurate focus on needs. The needs of individuals and communities after mass violence will correspond to what we might otherwise express as many of the aims of transitional justice: reparation; acknowledgment; truth. Focusing on harms in transitional justice without simultaneously addressing the needs that result from those harms is a hollow process. In the process of establishing shared aims, the needs of community members, victims and other stakeholders affected by violence should be uncovered and weaved into the design of transitional justice responses so that they can be better addressed.

In efforts to broaden our conception of transitional justice, it will be necessary to consider all mechanisms that could be employed. Step 2 described the process of developing shared aims. In order to better address expectations, we should use these shared aims to inform the selection and design of transitional justice institutions. The shape of any mechanism is likely to be more fit for purpose when devised and designed locally, with the input of those communities who are directly affected. The success of such mechanisms is likely to be strongest where they are contextually and culturally relevant. They need to reflect the community's understanding of justice, while being feasible to conduct given the local conditions. Those conditions will not be limited to cultural understandings; they also need to include human, financial, and even emotional resources.

In the content analysis, the problem of "lost opportunities" (where prosecution and conviction of high-profile figures are impossible) was raised. Although this sentiment was frequently expressed following the death of a senior figure considered responsible for atrocities, it is equally relevant in situations where war criminals cannot be identified; are unavailable for prosecution (perhaps because they are shielded from prosecution in a third country); or are unwilling to participate in a transitional justice process. In response, transitional justice should seek to employ mechanisms that can address the harms and needs of victims without the involvement of individual offenders. This relates to Johnstone's (2002, p. 79) suggestion for "clubbing together": "provid[ing] collective support for victims of crime". Johnstone conceives that a process for determining who is a victim is a necessary component of providing such support. As the Tribunal and Chambers are limited in their work to distinct prosecutions, representing a fraction of all crimes committed, they do not perform this task widely. Yet it is conceivable that such a process could be another function of international criminal tribunals. A process could be included where victims seek determination of their claim. The civil party process at the Chambers does perform this determination; however, it is an adjunct to criminal proceedings. It has also been problematic—especially when victims' applications for recognition are denied because they do not fit the particular case being prosecuted. While judges are evidently at pains to distinguish between being a victim and being a victim who may participate as a civil party, it is debatable whether such a distinction is satisfactory to those with unsuccessful applications. There may be some argument that the distinction compounds victimisation as well. Just as legal recognition vindicates victims, so legal denial diminishes them.

As the focus of activities at the Tribunals and Chambers is, by necessity, on other matters, the inclusion of a process to determine who is a victim could be unwise. Similarly, who is a victim after mass violence is itself difficult to answer. There are so many levels of direct and indirect victims in wars, and as many perpetrators will also be victims, distinctions will be blurred and difficult to make. Hence, it might be preferable to find alternative mechanisms to perform this function. The truth commission, for instance, is better suited to making such determinations: it is not as constrained by the relevance of victims to jurisdictional concerns or by reference to particular defendants and cases. Alternatively, efforts to recognise and address harms against victims could be incorporated into the proposal in the following section. While Johnstone conceives of "clubbing together" as the collective responsibility for the support of victims, the next section argues that collective responsibility needs to be adopted more broadly.

Broadening our conception of responsibilities in transitional justice may provide another way to address more expectations. The term *responsibilities*, as it is used here, is distinct from *responsibility*. This proposal does not seek to broaden our understanding of who is criminally responsible. This would be a problematic suggestion. Criminal responsibility for crimes against humanity is a well-developed area of jurisprudence. Rather, it is proposed that we broaden our understanding of responsibilities in the wake of mass violence and as a component of transitional justice. Responsibilities, in this sense, are steps that individuals, communities, businesses, industries, governments, militias and others ought to take to rectify past wrongs and contribute to ongoing justice and rebuilding efforts. An oft-cited justification for the use of criminal trials in transitional justice is that they individualise guilt. The benefit of this, it is claimed, is to alleviate the burden of collective guilt from communities and to encourage communities to see crimes as having been perpetrated by individuals, not groups or entire communities, thereby promoting reconciliation. The true extent that this has taken place in either the former Yugoslavia or Cambodia is difficult to assess. It appears, however, to have been more of a dream than a reality. For instance, Nettlefield's (2010) research showed that members of the Bosnian military were more likely to believe that other ethnicities, not their own, were most responsible for atrocities. Evidence of segregation in schools (Clark 2010), competing histories, the division in politics along ethnic lines from the conflict, and the persistence of ethnic identities since conflict, suggest that little deep reconciliation has taken place. Two participants described the current situation as the continuation of the war through politics and the media (Tribunal Outreach #1; Tribunal Outreach #2). Interviewees in Cambodia spoke of discrimination against the children of Khmer Rouge cadre by their non-Khmer Rouge teachers. Such evidence suggests that trials have not been successful in removing collective guilt from communities.

In response, it is proposed that to broaden transitional justice, we also need to conceive of responsibilities that stem from mass violence more broadly. There is a benefit in avoiding the attachment of guilt to communities in transitional societies, as outlined by the advocates for individualising guilt. What should be encouraged is collective ownership of harms. This means that communities, government agencies or departments, businesses and industries, militias and security forces would accept responsibility to perform acts that will address the impact of conduct or complicity by such groups during conflict. This will respond to situations where individual perpetrators may not be identified. It may also address the complicity of those who supported or encouraged abuses without perpetrating them themselves, as Fletcher and Weinstein (2002) have discussed. These are both areas that the current, retributive approach to transitional justice fails to address. To function, trials require a defendant. Yet the identification, location and apprehension of a defendant may prove to be impossible tasks in transitional societies and for the types of crimes transitional justice addresses. Similarly, many people will have various levels of complicity in human rights abuses and war crimes. Trials will only address those whose complicity falls within narrowly defined legal criteria (and from a due process perspective, this is appropriate). This will frequently mean that the conditions that permitted, and the support that was given to, the commission (and committers) of abuses are left untouched. It is reasonable to be concerned that a moral taint between communities may exist. This process should be considered a part of cleansing that moral taint.

One way that this might be conducted would be for leaders to express regret in an appropriate forum and provide apologies on behalf of their group to those who were victims (for a discussion of the role of apology in transitional justice, see Celermajer 2013). Given the plurality of violence and abuses in conflict, this would ideally be offered by all sides. The responsibility cannot end there: once accepting the responsibilities that flow from violence, communities should be encouraged to make gestures of goodwill, repair and restoration to one another to demonstrate the sincerity of their self-reproach. This represents recognition of the obligations that stem from widespread violence between communities—a feature of a more restorative lens for viewing transitional justice. For example, militias might contribute to building women's health clinics for the victims of rape and sexual trauma. Such gestures in the context of Bosnia might be the assistance in rebuilding places of worship that were destroyed as a part of ethnic cleansing. In Cambodia, where the identification of a "community" of Khmer Rouge cadres may be more difficult 30 years on, such gestures could involve the volunteering of time to maintain a *stupa* dedicated to victims. The imposition that such activities may have on communities would be a further demonstration of their sincerity.

Examples of similar activities to those proposed above have occurred during peacebuilding and reconciliation efforts elsewhere. The notion advanced here of collective responsibility that builds upon and draws from successful practices of group reconciliation efforts in Bougainville, where reconciliation between groups was observed to create paths to reconciliation between individuals (Braithwaite and Nickson 2012). The rebuilding of houses and places of worship is not a new manifestation of collective efforts at reconciliation: such activities occurred in Indonesian peacebuilding and were seen to encourage the return of victims to former communities (Braithwaite et al. 2010). These group reconciliation efforts highlight something that has been lacking at the official level of transitional justice in the former Yugoslavia and Cambodia. What is needed in both locations—and in all transitional societies—is the introduction of collective responsibilities, possibly within a restorative justice framework. Activities conducted under this rubric are likely to go a long way in achieving many aims of transitional justice that are often neglected in a focus on prosecutions and trials.

Offenders may find living with their crimes difficult and employ techniques of rationalisation and neutralisation to justify their behaviour (Sykes and Matza 1957). In a domestic criminal setting, offenders will argue that: their victims deserved it or invited the offence; the victims could afford to be deprived of their property or rights; the criminal conduct was not particularly harmful; or the offender themselves is the true victim of the situation (Sykes and Matza 1957). Such techniques are used to diminish feelings of guilt that would otherwise be experienced as a result of criminal conduct. Trials are said to address such rationalisation and neutralisation quite poorly (Zehr 2002). Instead of encouraging offenders to dispense with rationalisation and neutralisation techniques—to accept the harms committed and recognise the impact of their behaviour and the suffering of victims—prosecutions and trials have quite the opposite effect. The adversarial nature of criminal proceedings encourages the maintenance of rationalisation and neutralisation techniques. Similarly, the removal of—or limited role for—victims from the process does little to facilitate any realisation of the impact of offending on them. There is very little in prosecutions and trials that confronts the offender directly with the harm of their offending and that consequently challenges their rationalisations and neutralisations.

This is directly relevant to transitional societies. In such societies, rationalisation and neutralisation techniques are manifested in the process of othering. Here, groups are divided by some form of identity (such as ethnicity) and encouraged to view others in opposition to that identity. These "others" are the enemy and atrocities and human rights abuses against them are both rationalised and neutralised by reference to this identity framework (Stanley 2004). Problematically, at the Tribunal and Chambers, these rationalisations and neutralisations continue. It has not been uncommon for defendants to maintain their neutralisation fictions during trials at either institution. In many trials, the actions are still maintained as saving, liberating, reforming, protecting. Or the extent and nature of the abuses is denied. Such conduct during trials can further entrench social division in transitional societies.

This is because the various sides still see the enemy-other: there is nothing to bring communities together in this landscape. It is an impediment to peaceful co-existence and reconciliation.

An approach that directly confronted these rationalisation and neutralisation techniques could go much further in aiding shared aims of peaceful co-existence and reconciliation. What may be required is a process that re-humanises the victim who has become the enemy-other through rationalisation and neutralisation. Although such re-humanisation must take place from the offender's (and preferably also the offender community's) perspective, it places the dignity and inviolability of the victim at its centre. A shift from viewing the victim as the enemy-other to considering them a fellow citizen worthy of the same respect and rights is an important step towards reconciling individuals and communities. One way would be to focus on harms, but it also requires greater inclusivity. Even if reconciliation is too hopeful, there is still the prospect of contributing to an easing of tensions and the reduction of embedded violence by fostering a climate of greater mutual respect. These are steps toward peaceful co-existence between formerly opposed groups. Additionally, goals such as acknowledgment, truth, and healing are also likely to be more adequately addressed when rationalisation and neutralisation are more directly challenged. For example, acknowledgment is more likely if rationalisation and neutralisation techniques are removed: the purpose of such efforts is primarily one of acknowledgment of suffering and the worth and inviolability of the victim. Truth is also likely to be advanced when abusers no longer maintain rationalisation and neutralisation fictions. For the former Yugoslavia and Cambodia, such changes would be very beneficial in light of the manipulation through propaganda and other means that drove people to commit human rights abuses: ethnic nationalism in Yugoslavia; and the volatile mix of rabid nationalism and communism in Cambodia.

Deepening our conception of transitional justice means providing greater opportunities for meaningful engagement in the process. This should begin with steps 1 and 2 of this proposal. At step 1, the task of identifying which expectations are held is an important foundation for deeper transitional justice. It should demonstrate to stakeholders that their needs as a result of mass violence are being considered. Of course, step 2 takes this even deeper as it seeks a collaborative and dialogic development of shared aims between all stakeholders in transitional justice. Meaningful participation in both these steps illustrates significant examples of how transitional justice can be conceived more deeply. These two solutions enable deeper transitional justice. The first builds upon the suggestion for developing shared aims and including them in the design of transitional justice responses (as a component of broadening transitional justice). It argues that this method of institution design, "outside-in" design, is a more participatory and stakeholder inclusive method (Braithwaite 2005). The second solution is the establishment for Boards of Transition. Importantly, these boards would be well-equipped to undertake the first (identifying expectations that need to be managed) and second (developing shared aims) steps of the entire process. Boards of Transition, it is suggested, can provide meaningful forums for deeper engagement of stakeholders (and especially local community members) in transitional justice.

When discussing the need to broaden our conception of transitional justice, it was suggested that shared aims should inform the design of transitional justice institutions. This reflects an "outside-in" approach to the design of an institution where the design reflects the needs and preferences of users rather than administrators (Braithwaite 2005). Braithwaite (2005) notes, in relation to tax systems and risk management, that inside-out design (designed with administrative purposes in mind) institutions can often be too inflexible. A similar practice exists in transitional justice: mechanisms are often designed to reflect the capacities of donors or goals of elites. An "outside-in" design for transitional justice, a "bespoke" tailoring of transitional justice (Ramji-Nogales 2010), would incorporate many more shared aims in this process. There are several benefits for transitional justice from this. First, it makes transitional justice far more inclusive than its current practice at the official level. Communities would be aware that they have involvement in the process and that their ideas are considered. Second, it should assist in refocusing the purpose of transitional justice on achieving shared aims. In this way, the level of expectation disappointment could be further reduced. Such an approach would both broaden and deepen transitional justice in affected communities.

A new addition to transitional justice practice that could help this process would be Boards of Transition. These could be established at local/communal levels, as well as at state and national levels. Local boards would be well-placed to encourage direct efforts in transitional justice, facilitating grassroots projects and acting as a forum for local stakeholders. A national board would build upon this grassroots work and steer wider transitional justice efforts. It may conduct such activities as producing reports on transitional justice progress, but its primary task would be the selection and establishment of transitional justice mechanisms. Boards of Transition suit the three steps outlined to better address transitional justice expectations: they are well-placed to perform the tasks that each step entails. Adoption of the boards could also be done incrementally if the steps are only undertaken that way. A local board, for example, would act as a dialogic and consultative forum where local expectations could be identified. Boards at a local level, feeding up to a national level board, would facilitate the development of shared aims between local and international stakeholders (who may sit on boards and provide expertise). This process will itself deepen and broaden transitional justice, both parts of the third step. Such bodies may improve the capacity of transitional justice to achieve the various shared aims. The national level Board of Transition would design and implement transitional justice mechanisms that have been selected for their suitability in achieving the aims expressed by communities. The membership of the board would need to draw widely from a variety of groups within the affected community, as well as from transitional justice experts from NGOs, and representatives of political and/or religious groups that are contextually relevant to the transitional society. It has been suggested that local "moral leaders" should be given greater participation in transitional justice design and practice, with the aim of enhancing legitimacy (Ramji-Nogales 2010). In the same way, respected local leaders who are committed to the values of transition should be sought to work with and on the boards. These members might be elected or nominated. The Boards of Transition could exist for at least as long as transitional justice activities take place, but ideally longer.

In a broadened, deepened and lengthened form of transitional justice, they may exist permanently, their role evolving over time to perhaps one of stewardship or curatorship for memorialisation projects (Nickson and Braithwaite 2014).

Importantly, the flow of information must occur horizontally and vertically between boards. That is, information and resource sharing ought to be facilitated between local boards and a national board. The flow cannot be unidirectional: information must flow up and down to truly enhance the capacity of transitional justice measures to achieve aims. This should also be seen as an organic form of informing and educating. The optimal time for the creation of such boards would be when a peace process is far enough under way that confidence exists that details of the process will soon be settled. Once the peace process has been settled, the transitional justice phase proper will commence. A similar type of body would be the Peace Committees that have operated in a number of post-conflict societies (Odendaal 2010). The South African Peace Committees are a salient example. They were established as part of the National Peace Accord in 1991 at national, regional and local levels (U.S. Agency for International Development 1998). The Peace Committees, while not without their shortcomings, were seen to perform six functions as part of the peace process:

> 1) opening channels of communication; 2) legitimizing the concept of negotiating; 3) creating a safe place to raise issues that could not be addressed in other forums; 4) strengthening accountability; 5) helping equalize the power balance; and 6) helping reduce the incidence of violence. (U.S. Agency for International Development 1998, p. vii)

All these functions are relevant to transitional justice. The most obvious for addressing the expectation dilemma, however, are 1, 3, and 4. Boards that can open channels of communication may facilitate the identification of expectations and the effectiveness of expectation management; provide a space for developing shared aims through dialogue and collaboration; and allow space for repeated conversations about the work of transitional justice that permit new responses to be crafted as societies move forward from conflict. A safe place for these issues to be discussed is fundamental in this process: expectations may be managed more adequately in an environment of trust rather than suspicion; and dialogue and collaboration and the deep engagement necessary to achieve them require a safe space for them to take root and grow. These efforts should all be seen as measures to strengthen accountability and Boards of Transition would need to advocate for accountability, while being open to the shape and form of how accountability is both recognised and sought. In South Africa, the Peace Committees are credited with "demonstrat[ing] to many South Africans for the first time in their lives what it means to hold public officials accountable" (U.S. Agency for International Development 1998, p. 18). This was achieved by monitoring public officials' conduct in light of the National Peace Accords, police codes of conduct, and other relevant standards (U.S. Agency for International Development 1998). Transitional justice could benefit from greater accountability to the spirit and letter of transitional justice efforts, and boards could promote that accountability through monitoring. Boards can also promote and facilitate other projects that are part of wider transitional justice efforts. Where South African Peace Committees were often successful in diffusing tensions that could erupt in violence, Boards of Transition can promote projects at national, regional, and local levels designed to address significant expectations, including reconciliation, education, reparations, and peace. Local transitional justice projects, such as the rebuilding of places of worship in Indonesia (Braithwaite et al. 2010), or the reconciliation ceremonies performed in East Timor (Braithwaite et al. 2012), are examples of the sorts of efforts that Boards of Transition can encourage and develop. The success, for example, of reconciliation ceremonies in East Timor, was largely a result of their going to the spiritual heart of what the communities most cared about and what was central to holding the fabric of society together (Braithwaite et al. 2012).

Boards of Transition would not necessarily be limited in their role to direct transitional justice efforts. Indeed, they could perform functions similar to those of a Peace Committee in smothering sparks of conflict re-ignition. They can also build legitimacy for transitional justice efforts by undertaking projects that may have an immediate and direct impact locally. For example, an often under-addressed dimension in the practice of transitional justice is the role that local rebuilding can play in promoting social and distributive forms of justice. Such efforts might include rebuilding a school so that students may return; repairing a bridge; or re-opening a market. While not traditionally part of the transitional justice rubric, these activities may address significant expectations, especially expectations that seek a better future from transitional justice. A re-opened market can also be a confidence-building space between distrustful former enemies who begin to trade in peace, and a quick impact project in terms of job creation. Some projects (e.g. market openings) also have more deeply catalytic effects on peacebuilding in communities than others. Additionally, boards can work towards promoting disarmament: for example, combatants might relinquish their weapons in reconciliation ceremonies that provide a symbolic gesture to victims and communities (with the tangible benefit of a reduction in weapons). Early activities that disarm will contribute to later transitional justice endeavours: trials are less likely to be derailed by threats of renewed violence, for instance. Evidence of a quick dividend from transitional justice initiatives may work to build support for the aspects of transitional justice that require deeper engagement and longer commitment (including trials).

Lessons from the South African Peace Committees may give some indication regarding obstacles to the success of Boards of Transition. It was noted that in South Africa, Peace Committees were dependent "on the quality and personal characteristics of the staff" (U.S. Agency for International Development 1998, p. 12). The same is likely to be true for Boards of Transition, where the ability to communicate effectively and persuasively will be key to the performance of a board's work. In many transitional societies, there will be individuals who have dedicated themselves to tasks relevant to transitional justice, such as advocating for victims' rights, promoting accountability, or campaigning for judicial reform. Finding the right board members will not necessarily be easy, but it would be an uncommon circumstance if none were available. Board members would need to be committed to incorporating local communities into the transitional justice process, and a balance of approaches and ideals (or at least a variety) among board members is most likely to be preferable. Eight factors were identified that influenced the effectiveness of South African Peace Committees and are also relevant in the design of Boards of Transition. Those factors were as follows:

> 1) political will at the national level to see the peace process through; 2) the attitude adopted by the security forces to the work of the peace committees; 3) the development of constructive relationships among key actors; 4) the capacity of civil society to make a constructive contribution; 5) the perceived legitimacy of the peace committees; 6) the ability to communicate the objective of the peace process and provide an objective view of events; 7) the financial and structural flexibility of the peace committees; and 8) the role of two international actors: international monitors and development cooperation agencies. (U.S. Agency for International Development 1998, p. 24)

For many of these factors, "peace process" could be replaced with "transitional justice" and the observation would make intuitive sense regarding the new focus. It would be no surprise, for instance, for transitional justice to be influenced at the national level by political will. In respect to addressing the expectation gap, factors 3, 4, 5, and 6 are particularly pertinent. Constructive relationships will be important in identifying and managing expectations, as well as in the development of shared aims. In a broadened and deeper conception of transitional justice, civil society must be capable of making numerous, and sustained, contributions. Legitimacy of any transitional justice activity will be key to its perceived success, and therefore to the perception that it has addressed expectations (Ramji-Nogales 2010). Additionally, if a motivation for the establishment of boards is their contribution to procedural forms of justice (when other forms of justice may be difficult to attain through trials or other traditional approaches to transitional justice), then their legitimacy is paramount in providing a sense of procedural justice. Finally, the ability to communicate objectives of the transitional justice process has clear ramifications for expectation management, as well as expectation satisfaction. Bell notes that peace committees must be able "to break the warring parties' monopoly over information" (U.S. Agency for International Development 1998, p. 54). The experience of the former Yugoslavia, with attitudes to the Tribunal shaped largely by political elites and ethnic-biased media outlets, provides a clear case of a need for transitional justice institutions that challenge this monopoly of information.

Boards could initially seek to publish a report regarding the consultation stage of the transitional justice process. This report would cover the shared aims of transitional justice, providing an early product of transitional justice efforts. The ongoing work of the board—once institutions have been established—would be to assess the progress of transitional justice in achieving aims. They would also serve as a conduit between institutions and the community. They may act as a forum for community groups to express dissatisfaction with current transitional justice. Consequently, they should be empowered to generate new transitional justice responses as the transitional justice landscape evolves. This would create a dynamic form of transitional justice that is not limited to the contributions of a single mechanism. This could overcome problems that may flow from decisions made early in a transitional process that were more applicable to conditions at that point than they are in the future. Independence between the board and the institutions designed and established by them should be maintained. Oversight would not necessarily entail direct involvement in the day-to-day functions of a mechanism. For example, there would still need to be a sufficient level of independence for judges, prosecutors, and investigators if trials are adopted. Importantly, the board should instead consider what progress has been made in achieving the aims of transitional justice and what other ways efforts in that direction might be advanced.

A valid concern with such a suggestion is the time it would add to transitional justice activities, as well as the increased risk that efforts might get bogged down or stall. Such a proposal, if adopted, would add time to the process. This is not necessarily a negative. This research has shown that certain institutions are unable to address all the aims of transitional justice. It was the case for the Tribunal, where the decision was made relatively quickly to adopt prosecutions in response to ongoing violence, and for the Chambers, where the decision for prosecutions was made early despite negotiations for the establishment of a court taking considerable time. Greater time for considering the suitability of a mechanism in the earliest stages of transitional justice will increase the possibility of satisfying more aims in the long haul (Karstedt 2010). Similarly, it hardly seems a fair criticism that the steps proposed here are necessarily any longer than the decades it took to establish a court to try the leaders of the Khmer Rouge. The time required for a consultative period as proposed here will vary in length between transitional justice enterprises. There is no immediate reason to suspect it would represent an unrealistic burden for transitional justice.

A second criticism is likely to be that to broaden, deepen and lengthen transitional justice in these ways may increase the number of unsatisfied and disappointed expectations. This argument would suggest that due to increased involvement and the suggestion of addressing more aims, more people will be disappointed when transitional justice does not deliver on those aims (Nickson and Braithwaite 2014). This is a risk involved in the proposal. Yet the greater opportunities for stakeholders to receive some justice, along with deeper engagement in a process that can constitute a meaningful form of procedural justice, obviate some of that risk (Nickson and Braithwaite 2014). The participants in this research made it clear that expectations existed within the communities they worked with as a matter of course. This corresponds to how we would think intuitively about transitional societies: it is no surprise that they hold hopes for what any transitional justice process will provide. Given that expectations will exist irrespective of our approach to transitional justice, this criticism seems less valid. Rather than raising expectations further, this approach provides outlets for the expression of expectations and their transformation into shared aims. Not all aims are likely to be addressed, or addressed as completely as some may wish. A further risk is that, under this proposal, expectations are more likely to be disappointed for people with an expectation that transitional justice will provide nothing for them. Their expectations are negative expectations—as opposed to the positive expectations assumed above. If the process described here transforms negative expectations into positive ones, there is a greater chance of disappointing them. The proposal advanced here, however, seeks to incorporate in the process of transitional justice the aims those expectations represent and involve those who hold them. The potential and likely benefits of this approach outweigh the risks of changing negative expectations into positive expectations in the process.

Another problem demonstrated by this research was media coverage of expectations. While the local media was a primary source for information regarding trials, it did not accurately convey information regarding those trials; was frequently hostile to transitional justice institutions; discussed topics in superficial ways or from a tabloid perspective; and/or was event-driven, covering issues of high drama but without sustained coverage. While a free press is an important feature for transitional societies, it is not necessarily a suitable single source of information for communities. Of course, a plurality of new media sources will not ensure that these problems are overcome. For instance, although sites such as Twitter will be bottom-up nodes of communication, their brevity, lack of any professional media code and ease of misuse may mean they are often worse in this regard than traditional media. Reliance on media is in many respects the result of insufficient direct involvement in proceedings. The tireless efforts of Outreach at both the Tribunal and Chambers have gone some way to creating greater opportunities for involvement in proceedings by local communities. As we were told by staff at the Outreach section of Chambers, tens of thousands of Cambodians have been brought to experience the court first-hand through Outreach and NGO efforts. This was one distinct advantage that the Chambers displayed over the Tribunal: access and ownership of the proceedings were enhanced by being located within the country. One participant, however, questioned how meaningful it was for Cambodians to spend two hours watching proceedings they most likely could not understand (Cambodia NGO #9). Despite potential shortcomings, it seems reasonable to assume that such engagement was a positive avenue of communication between transitional justice institution and community. To truly overcome the limitations of a small number of information outlets, transitional justice needs to broaden, deepen, and lengthen its engagement with local communities. In particular, if transitional justice becomes more inclusive, then a greater number of nodes of communication exist. This creates a plurality of opportunities for contact and information sharing between community members and institutions.

It has been noted that current conceptions of transitional justice favour speedy trials and time-limited truth commissions (Nickson and Braithwaite 2014). Operating within tight timeframes may make fiscal sense, but there is a trade-off in satisfied expectations as a result. For many victims of mass violence, the decade within which a great deal of transitional justice might occur after conflict is too narrow a window. Victims, and perpetrators may not be physically, mentally, or emotionally prepared to engage in a transitional justice process that occurs immediately after violence. Those victims who are not immediately ready should not be excluded from official forms of transitional justice, and this is where lengthening our conception of transitional justice can assist.

Part of lengthening should be to not limit the work of Boards of Transition to defined time periods. Boards of Transition may be instrumental in selecting prosecutions (from all the available transitional justice options) to redress past wrongs, but their work does not need to end when prosecutions do. When continued scope for the operation of transitional justice exists, the boards will have a role as a forum for dialogue and interaction among stakeholders. They will be well placed to create legacy projects in coordination with local communities and can play a significant role in memorialisation efforts. The ideal time for their work to cease will be when communities feel that time has come, and not before. Bell's research on peace committees in South Africa provides support for a lengthened approach to the work of boards of transition. Bell found as follows:

> Enduring change probably cannot be achieved in less than a generation. The South African experience points to the need for some type of continuing forum to promote intergroup and interpersonal dialog and problem-solving at all levels of society. (U.S. Agency for International Development 1998, p. 56)

Boards should reflect this experience, as should transitional justice. That is not to say that there is no benefit in limiting the scope of certain institutions. It may be prudent for courts to have defined mandates and jurisdictions. Consequently, when those have been satisfied, the court may leave other institutions to carry on the work of transitional justice. Courts are costly: they consume vast amounts of financial and personnel resources. The burden of staffing and maintaining an international tribunal may therefore not provide a sufficient dividend on investment beyond a limited number of trials for senior figures. Subsequently, it may fall on local courts and other transitional justice institutions to continue transitional justice. What appears to be clear from this research is that if official efforts end with the trials, many expectations will not have been adequately addressed or incorporated.

Another way to lengthen transitional justice would be to make a truth commission permanent (if one has been adopted based on shared aims). A problem experienced by time-limited truth commissions—with relevance to most, if not all, transitional justice institutions—"is that the most traumatized victims often take longest to be ready to participate in transitional justice" (Nickson and Braithwaite 2014, p. 455). The permanent truth commission, as proposed by Braithwaite and Nickson (2012), must be distinguished from Scharf's (1996) proposed permanent truth commission. Scharf conceives of a permanent truth commission as an adjunct to the permanent international criminal court. For Scharf (1996, p. 380), the benefits to this model are: "(1) superior sufficiency in funding; (2) a greater perception of neutrality; (3) less susceptibility to domestic influences; and (4) greater speed in launching investigations." Scharf's recommendation has merits and without having been implemented it is impossible to assess whether gains in neutrality and a reduction in domestic influences exceed the losses associated with de-localising truth commissions. The proposal advanced by Braithwaite and Nickson is for the following:

> Truth and Reconciliation Commissions that are permanent institutions, keeping their doors open to assist with truth, reconciliation, and justice at whatever point in time victims and perpetrators are emotionally ready. (Nickson and Braithwaite 2014, p. 444)

A permanent truth commission can operate beyond the generation of direct victims, shifting its function to memorialisation or a museum, a repository for testimony, artefacts and documents, and as a hub for education about past violence and abuses (Nickson and Braithwaite 2014). A permanent truth commission is but one example of an institution whose scope for contribution is enhanced through a lengthened conception of transitional justice. In the consultations and dialogues that should constitute a foundation for transitional justice activities, stakeholders will be able to design and create their own lengthened justice mechanisms. A truth commission may not be favoured or appropriate in all settings. Yet, the example is still valid for transitional societies who believe that other institutions will better address their expectations and will inevitably need significant periods of time to address violence, suffering, and human rights abuses.

Transforming Justice

The difficulty that recent transitional justice has encountered in achieving the aims of affected communities has exposed the necessity of reconsidering our approach. With justice after conflict and mass atrocity, the "transition" label refers to the political context that these efforts occur in. If one can recall the definitions of transitional justice that were provided at the beginning of this book, it is clear that "transition" has little to do with the type of justice. Rather, it denotes transitions from periods of authoritarianism to democracy (or war to peace). As a result, the label does not describe the quality, type, or form of justice that societies in transition should seek to pursue. This permits us the opportunity to invest transitional justice with the qualities, type and form that are seen as most appropriate and desirable. In this sense, we ought to consider transitional justice as transformative. Lambourne (2009, p. 30) draws a similar conclusion, recommending that we "think instead in terms of 'transformation,' which implies long-term, sustainable processes embedded in society and adoption of psychosocial, political and economic, as well as legal, perspectives on justice." We want justice that will transform violence into peace; unrest into dialogue; and warring enemies into neighbours.

A criticism of criminal justice is that it often does little to address the underlying causes of conflict in societies. A transformational approach, however, would seek to address those underlying causes. This is perhaps more important for transitional societies than established democracies. In transitional societies, much violence is seen as embedded and endemic. Research has shown that the risk that a country emerging from war returns to conflict within ten years is 38% (Collier 2009). At the same time, the poorest countries in the world face a one in six chance of falling into civil war in any five-year period (Collier 2007). Similarly, many current conflicts have been raging for years, with a significant number having continued for decades (Human Security Report Project 2012). In authoritarian regimes, discrimination and violence often become central features of the State's manifestation of power. In these circumstances, it is especially important to examine the underlying causes and context of human rights abuses. Failing to do so may well ensure that seething animosities between formerly warring factions are never dispelled. Instead, they may permeate and undermine other areas of a transitional society's rebuilding. This is to say nothing of their potential contribution to future outbreaks of violence.

Taking a transformative approach to transitional justice borrows from the peacebuilding literature, particularly the work of Lederach, who conceives of transformation as a more secure and far-sighted approach to peacebuilding:

> Transformation envisions the presenting problem as an opportunity to engage in a broader context, to explore and understand the system of relationships and patterns that gave birth to crisis. (Lederach 2003, p. 30)

Within the rubric of conflict transformation, Lederach (2003, 2010) has described the need for a "transformational platform." This platform provides the base for generating processes as solutions to short-term needs while simultaneously working towards strategic, long-term constructive change. Transitional justice needs to adopt a similar approach. Too often, transitional justice mechanisms are designed as solutions to short-term needs without considering how they will contribute to strategic and long-term aims of transitional justice. This is especially true of the transitional justice trial. It seems that most often trials are instituted to address immediate needs: for punishment; or simply to be seen to be doing something. In such circumstances one is reminded of Ernest Hemingway's warning: never mistake movement for action.

If transitional justice were to adopt a "transformational platform", it would provide a basis for designing mechanisms to meet immediate needs, while fitting within a transitional justice framework where the overarching aims have been articulated. To some extent, this has already occurred in transitional justice. It appears, however, that most frequently the connection between any overarching aims for transitional justice and the resolution of immediate needs is assumed, rather than examined and considered. Sometimes the mechanisms that are established this way do contribute to broader aims. The research suggests that those contributions are limited. Without any clear articulation of aims beforehand, it is possible to debate whether those contributions were made to the most pressing aims for that transitional society—or if advocates have simply highlighted contributions to any aims that we can apply *ex post facto*. When single institution responses are implemented, it is questionable how much these have been designed to meet immediate expectations in any event. Transitional justice trials can only ever meet a few of the great many expectations of individuals and communities in transitional societies. For these reasons, mechanisms should not be employed based solely on their perceived capacity to address an immediate expectation.

The failure of transitional justice to achieve many aims is represented here in two ways. First of all, the establishment of transitional justice mechanisms has rarely, or poorly, considered the link between short-term needs and long-term aims. Second, transitional justice is conceived in practice as a short-term operation. This leads many transitional justice advocates—frequently of the retributive or legalist persuasion—to dismiss long-term aims as either being outside the scope of their work, or as things that will be realised as a result of their work, but only in the distant future. What this attitude might be replaced with is one where all those involved in transitional justice consider the aims of that particular endeavour (especially from a local perspective) and consider what mechanisms will facilitate achieving those aims. This is to be contrasted with a process that looks at the crimes and focuses first on responding to them, while only vaguely thinking about how that response will contribute to the greater aims.

Lederach's considerable practical experience of peacebuilding has informed his view of the need to eschew conflict resolution in favour of conflict transformation. As part of generating a greater level of reconciliation between former groups, Lederach (2010, p. 55) observed that local processes are far more successful than elite processes:

> From personal experience I can attest to the fact that the process of advancing political negotiation at polished tables in elite hotels, while very difficult and complex in its own right, is both a more formal and a more superficial process than the experience of reconciliation in which former enemies are brought together at the village level.

Although it would be an error to label the official transitional justice processes that occurred in The Hague and Phnom Penh as superficial, much of this passage is relevant. Local transitional justice initiatives and mechanisms can be meaningful, powerful and transformative for the communities involved. Those aims identified in this research as being unfulfilled may have a greater chance of fulfilment with a focus that is less distant and more local and integrative. Similarly, the process that Lederach describes as more meaningful is a more restorative process.

Conclusion

Three complementary steps have been proposed to address the expectation dilemma of transitional justice. Taken together, these steps comprise a holistic approach to narrowing the expectation gap. The first step calls for developing more robust and multidimensional strategies of expectation management. To do this well, it is suggested that efforts to identify stakeholder expectations should occur before transitional justice institutions have been established, and at least before there has been sufficient opportunity for expectations to be disappointed. This will require more proactive efforts, as opposed to the reactive approach that currently dominates. It will frequently be necessary for numerous expectations to be managed, particularly when they relate to justice dividends that cannot be accommodated, such as executions. Managing expectations will require transitional justice to develop more diverse methods of communicating with local communities, as well as fostering more collaborative relationships with news media outlets.

Expectation management, when done well, provides a sound foundation for developing shared aims among all stakeholders in transitional justice. This is because a sound expectation management strategy will likely involve consultation and engagement between transitional communities and transitional justice elites. Developing shared aims improves on the work of expectation management by taking a collaborative and dialogic approach to establishing the goals of transitional justice. This allows for deeper and (potentially) more meaningful engagement than frequently occurs in current practice. Developing shared aims should inform the creation and establishment of transitional justice institutions. In this way, we may fashion mechanisms more responsive to the context and aims in disparate transitional societies. The adoption of Boards of Transition could aid this process considerably, providing a forum for dialogue as well as a body with the capacity to promote local and national transitional justice efforts. Finally, by conceiving of transitional justice more broadly, deeply, and longer we can provide greater opportunities for justice to meet the expectations of stakeholders. In a process that is broader, the expectations of stakeholders can be addressed in a greater variety of ways. Deeper engagement aids in narrowing the expectation gap by encouraging greater understanding among stakeholders of the limits of different mechanisms; allowing for a greater number of communication nodes between stakeholders and institutions; providing a level of procedural justice when other dimensions of justice are unavailable; and allowing stakeholders an opportunity to influence the design and focus of transitional justice. A longer conception of transitional justice may narrow the expectation gap by permitting participation in the process when stakeholders (particularly victims) feel ready. It can also encourage us to consider justice as a long-term goal and discourage a feeling of dissatisfaction in short timeframes for expectations that may genuinely take years, decades, and generations to meet.

As a proposal, this whole process should be considered aspirational. It may not be feasible to adopt all of the suggestions made here in a transitional justice setting. Ideally, the proposal should be seen as a whole, but it would be better for transitional justice to adopt at least parts of it than to ignore it as a whole. Indeed, the proposal lends itself to incremental adoption. For instance, the adoption of a board should be possible in almost all transitional settings. Such a board could be adopted in Bosnia, Croatia, Serbia, and Kosovo individually or regionally, even now, to steer the legacy effort involved in sustaining the work of the Tribunal for future generations, as well as to look for new avenues to implement transitional justice. The same is possible for Cambodia, where the work of transitional justice should not end after the trials conclude at the Chambers.

References

Afri-Forum and Another vs. Malema and others, no. 20968/2010 S.A. Eq. Ct., [2011] ZAEQC 2 [11–12].

Akhavan, P 1998, 'Justice in The Hague, peace in the former Yugoslavia? A commentary on the United Nations war crimes tribunal', *Human Rights Quarterly*, vol. 20, no. 4, pp. 737–816.

Aukerman, MJ 2002, 'Extraordinary evil, ordinary crime: A framework for understanding transitional justice', *Harvard Human Rights Journal*, vol. 15, pp. 39–98.

Balint, JL 1996, 'The place of law in addressing internal regime conflicts', *Law and Contemporary Problems*, vol. 59, no. 4, pp. 103–126.

Braithwaite, J 2005, *Markets in vice, markets in virtue*, Federation Press, Annandale, NSW.

Braithwaite, J, Braithwaite, V, Cookson, M and Dunn, L 2010, *Anomie and violence: Non-truth and reconciliation in Indonesian peacebuilding*, ANU E-Press, Canberra, Australia.

Braithwaite, J, Charlesworth, H and Soares, A 2012, *Networked governance of greedom and tyranny: Peace in Timor-Leste*, ANU E-Press, Canberra, Australia.

Braithwaite, J and Nickson, R 2012, 'Timing truth, reconciliation, and justice after war' *Ohio State Journal on Dispute Resolution*, vol. 27, no. 3, pp. 443–446.

Celermajer, D 2013, 'Mere ritual? Displacing the myth of sincerity in transitional rituals', *International Journal of Transitional Justice*, vol. 7, no. 3, pp. 286–305.

Clark, JN 2010, 'Education in Bosnia-Hercegovina: The case for root and branch reform', *Journal of Human Rights*, vol. 9, no. 3, pp. 344–362.

Cockayne, J 2005, 'Hybrids or mongrels? Internationalized war crimes trials as unsuccessful degradation ceremonies', *Journal of Human Rights*, vol. 4, no. 4, pp. 455–473.

Collier, P 2007, *The bottom billion: Why the poorest countries are failing and what can be done about it*, Oxford University Press, New York.

Collier, P 2009, *Wars, guns and votes: Democracy in dangerous places*, Bodley Head, London.

Drumbl, MA 2007, *Atrocity, punishment, and international law*, Cambridge University Press, Cambridge.

Eriksen, EO 1994, 'Deliberative democracy and the politics of plural society', Paper presented at the Arena Conference on the Europeanization of Normative Theory, Oslo, Norway.

Fletcher, LE and Weinstein, HM 2002, 'Violence and social repair: Rethinking the contribution of justice to reconciliation', *Human Rights Quarterly*, vol. 24, no. 3, pp. 573–639.

Ivkovic, SK 2001, 'Justice by the International Criminal Tribunal for the Former Yugoslavia', *Stanford Journal of International Law*, vol. 37, no. 2, pp. 255–265.

Human Security Report Project 2012, *Human Security Report 2012: Sexual Violence, Education and War: Beyond the Mainstream Narrative*, Human Security Press, Vancouver.

Johnstone, G 2002, *Restorative Justice: Ideas, Values, Debates*, Willan Publishing, Portland, Oregon.

Karstedt, S 2010, 'From absence to presence, from silence to voice: Victims in transitional justice since the Nuremberg trials', *International Review of Victimology*, vol. 17, no. 1, pp. 9–30.

Lambourne, W 2009, 'Transitional justice and peacebuilding after mass violence', *The International Journal of Transitional Justice*, vol. 3, no. 1, pp. 28–38.

Lederach, JP 2003, *The little book of conflict transformation*, Good Books, Intercourse, PA.
Lederach, JP 2010, *Building peace: Sustainable reconciliation in divided societies*, 9th Printing, United States Institute of Peace, Washington.
Llewellyn, JL and Philpott, D 2014, 'Restorative justice and reconciliation: Twin frameworks for peacebuilding', in Llewellyn, JL and Philpott, D (eds) *Restorative Justice, Reconciliation and Peacebuilding*, Oxford University Press, New York.
Nettlefield, LJ 2010, 'From the battlefield to the barracks: The ICTY and the armed forces of Bosnia and Herzegovina', *International Journal of Transitional Justice*, vol. 4, no. 1, pp. 87–109.
Nickson, R and Braithwaite, J 2014, 'Deeper, broader, longer transitional justice', *European Journal of Criminology*, vol. 11, no. 4, pp. 445–463.
Odendaal, A 2010, *An architecture for building peace at the local level: A comparative study of local peace committees*, United Nations Development Programme, New York.
Ramji-Nogales, J 2010, 'Designing bespoke transitional justice: A pluralist process approach', *Michigan Journal of International Law*, vol. 32, no. 1, pp. 1–72.
Scharf, MP 1996, 'The case for a permanent international truth commission', *Duke Journal of International and Comparative Law*, vol. 7, pp. 375–410.
Stanley, E 2004, 'Torture, silence and recognition', *Current Issues in Criminal Justice*, vol. 16, no. 1, pp. 5–25.
Sunstein, C 1995, 'Incompletely theorized agreements', *Harvard Law Review*, vol. 108, no. 7, pp. 1733–1772.
Sunstein, C 1996, *Legal Reasoning and Political Conflict*, Oxford University Press, New York.
Sykes, GM and Matza, D 1957, 'Techniques of neutralization: A theory of delinquency', *American Sociological Review*, vol. 22, no. 6, pp. 664–670.
U.S. Agency for International Development 1998, *Managing Conflict: Lessons from the South African Peace Committees*, USAID Evaluation Special Study Report No. 78.
Zehr, H 1995, *Changing lenses: A new focus for crime and justice*, Herald Press, Scottdale, PA.
Zehr, H 2002, *The little book of restorative justice*, Good Books, Intercourse, PA.

8

Conclusion

Expectations of the Tribunal and Chambers were frequently seen as "too high", "unrealistic", and "inappropriate". Yet the expectation dilemma is by no means limited to these two institutions and exists for transitional justice more broadly. An expectation gap—between likely and expected contributions—may influence a variety of factors that are important in aiding recovery after mass violence. Unsatisfied expectations may have a distinct impact on the contribution that institutions can make in transitional societies. While it is impossible to meet every expectation, better strategies for expectation realisation are needed.

An expectation gap is what we might expect when turning our minds to the hopes that are held for transitional justice and the practical limitations these endeavours encounter. Part of the problem is the current application of expectation management. This is frequently reactive, ad hoc, and unfocused. When practitioners spoke of managing expectations, it was conceived almost exclusively in terms of court outreach. This normative construction sees expectations managed by the provision of information once institutions are operating. Often, expectations are managed once they have already been disappointed. We were told

R. Nickson and A. Neikirk, *Managing Transitional Justice*,
Palgrave Studies in Compromise after Conflict,
https://doi.org/10.1007/978-3-319-77782-5_8

that in education and communication strategies, Outreach could not pre-empt decisions. Yet, better expectation management does not have to transcend the boundary between information and prediction. A dialogue regarding the scope of sentences, the possibility of acquittals, and other significant points of contention should begin when transitional justice efforts are in their infancy. Institutions can and ought to be more innovative in their approach to outreach regarding expectations.

The need for modesty about what limited interventions and mechanisms can achieve remains crucial. In some cases, transitional justice institutions have directly (though inadvertently) raised expectations. This has necessitated reactive management efforts that divert important resources from other court activities. Raised expectations occur both generally and specifically. In a specific context, it applies to particular tools that various mechanisms employ. When the Chambers instituted a policy of reparations without explaining its unique features—the most significant being that no one could receive any reparation payments under the scheme—staff should have anticipated confusion and the need to inform eligible victims about the available orders. Information given proved insufficient, and many victims were disappointed as a result of expectations that were not matched by the reparations orders.

In a general way, expectations are unwittingly raised by the promotion of certain offences (genocide) above others (crimes against humanity); this was a clear frustration for some respondents. It may also take place when certain concepts are promoted or advanced without sufficient consideration of the transitional context. This commonly occurred with the overuse (and perhaps uncritical use) of reconciliation. A media officer at the Tribunal explained it to us in this way:

> And then the reconciliation one … I think the word became so much a synonym to a goal that is achievable. So if you lived at any time … if you lived in any of these countries, and you belonged to any of these people at any time, and you had any interaction with the international community they would always say, 'Well what are we doing? We are doing this because we are going to achieve reconciliation.' Or you are writing a report about rebuilding a house in Foca, you are writing an application for the funds: what is the end goal? Everything became reconciliation …

> and in some way it became accepted that one act, or one institution, or one segment of the society, or one side of the war can bring out reconciliation, which is I think very, very far from the truth… you cannot forcibly reconcile people. You can't all of a sudden turn everyone into academics and draw them their little model and say, 'This is what you need to have in order to reconcile and therefore you should almost be there.' You know, they don't function like that. And I view it again much more as an individual. I view it as a very personal exercise. And the only thing that you can do, whether you are the ICTY, whether you are the War Crimes Chamber in Sarajevo, whether you are the coalition for missing persons or ICMP and looking for missing bodies, whichever one of those you are, you can only contribute so that those people standing above that mass grave can say, 'Okay. I'm ready to forgive now.' But I can't come to him and come to the guy in Brutanac and say 'Shake hands and reconcile because these guys have been put on a trial and we have established facts.' It doesn't work like that … It has resulted in this word just being thrown out and thrown about for anything. You know, I want to grow 10 plum trees by the river of the Drina and I will send an application to the regional embassy and then say, 'Well, it will help the returnees and therefore it will aid reconciliation.' No it won't. You know, if we don't have the other elements, then the Serb kid from the other side of the Drina will come over and cut my bloody plum tree down! So it's not going to aid reconciliation. (Tribunal Media #1)

Unfortunately, experiences like this represent the best of intentions leading to disappointed expectations. Such incidents highlight the need for a better understanding of the role of expectations in transitional justice, as well as the need for a more focused and better-developed understanding of expectations. Disappointed specific expectations are a synecdoche of the wider expectation dilemma in transitional justice: hopes are raised when something is offered and then disappointed when that something is not well explained or understood. Many transitional justice expectations attach to trials when this mechanism is ill suited to meet them. The failure to adequately explain the role of trials and their limitations (as well as providing only trials without other responses) contributes significantly to an expectation dilemma. The hazard of relying on a single mechanism whose role, benefits, and limitations are not well explained or understood does not attach solely to trials. It occurs for other transitional justice mechanisms (for example, truth commissions) that equally suffer from the burden of expectations they are ill suited to meet.

Transitional justice institutions need to be active in identifying what expectations exist, preferably before those expectations are disappointed. Although expectations outside of traditional trial goals were widely held, these were not considered in the design of transitional justice responses for the former Yugoslavia or Cambodia. This is illustrated by the experience of mothers' testifying at the Tribunal. They ask: Where is my son? Where is he buried? Where can I collect his remains so that he can be buried beside his father? They sometimes offer to forgive everything for the opportunity to locate their loved ones. But why would a General, or a militia leader, want to reveal the location of a mass grave during his own prosecution? It is likely to jeopardise his defence. If this information has not been revealed during investigations, it is unlikely to be revealed during a trial. Furthermore, the person with that knowledge may never be investigated or prosecuted. The need and expectation to know the fate of family members should be considered more centrally. Mechanisms designed to encourage participation and revelation by all sides to a conflict would be more successful at meeting such expectations. To achieve this, it will generally mean earlier and more considered engagement with local stakeholders to determine what their expectations are.

Interviews demonstrated that an expectation overload can lead to nihilism among transitional justice practitioners. This was observed at both the Tribunal and Chambers. It is probable this arose because these were isolated official mechanisms that had been saddled with most of the hopes for transitional justice. Nihilism sometimes found expression when respondents stated that the only appropriate goal for either institution was to establish the guilt or innocence of an accused. Those same respondents dismissed many alternative goals, such as the establishment of an historical record, or the contribution that trials might make to deterrence. During fieldwork in The Hague, we spoke with a senior member of staff at the International Criminal Court (ICC) who vehemently opposed any expectation except that the court would establish guilt or innocence (ICC #1). This participant would not entertain the idea that the ICC could perform other tasks. This attitude is itself an unrealistic expectation: the influence of courts extends beyond the defendant, and indeed beyond immediate victims. Additionally, this attitude is unfair to stakeholders who want and need more than a determination of guilt. To dismiss a trial's wider significance is a disservice that may fail to fulfil a trial's greater transformational, educative, deterrent, and restorative potential. This also serves to illustrate that expectations are not purely a local problem requiring external management. The expectation dilemma exists in all directions: international elites as well as local stakeholders hold unrealistic expectations. Expectations of speedy reconciliation, that court determinations regarding recent history will be accepted, or that prosecutions will symbolically satisfy victims, can constitute unrealistic expectations. While we recognise, for example, that expectations of non-cooperation may exist that require management, it is also true that an elite expectation that locals will cooperate simply because they are required to is similarly unrealistic.

The number and diversity of expectations should be considered in the development of any expectation management strategy. Failure to do this is likely to limit the realisation of expectations, particularly if they are overlooked. This failure also constrains the option of compensating for the impossibility of realising one expectation by delivering another. This perspective is important given the reality that there is no expectation that can be delivered so well as to make up for the loss of a partner, a child, a parent. As one respondent remarked, responses to atrocities—like the atrocities themselves—need to be "widespread and systematic". This study observed expectations in three broad categories: the scope of justice; the search for answers; and forward-looking expectations. As respondents made clear, different expectations may be held by different groups and between members of the same group. Yet, there is no consensus among scholars, practitioners, advocates or stakeholders about which are appropriate or realistic expectations. The dominant understanding of expectations and their management appears to be a unidirectional, top-down approach. What is needed is a more collaborative and consultative approach. It is evident that expectations have to be managed bottom-up: an expectation that warring groups will reconcile after a handful of trials is an elite expectation requiring a reality check. Similarly, an expectation that a particular type of justice will *always* be suitable may need management from bottom-up impulses emanating from local communities. Indeed, any expectation that we can successfully manage all (and even most) expectations in transitional justice is itself an unrealistic expectation. Current practices of expectation management—and transitional justice broadly—are not conducive to multi-directional expectation realisation.

A variety of external factors are observed to influence expectations. The Tribunal had to contend with suspicions that it was (a) instituted solely to demonise Serbs and (b) with conspiracy theories that it was an American/CIA institution created to further US imperialism (Belgrade Center for Human Rights 2004). These attitudes reflected the way in which the Tribunal had been established (Belgrade Center for Human Rights 2004). A more participatory system that designed transitional justice responses following consultation and dialogue would provide less traction for these ideas. At the same time, responses could better reflect the multitude of motivations and expectations in transitional justice: respondents made clear that a wide variety of expectations were held across all stakeholders. If stakeholders have a greater sense of ownership of transitional justice institutions, these problems may be reduced.

The pitfalls of a distant process with limited opportunities for stakeholder participation are exemplified by media coverage in the former Yugoslavia regarding the Tribunal. The population of the former Yugoslavia, for the most part, had little or no direct experience with the Tribunal. Consequently, media coverage was instrumental in informing people about the Tribunal's work. When that media was hostile to and biased against the Tribunal, many local attitudes reflected this. It was observed that media outlets did not cover trials when members of their own community were victims, and instead focused on how members of their community were prosecuted. Yet it was described how direct engagement between the Tribunal and media outlets from the region greatly facilitated a more balanced media portrayal. Journalists and editors from the region would experience a revelation during organised media visits to the Tribunal. They were surprised that prosecutors were so "nice", that the Tribunal was not a centre for persecuting particular ethnicities, and they vowed to ensure coverage reflected their new impressions of the Tribunal (Tribunal Outreach #1). What should be remembered in transitional justice efforts, is that institutions and mechanisms are not only working *for* transitional societies, but are working *with* transitional societies.

News media are constrained by their own professional rules, their articles may elevate certain expectations above others and attach those expectations to specific individuals rather than the work of an institution as a whole. In *NY Times* coverage it was observed that many expectations were expressed more favourably in connection to trials of the big fish. Early coverage was critical of the Tribunal for failing to prosecute major figures. At the same time, multiple expectations were raised in years relating to big fish events (e.g. the arrests of Milosevic and Mladic). While coverage tended to suggest that the Tribunal made positive advances towards meeting expectations when big fish were prosecuted, coverage also encumbered big fish prosecutions with a great variety of expectations that were more difficult to realise. This suggests that prosecutions of senior figures are important for achieving multiple expectations. Yet it is also problematic, as the success of transitional justice becomes intimately connected to a handful of senior prosecutions. Indeed, one of the consequences of a preference for trials is that anything other than a trial may be cast as "dreadful impunity" (Waters 2009). The media appear to highlight impunity so that they may express outrage. So, when "war criminals" are sunbathing on tropical beaches or sipping coffee on a terrace (in front of international police), this will be covered, and scathingly. While the media emphasise that senior impunity, the direct perpetrator's (or the small fish's) impunity is felt by his or her victims, who must see him or her at the market and living on the same street. Impunity is galling, and when prosecutions are desired, just, and possible, they should be pursued. Transitional justice needs, however, to think of alternative ways to satisfy calls to end impunity and needs for acknowledgment when prosecutions are not possible or desired. It was said that by not prosecuting Pol Pot, the message the international community communicated to Cambodians was that the Khmer Rouge did not commit crimes and hence there was no acknowledgment of suffering (Becker 1998). This is, perhaps, an overstatement. Yet in a "trying paradigm" where non-prosecutorial alternatives are portrayed as forms of impunity, it is less an overstatement than it should be. In conceiving of justice in times of transition we should eschew black and white notions of what constitutes justice, redress, and acknowledgment. Reports that treat the deaths of apex war criminals as irretrievably lost opportunities diminish the contributions that institutions make over a number of trials of senior and other perpetrators, with each trial contributing to expectations like accountability and acknowledgment. It may also do a disservice to alternative dimensions of justice that may be feasible when big fish prosecutions are impossible. This is compounded by coverage that readily assumes the guilt of big fish and casts them as demonstrably evil. Not only does this present a feature of transitional justice in need of considered management but also a shortcoming of transitional justice as it has been practised at the Tribunal and Chambers: when prosecutions are the only dimension of justice on offer, an opportunity *is* lost when trials become impossible. When additional dimensions of justice are available, the impossibility of one does not preclude other opportunities for justice.

Given the limitations of transitional justice trials identified by others, it is perhaps not surprising that an expectation gap was found to exist. Had the study been conducted of more holistic transitional justice activities, the expectation issue may have been expressed differently, or possibly not have been observed as problematic. Still, any singular activity will encounter limitations, and multiple combinations of transitional justice activities will not address every expectation completely. Consequently, expectation management will frequently be required. To an extent, the nature of expectation management expressed in the data in this volume mirrors the institution: the problems of transitional justice reflect the problems of transitional justice trials. It would be a fallacy, however, to understand it only in this way. The dominance of legalism and the preference for prosecution is reflected in the construction of expectation management. Significantly, expectations that do not readily fit with legalism are still apparent. This suggests that to adequately address expectations, we must consider employing responses beyond prosecutions. For example, when victims are frustrated that their expectations of punishment are not met, there may well have been a failure to manage expectations. There may also have been a failure to provide alternatives that would assist in alleviating what may be inevitable disappointment (as it is difficult to imagine, and inappropriate to adopt, a punishment commensurate with the offending). Picture the elderly survivor of Srebrenica, who though distraught and full of grief takes a plane flight (for the first time in her life) to attend The Hague and relive her trauma through her testimony. She then feels outraged and makes a special effort to call staff at the Tribunal to declare that she never would have agreed to participate had they known that the sentence "would be so low" (Chambers Victim Support #1). To improve upon current expectation management efforts, it is important to consider why a gap exists and what institutional weaknesses are reflected in that gap when developing responses. Management should be more than a simple declaration that an expectation will not be achieved (and in fairness, most Outreach activities do more than this). Instead, transitional justice needs a greater number of, as well as more innovative, expectation management responses.

Courts are capable of meeting various expectations. This was suggested by coverage in the *NY Times*. Though not amounting to proof that expectations were met, shifts from negative to positive coverage may indicate that (at least) journalists and editors felt the Tribunal had gone some way to satisfying certain expectations. This can occur despite disappointing the same expectations during early phases in the operation of transitional justice mechanisms. Shifts in the coverage of impunity and the role of big fish represent positive impacts that the Tribunal and Chambers made in addressing certain expectations. How the issue of big fish was approached at the Tribunal and Chambers provides a salient lesson in expectation management. The Tribunal made representations to the effect that its role was to try the most responsible criminals. Early trials, however, were criticised for prosecuting defendants who many saw were not the most responsible. The disparity between expected and actual defendants resulted in dissatisfaction with the Tribunal. The Chambers avoided this criticism by focusing solely on defendants who could be classified as most responsible and most senior, as had been their stated intention. Putting aside the practical dimensions that influenced who was prosecuted at either institution, the benefit of adhering to a clear prosecutorial strategy is evident. When the Tribunal was later able to prosecute more senior figures, this was recognised with a decrease in media criticism and an increase in favourable coverage on issues of impunity and seniority of defendants. Indeed, impunity (and combating it) were observed as significant expectations in all the sources of data for this research. A positive impact in reducing impunity is an important contribution that transitional justice can make. Individual prosecutions may represent only small steps, but collectively these can amount to profound strides in efforts to meet expectations regarding impunity. In addition, these positive contributions counsel against the nihilism that was observed with respect to "broader" expectations.

Management is not the only possible measure in responding to the expectation gap. There are limitations to what expectation management can achieve: it is restricted to shaping and informing expectations to fit institutions. Instead, we should aim for greater expectation realisation. The need for participatory and consultative processes in transitional justice has been discussed. A process that seeks to address, support, and meet as many expectations as possible would be an improvement. The next logical step is to develop shared aims. In the process of devising robust expectation management strategies, a great deal of groundwork for developing shared aims may already be completed: it is necessary that stakeholder expectations are identified (and given a "reality check" when appropriate). Developing shared aims goes further, however, in that it seeks to incorporate expectations into the design of transitional justice responses. In transitional justice, it will be impossible to adopt mechanisms to address local expectations wholesale—this is not what is being advocated. Rather, developing shared aims is a collaborative process where lofty expectations of local and international communities are tempered by each other. In this way, local expectations for executions will be moderated by international opposition to capital punishment; international expectations of speedy reconciliation will be chastened by local needs for time to heal, and so on. The benefit of developing shared aims is premised on the argument that transitional justice is improved the more it reflects the informed expectations of all stakeholders. We have seen in the preceding chapters how expectations uninformed by transitional justice and transitional justice uninformed by expectations are problematic. Developing shared aims is a method for overcoming these problems as far as possible.

Shared aims represent goals that recognise bottom-up impulses for transitional justice, moderated by the realities faced in the practice of transitional justice. Shared aims may be established in multiple ways. This research has proposed that consultations occur before the creation of a transitional justice institution or adoption of a mechanism. Such consultations should be seen as an important method for enhancing the inclusivity and engagement of transitional justice with affected communities. This in itself may serve several important shared aims. For example, in societies familiar with violence as a means of political expression deeper engagement may encourage greater participation in democratic processes.

This book recommends that transitional justice efforts employ boards that provide forums for deeper engagement. These boards, similar in many respects to peace committees (see Odendaal 2010), provide a space to develop shared aims in consultation. Boards of Transition can also work in the design and implementation of transitional justice, encouraging local and national activities that promote transitional justice goals. In the formative stages of transitional justice, boards can conduct or oversee many activities that will be catalytic for future transitional justice, such as communities rebuilding places of worship, or ceremonies where communities express regret and sorrow and accept responsibilities. It is fundamental that shared aims be an important consideration when designing transitional justice. Instead of designing transitional justice as primarily a response to events of the past, we might conceive transitional justice as providing steps on a path to a brighter future (Shearing and Froestad 2007). This means understanding aims and working towards them. The gulf between expectations and transitional justice is at present a perilous sea, beset with shoals, whirlpools, and reefs. Developing shared aims helps to chart a path through the turbulent waters of transition. Shared aims are the navigational stars: they are what we look up to and guide us to our destination. In this way, we might design institutions that are appropriate to expectations as well as, and perhaps before, considering whether expectations are appropriate to the institution. This approach to creating transitional justice institutions reflects an "outside-in" design model (Braithwaite 2005). It facilitates the design of institutions that are not only informed by stakeholder expectations but are also more reflective and responsive to those expectations.

Developing shared aims will itself be an important feature of a broader, longer and deeper conception of transitional justice. In the process of developing shared aims, an important form of procedural justice will be provided to participants. This sort of procedural justice may not be the justice they desire most. Victims, for example, could very likely desire other forms of retributive or restorative justice. Ideally, those victims will receive the justice that is most desired. Experience, however, tells us that many will not. A Judge at the Tribunal provided a telling hypothetical: two children are forced to watch their mother raped and both parents killed before the destruction of the family farm (Tribunal Judge #1). They can only sigh an exasperated "Fuck!" and wonder how their suffering will be addressed when those crimes are not prosecuted. For those, participation in a process that seeks to understand their expectations and includes their voice in discussions may provide justice opportunities they would otherwise have missed. It is only one dimension of justice, and not likely the dimension that many will initially expect. But it can be a meaningful dimension of justice for many. Deep engagement in this way could provide a spoonful of procedural justice rather than the empty plate of retributive justice they might have otherwise received.

If we truly hope to address the expectation dilemma, it is necessary to conceive of transitional justice more broadly, deeply, and longer. When there are more available dimensions of justice, there are more opportunities to meet expectations. In conceiving of transitional justice more broadly, we can heed the calls for a holistic approach to transitional justice. We could also expand our notions of transitional justice to include more understandings of justice: traditional justice; indigenous justice; and restorative justice, to name a few. In responding more adequately to expectations, transitional justice should delve deeper and promote greater and more meaningful engagement with members of affected communities. In a prosecutorial approach, there is limited scope for engagement: even direct involvement as a victim-witness is restricted to a few victims and provides only limited engagement. When other forms of justice are included, there are greater opportunities for people to directly engage with transitional justice. Most obviously, by considering shared aims as building blocks for successful transitional justice, an important opportunity for deeper engagement is created. Deeper engagement also means more nodes of communication. This may overcome some of the limitations that a reliance on news media imposes on transitional justice and transitional societies. It may also serve to organically ease expectations: affected community members are likely to have a better understanding of the function, work and constraints of transitional justice mechanisms through greater involvement. This is not a guarantee that people will be more satisfied with outcomes, but they may better understand why certain outcomes have been achieved and not others.

Transitional justice can, and does, provide important benefits to societies emerging from the throes of conflict and the oppression of dictators. There will be a continued need for transitional justice activities into the twenty-first century. In those transitions, perhaps we can meet a greater number of expectations, exceed a few, and provide justice to a greater number of people over longer periods through engagement in a wide variety of possible responses. Stakeholders from affected communities have lacked voices in the design of official transitional justice. Placing more trust in conversations with those groups will be an important step to more satisfactory transitional justice.

References

Becker, E 1998, 'Death of Pol Pot: The diplomacy; Pol Pot's end won't stop U.S. pursuit of his circle', *The New York Times*, April 17.

Belgrade Center for Human Rights 2004, *Attitudes towards the International Criminal tribunal for the Former Yugoslavia 2004*, Belgrade Center for Human Rights, Belgrade.

Braithwaite, J 2005, *Markets in vice, markets in virtue*, Federation Press, Annandale, NSW.

Odendaal, A 2010, *An architecture for building peace at the local level: A comparative study of local peace committees*, United Nations Development Programme, New York.

Shearing, C and Froestad, J 2007, 'Beyond restorative justice—Zwelethemba, a future-focused model using local capacity conflict resolution' in Mackay, R, Bosnjak, M, Deklerck, J, Pelikan, C, Van Stokkom, B and Wright, M (eds), *Images of Restorative Justice Theory*, Verlag fur Polizeiwissenschaft, Frankfurt, Germany.

Waters, TW 2009, 'Seeking justice decades later: Hear the victims' voices', *The New York Times*, February 4.

Bibliography

Afri-Forum and Another vs. Malema and others, no. 20968/2010 S.A. Eq. Ct., [2011] ZAEQC 2 [11–12].

Akhavan, P 1993, 'Punishing war crimes in the former Yugoslavia: A critical juncture for the new world order', *Human Rights Quarterly*, vol 15, no. 2, pp. 262–289.

Akhavan, P 1998, 'Justice in The Hague, peace in the former Yugoslavia? A commentary on the United Nations war crimes tribunal', *Human Rights Quarterly*, vol. 20, no. 4, pp. 737–816.

Aukerman, MJ 2002, 'Extraordinary evil, ordinary crime: A framework for understanding transitional justice', *Harvard Human Rights Journal*, vol. 15, pp. 39–98.

Balint, JL 1996, 'The place of law in addressing internal regime conflicts', *Law and Contemporary Problems*, vol. 59, no. 4, pp. 103–126.

Barria, LA and Roper, SD 2005, 'How effective are international criminal tribunals? An analysis of the ICTY and the ICTR', *The International Journal of Human Rights*, vol. 9, no. 3, pp. 349–368.

Bassiouni, MC 1996, 'Searching for peace and achieving justice: The need for accountability', *Law and Contemporary Problems*, vol. 59, no. 4, pp. 9–28.

Becker, E 1997, 'Videotape shows Pol Pot facing Khmer Rouge justice', *The New York Times*, July 29.

R. Nickson and A. Neikirk, *Managing Transitional Justice*,
Palgrave Studies in Compromise after Conflict,
https://doi.org/10.1007/978-3-319-77782-5

Becker, E 1998, 'Death of Pol Pot: The diplomacy; Pol Pot's end won't stop U.S. pursuit of his circle', *The New York Times*, April 17.

Becker, E 1999. 'Crisis in the Balkans: The overview; NATO says new bombing is the strongest effort yet', *The New York Times*, May 1.

Becker, E 2009, 'When justice is delayed', *The New York Times*, March 14.

Belgrade Center for Human Rights 2004, *Attitudes towards the International Criminal tribunal for the Former Yugoslavia 2004*, Belgrade Center for Human Rights, Belgrade.

Belgrade Center for Human Rights 2009, *Attitudes towards the International Criminal tribunal for the Former Yugoslavia 2009*, Belgrade Center for Human Rights, Belgrade.

Bell, C 2009, 'Transitional justice, interdisciplinarity and the state of the 'field' or 'non-field'', *International Journal of Transitional Justice*, vol. 3, no. 1, pp. 5–27.

Bertelman, H 2010, 'International standards and national ownership? Judicial independence in hybrid courts: The Extraordinary Chambers in the Courts of Cambodia', *Nordic Journal of International Law*, vol. 79, no. 4, pp. 341–382.

Bilefsky, D and Simons, M 2008, 'Bosnian Serb under arrest in war crimes', *The New York Times*, July 22.

Bonner, R 1999a, 'Conflict in the Balkans: The tribunal; tactics were barrier to top Serb's indictment', *The New York Times*, March 29.

Bonner, R 1999b, 'Crisis in the Balkans: The tribunal; Crimes court not ready to punish Kosovo violence', *The New York Times*, March 31.

Bonner, R 1999c, 'Crisis in the Balkans: The outlook: Despite indictment, politicians and diplomats control Milosevic's future', *The New York Times*, May 28.

Boyle, D 2006, 'The rights of victims: Participation, representation, protection, reparation', *Journal of International Criminal Justice*, vol. 4, no. 2, pp. 307–313.

Braithwaite, J 2005a, 'Between proportionality and impunity: Confrontation, truth, prevention', *Criminology*, vol. 43, no. 2, pp. 283–306.

Braithwaite, J 2005b, *Markets in vice, markets in virtue*, Federation Press, Annandale, NSW.

Braithwaite, J, Braithwaite, V, Cookson, M and Dunn, L 2010, *Anomie and violence: Non-truth and reconciliation in Indonesian peacebuilding*, ANU E-Press, Canberra, Australia.

Braithwaite, J, Charlesworth, H and Soares, A 2012, *Networked governance of greedom and tyranny: Peace in Timor-Leste*, ANU E-Press, Canberra, Australia.

Braithwaite, J and Nickson, R 2012, 'Timing truth, reconciliation, and justice after war' *Ohio State Journal on Dispute Resolution*, vol. 27, no. 3, pp. 443–446.

Brdar, M and Vukovic, S 2006, 'A semiotic analysis of 'enemy' management: 'Serbs' in the Western media', *International Journal for the Semiotics of Law/ Revuew Internationale de Semiotique Juridique*, vol. 19, no. 4, pp. 435–456.

Burke-White, W 2008, 'The domestic influence of international criminal tribunals: The International Criminal Tribunal for the Former Yugoslavia and the creation of the State Court of Bosnia and Herzegovina', *Columbia Journal of Transnational Law*, vol. 46, no. 2, pp. 279–350.

Call, CT 2004, 'Is transitional justice really just?', *Brown Journal of World Affairs*, vol. 11, no. 1, pp. 101–113.

Cassese, A 1998, 'Reflections on international criminal justice', *Modern Law Review*, vol. 61, no. 1, pp. 1–10.

Castle, S 2011, 'Mladic arrest opens door to Serbia's long-sought European Union membership', *The New York Times*, May 26.

Celermajer, D 2013, 'Mere ritual? Displacing the myth of sincerity in transitional rituals', *International Journal of Transitional Justice*, vol. 7, no. 3, pp. 286–305.

Chandler, D 2008, *A History of Cambodia*, 4th ed., Westview Press, Boulder, Colorado.

Chibnall, S 1977, *Law and Order News: An Analysis of Crime Reporting in the British Press*, Tavistock Publications, London.

Clark, JN 2009a, 'Judging the ICTY: Has it achieved its objectives?', *Southeast European and Black Sea Studies*, vol. 9, no. 1, pp. 123–142.

Clark, JN 2009b, 'The limits of retributive justice: Findings of an empirical study in Bosnia and Hercegovina', *Journal of International Criminal Justice*, vol. 7, no. 3, pp. 463–487.

Clark, JN 2009c, 'International war crimes tribunals and the challenge of outreach', *International Criminal Law Review*, vol. 9, no. 1, pp. 99–116.

Clark, JN 2010, 'Education in Bosnia-Hercegovina: The case for root and branch reform', *Journal of Human Rights*, vol. 9, no. 3, pp. 344–362.

Cockayne, J 2005, 'Hybrids or mongrels? Internationalized war crimes trials as unsuccessful degradation ceremonies', *Journal of Human Rights*, vol. 4, no. 4, pp. 455–473.

Cohen, R 1995a, 'Tribunal to cite Bosnia Serb chief as war criminal', *The New York Times*, April 24.
Cohen, R 1995b, 'U.N. in Bosnia: Black robes clash with blue hats', *The New York Times*, April 25.
Cohen, R 1995c, 'Bosnian Serb denies all at a war crimes tribunal', *The New York Times*, April 27.
Cohen, R 2001, 'Milosevic to Represent Himself at His Arraignment Today', *The New York Times*, July 3.
Cole, EA 2007, 'Transitional justice and the reform of history education', *International Journal of Transitional Justice*, vol. 1, no. 1, pp. 115–137.
Collier, P 2007, *The bottom billion: Why the poorest countries are failing and what can be done about it*, Oxford University Press, New York.
Collier, P 2009, *Wars, guns and votes: Democracy in dangerous places*, Bodley Head, London.
Cowell, A 1995, 'Nuremberg journal: War crimes and punishments, then and now', *The New York Times*, November 20.
Cowell, A 1997, 'German court sentences Serb to life for genocide in Bosnia', *The New York Times*, September 27.
Crocker, DA 1999, 'Reckoning with past wrongs: A normative framework', *Ethics & International Affairs*, vol. 13, no. 1, pp. 43–64.
Crosette, B 2001, 'Long-range justice raises fears for sovereignty'. *The New York Times*, July 1.
'Deal Reached on Trials for Khmer Rouge' 2003, *The New York Times*, March 17.
Drumbl, MA 2002, 'Restorative justice and collective responsibility: Lessons for and from the Rwandan genocide', *Contemporary Justice Review*, vol. 5, no. 1, pp. 5–22.
Drumbl, MA 2003, 'Toward a criminology of international crime', *Ohio State Journal on Dispute Resolution*, vol. 19, no. 1, pp. 263–281.
Drumbl, MA 2007, *Atrocity, punishment, and international law*, Cambridge University Press, Cambridge.
Dzihana, A and Hodzic, S 2011, 'The Karadzic case: The analysis of media reporting about Radovan Karadzic's arrest and trial' in Dzihana, A and Volcic, Z (eds), *Media and national ideologies: Analysis of reporting on war crime trials in the former Yugoslavia*, Media Centar Sarajevo, Sarajevo, Bosnia and Herzegovina.
Dzihana, A and Volcic, Z (eds) 2011, *Media and national ideologies: Analysis of reporting on war crime trials in the former Yugoslavia*, Media Centar Sarajevo, Sarajevo, Bosnia and Herzegovina.

Eckstein, H 1975, 'Case studies and theory in political science' in Greenstein, F and Polsby, N (eds), *Handbook of Political Science, Vol. 7*, Addison-Wesley, Boston.

Editorial 1998, 'Pol Pot escapes justice', *The New York Times*, April 17.

Editorial 2001, 'The prosecution of Mr. Milosevic', *The New York Times*, January 16.

Editorial 2004, 'International justice', *The New York Times*, February 27.

Editorial 2006a, 'The death of Milosevic', *The New York Times*, March 14.

Editorial 2006b, 'The Killing Fields', *The New York Times*, July 6.

Editorial 2009, 'Trial on trial', *The New York Times*, March 11.

Editorial 2011, 'End of the line', *The New York Times*, May 26.

Engelberg, S 1995, 'Panel seeks U.S. pledge on Bosnia war criminals', *The New York Times*, November 3.

Eriksen, EO 1994, 'Deliberative democracy and the politics of plural society', Paper presented at the Arena Conference on the Europeanization of Normative Theory, Oslo, Norway.

Erjavec, K 2011, 'The case of Dobrovoljacka: An analysis of the Serbian and Bosnian-Herzegovinian daily press' in Dzihana, A and Volcic, Z (eds), *Media and national ideologies: Analysis of reporting on war crime trials in the former Yugoslavia*, Media Centar Sarajevo, Sarajevo, Bosnia and Herzegovina.

Erjavec, K and Volcic, Z 2009a, 'Journalistic (re)production of history: Televized coverage of Radovan Karadzic's arrest in Serbia', Solsko Polje, vol. 20, no. 5/6, pp. 75–99.

Erjavec, K and Volcic, Z 2009b, 'Rehabilitating Milosevic: Posthumous coverage of the Milosevic regime in Serbian newspapers', *Social Semiotics*, vol. 19, no. 2, pp. 125–147.

Erlanger, S 1999, 'Crisis in the Balkans: Belgrade; Word of indictment stuns Serbs and blights hopes', *The New York Times*, May 27.

Erlanger, S 2000, 'Showdown in Yugoslavia: The overview; Milosevic concedes his defeat; Yugoslavs Celebrate New Era', *The New York Times* (New York), 7 October 2000.

Erlanger, S 2001, 'The handover of Milosevic: News analysis; Milosevic trial; Test on many levels', *The New York Times*, June 29.

Erlanger, S and Wren, CS 1999, 'Early count hints at fewer Kosovo deaths', *The New York Times*, November 11.

Etcheson, C 2005, *After the killing fields: Lessons from the Cambodian genocide*, Praeger, Westport, Connecticut.

Filipovic, Z 2006, *Zlata's diary: A child's life in wartime Sarajevo*, Penguin, New York.

Fisher, I 2001, 'Opinion is divided in Serbia over handover of Milosevic', *The New York Times*, June 30.

Fisher, I and Simons, M 2002, 'Milosevic, 'the biggest fish', on eve of war crimes trial', *The New York Times*, February 12.

Fletcher, LE and Weinstein, HM 2002, 'Violence and social repair: Rethinking the contribution of justice to reconciliation', *Human Rights Quarterly*, vol. 24, no. 3, pp. 573–639.

Frankel, M 1999, 'Our humanity vs. their sovereignty', *The New York Times*, May 2.

Galtung, J 1969, 'Violence, peace, and peace research', *Journal of Peace Research*, vol. 6, no. 3, pp. 167–191.

Gay, M 2011, 'Dark past in Balkan war intrudes on new life', *The New York Times*, April 3.

Glenny, M 1996, *The fall of Yugoslavia*, 3rd edition, Penguin, London.

Goldston, JA 2011, 'No justice in the Killing Fields', *The New York Times*, April 26.

Goodman, W 1996, 'Television review: Sorting out war crimes and tangles of history', *The New York Times*, May 13.

Hafner, D and King, E 2007, 'Beyond traditional notions of transitional justice: How trials, truth commissions and other tools for accountability can and should work together', *Boston College International and Comparative Law Review*, vol. 30, no. 1, pp. 91–109.

Haider, H 2009, '(Re)Imagining coexistence: Striving for sustainable return, reintegration and reconciliation in Bosnia and Herzegovina', *International Journal of Transitional Justice*, vol. 3, no. 1, pp. 91–113.

Hancock, V 2008, '"No self" at trial: How to reconcile punishing the Khmer Rouge for crimes against humanity with Cambodian Buddhist principles', *Wisconsin International Law Journal*, vol. 26, no. 1, p. 87.

Hazan, P 2004, *Justice in a time of war: The true story behind the International Criminal Tribunal for the Former Yugoslavia*, Texas A&M University Press, College Station, Texas.

Hedges, C 1996, 'Balkan war crimes: Bosnia is first to turn in its own', *The New York Times*, May 3.

Hinton, AL 2005, *Why did they kill? Cambodia in the shadow of genocide*, University of California Press, Berkeley, California.

Hodzic, R 2010, 'Living the legacy of mass atrocities: Victims' perspectives on war crimes trials', *Journal of International Criminal Justice*, vol. 8, no. 1, pp. 113–136.

Holsti, OR 1969, *Content analysis for the social sciences and humanities*, Addison-Wesley Publishing Co., Reading, Massachusetts.

Horsington, H 2004, 'The Cambodian Khmer Rouge tribunal: The promise of a hybrid tribunal', *Melbourne Journal of International Law*, vol. 5, no. 2, pp. 462–483.

Human Security Report Project 2012, *Human Security Report 2012: Sexual Violence, Education and War: Beyond the Mainstream Narrative*, Human Security Press, Vancouver.

Humphrey, M 2003, 'From victim to victimhood: Truth commissions and trials as rituals of political transition and individual healing', *The Australian Journal of Anthropology*, vol. 14, no. 2, pp. 171–187.

Hussain, V 2005, 'Sustaining judicial rescues: The role of outreach and capacity-building efforts in war crimes tribunals', *Virginia Journal of International Law*, vol. 45, no. 2, pp. 547–561.

International Criminal Tribunal for the Former Yugoslavia, *About the ICTY*, International Criminal Tribunal for the Former Yugoslavia http://www.icty.org/section/AbouttheICTY (accessed 16 March 2013).

Ivkovic, SK 2001, 'Justice by the International Criminal Tribunal for the Former Yugoslavia', *Stanford Journal of International Law*, vol. 37, no. 2, pp. 255–265.

Iyer, V 2007, 'Of prosecutions and amnesties: Does Fiji's experience suggest a reconsideration?', *Australian Journal of Asian Law*, vol. 9, no. 1, pp. 1–43.

Johnstone, G 2002, *Restorative Justice: Ideas, Values, Debates*, Willan Publishing, Portland, Oregon.

Joyner, CC 1993, 'Enforcing human rights standards in the former Yugoslavia: The case for an international war crimes tribunal', *Denver Journal of International Law and Policy*, vol. 22, no. 2 & 2, p. 235.

Karstedt, S 2010, 'From absence to presence, from silence to voice: Victims in transitional justice since the Nuremberg trials', *International Review of Victimology*, vol. 17, no. 1, pp. 9–30.

Keller, B 2002, 'The monster in the dock', *The New York Times*, February 9.

Kiernan, B 2004, *How Pol Pot came to power: Colonialism, nationalism and communism in Cambodia 1930–1975*, 2nd ed, Yale University Press, New Haven, Connecticut.

Kiernan, B 2008a, *The Pol Pot regime: Race, power, and genocide in Cambodia under the Khmer Rouge, 1975–79*, Yale University Press, New Haven, Connecticut.

Kiernan, B 2008b, *Genocide and resistance in South East Asia: Documentation, denial and justice in Cambodia and East Timor*, Transaction Publishers, New Brunswick, New Jersey.

Klarin, M 2009, 'The impact of the ICTY trials on public opinion in the former Yugoslavia', *Journal of International Criminal Justice*, vol. 7, no. 1, pp. 89–96.

Klein, KM 2006, 'Bringing the Khmer Rouge to justice: The challenge and risks facing the joint tribunal in Cambodia', *Northwestern Journal of International Human Rights*, vol. 4, no. 3, pp. 549–566.

Kong, SO 2008, 'Jurisdiction *ratione personae* of the Extraordinary Chambers in the Court of Cambodia: Peace vs. justice', *Forum of International Development Studies*, vol. 37, pp. 149–167.

Korac, M 1993, 'Serbian nationalism: Nationalism of my own people', *Feminist Review*, vol. 45 (Autumn), pp. 108–112.

Krippendorff, K 1980, *Content analysis: An introduction to its methodology*, Sage Publications, Beverley Hills, California.

Lambourne, W 2009, 'Transitional justice and peacebuilding after mass violence', *The International Journal of Transitional Justice*, vol. 3, no. 1, pp. 28–38.

Landsman, S 1996, 'Alternative responses to serious human rights abuses: Of prosecution and truth commissions', *Law and Contemporary Problems*, vol. 59, no. 4, pp. 81–92.

'Lawyer Scolds Cambodia Tribunal Judges' 2008, *The New York Times*, April 24.

Lederach, JP 2003, *The little book of conflict transformation*, Good Books, Intercourse, PA).

Lederach, JP 2010, *Building peace: Sustainable reconciliation in divided societies*, 9th Printing, United States Institute of Peace, Washington.

Leebaw, BA 2008, 'The irreconcilable goals of transitional justice', *Human Rights Quarterly*, vol. 30, no. 1, pp. 95–118.

Lewis, A 1995, 'Abroad at home: Never again', *The New York Times*, April 3.

Lewis, NA 1995, 'At the Bar: A South African jurist focuses on Bosnia', *The New York Times*, March 31.

Llewellyn, JL and Philpott, D 2014, 'Restorative justice and reconciliation: Twin frameworks for peacebuilding', in Llewellyn, JL and Philpott, D (eds), *Restorative Justice, Reconciliation and Peacebuilding*, Oxford University Press, New York.

Lloyd, A 2014, *My war gone by, I miss it so*, Penguin, New York.

Luftglass, S 2004, 'Crossroads in Cambodia: The United Nation's responsibility to withdraw involvement from the establishment of a Cambodian tribunal to prosecute the Khmer Rouge', *Virginia Law Review*, vol. 90, no. 3, pp. 893–964.

McEvoy, K 2007, 'Beyond legalism: Towards a thicker understanding of transitional justice', *Journal of Law and Society*, vol. 34, no. 4, pp. 411–440.

McEvoy, K 2008, 'Letting go of legalism: Developing a 'thicker understanding of transitional justice' in McEvoy, K and McGregor, L (eds), *Transitional justice from below: Grassroots activism and the struggle for change*, Hart Publishing, Portland, Oregon.

McFadden, RD 1998, 'Death of Pol Pot: The Witness; Survivor of Killing Fields is Resolute in Quest for Justice', *The New York Times*, April 17.

McMahon, PC and Forsythe, DP 2008, 'The ICTY's impact on Serbia: Judicial romanticism meets network politics', *Human Rights Quarterly*, vol. 30, no. 2, pp. 412–435.

Margolis, JE 2007, 'Trauma and the trials of reconciliation in Cambodia: View from the ground', *Georgetown Journal of International Affairs*, vol. 8, no. 2, pp. 153–161.

Markovic, P and Subasic, K 2011, 'The case of Vukovar: A comparative analysis of reports on trials for war crimes committed in Vukovar in 1991 in The Hague and Belgrade' in Dzhiana, A and Volcic, Z (eds), *Media and national ideologies: Analysis of reporting on war crime trials in the former Yugoslavia*, Media Centar Sarajevo, Sarajevo, Bosnia and Herzegovina.

Marks, SP 1994, 'Forgetting "the policies and practices of the past": Impunity in Cambodia', *Fletcher Forum of World Affairs*, vol. 18, no. 2, p. 17.

Meernik, J 2005, 'Justice and peace? How the international criminal tribunal affects societal peace in Bosnia', *Journal of Peace Research*, vol. 42, no. 3, pp. 271–289.

Meron, T 1993a, 'The case for war crimes trials in Yugoslavia', *Foreign Affairs*, vol. 72, no. 3, pp. 122–135.

Meron, T 1993b, 'Rape as a crime under international humanitarian law', *The American Journal of International Law*, vol. 87, no. 3, pp. 424–428.

Minichiello, V, Aroni, R, and Neville Hays, T 1990, *In-depth interviewing: Principles, techniques, analysis*, Longman Cheshire, Hong Kong.

Mydans, S 1997a, 'Cambodian rivals say they will bring Pol Pot to justice', *The New York Times*, June 22.

Mydans, S 1997b, 'A stalemate in Cambodia', *The New York Times*, July 2.

Mydans, S 1997c, 'In an interview, Pol Pot declares his conscience is clear', *The New York Times*, October 23.

Mydans, S 1998a, 'Reporter visits Pol Pot still held by Khmer Rouge', *The New York Times*, January 7.

Mydans, S 1998b, 'Khmer Rouge factions battle each other in the jungle', *The New York Times*, March 30.

Mydans, S 1998c, 'For Pol Pot, an endgame', *The New York Times*, April 13.

Mydans, S 1998d, 'Pol Pot is dead, Thai army says; Made Cambodia a "Killing Field"', *The New York Times*, April 16.

Mydans, S 1998e, 'Death of Pol Pot: The analysis; The demons of a despot', *The New York Times*, April 17.

Mydans, S 1998f, 'At cremation of Pol Pot, no tears shed', *The New York Times*, April 19.

Mydans, S 1999a, 'Two Khmer Rouge leaders spend beach holiday in shadow of past', *The New York Times*, January 1.

Mydans, S 1999b, 'Cambodia says it plans trial for jailed Khmer Rouge commander', *The New York Times*, March 8.

Mydans, S 1999c 'Captured Khmer Rouge leader to face charges in Cambodia', *The New York Times*, March 10.

Mydans, S 1999d 'Phnom Penh journal: Intrepid lawyer rises for first Khmer Rouge trial', *The New York Times*, May 14.

Mydans, S 2006, 'Former Cambodian leaders to face trial', *The New York Times*, January 23.

Mydans, S 2009a, 'Efforts to limit Khmer Rouge trials decried', *The New York Times*, February 1.

Mydans, S 2009b, 'Trial begins for Khmer Rouge leader', *The New York Times*, February 17.

Mydans, S 2009c, 'Accusations of corruption cast a shadow over the Khmer Rouge trials in Cambodia', *The New York Times*, April 10.

Mydans, S 2010, 'Anger in Cambodia Over Khmer Rouge Sentence', *The New York Times*, July 26.

Nettlefield, LJ 2010a, *Courting democracy in Bosnia and Herzegovina: The Hague tribunal's impact in a postwar state*, Cambridge University Press, New York, New York.

Nettlefield, LJ 2010b, 'From the battlefield to the barracks: The ICTY and the armed forces of Bosnia and Herzegovina', *International Journal of Transitional Justice*, vol. 4, no. 1, pp. 87–109.

Nickson, R 2017, 'Unmet expectations and the legitimacy of transitional justice institutions' in Karstedt, S and Brants, C (eds), *Engagement, contestation and legitimacy*, Hart Publishing, Portland, Oregon.

Nickson, R and Braithwaite, J 2014, 'Deeper, broader, longer transitional justice', *European Journal of Criminology*, vol. 11, no. 4, pp. 445–463.

Nikolaev, AG 2009, 'Images of war: Content analysis of the photo coverage of the war in Kosovo', *Critical Sociology*, vol. 35, no. 1, pp. 105–130.

O'Brien, JC 1993, 'The international tribunal for violations of international humanitarian law in the former Yugoslavia', *The American Journal of International Law*, vol. 87, no. 4, pp. 639–659.

O'Connor, M 1995, 'At one hotel in Bosnia, hunters and the hunted', *The New York Times*, December 29.

O'Connor, M 1996, 'Grim Reaper; Harvesting evidence in Bosnia's killing fields', *The New York Times*, April 7.

Odendaal, A 2010, *An architecture for building peace at the local level: A comparative study of local peace committees*, United Nations Development Programme, New York.

Olsen, TD, Payne, LA and Reiter, AG 2010, 'The justice balance: When transitional justice improves human rights and democracy', *Human Rights Quarterly*, vol. 32, no. 4, pp. 980–1007.

Open Society Justice Initiative 2012, *The future of cases 003/004 at the Extraordinary Chambers in the Courts of Cambodia*, Open Society Justice Initiative, New York.

Opinion 1997, 'A trial for Pol Pot', *The New York Times*, June 24.

Opinion 1998, 'Bringing Pol Pot to justice', *The New York Times*, April 10.

Opinion 2002, 'The trial of Slobodan Milosevic', *The New York Times*, February 11.

Orentlicher, D 1991, 'Settling accounts: The duty to prosecute human rights violations of a prior regime', *The Yale Law Journal*, vol. 100, no. 8, pp. 2537–2615.

Orentlicher, D 2010, *That someone guilty be punished: The impact of the ICTY in Bosnia*, The Open Society Justice Initiative, New York.

Parker, T 2004, 'Judgment at Baghdad', *The New York Times*, July 7.

Perlez, J 1996, 'War crimes tribunal on Bosnia is hampered by basic problems', *The New York Times*, January 28.

Pham, P, Vinck, P, Balthazard, M, Hean, S and Stover, E 2009, *So we will never forget: A population based survey on attitudes about social reconstruction and The Extraordinary Chambers in the Courts of Cambodia*, Human Rights Center, University of California, Berkeley, California.

Pham, PN, Vinck, P, Balthazard, M, Strasser, J and Om, C 2011. 'Victim participation and the trial of Duch at the Extraordinary Chambers in the Courts of Cambodia', *Journal of Human Rights Practice*, vol. 3, no. 3, pp. 264–287.

Philpott, D 2012. *Just and unjust peace: An ethic of political reconciliation*, Oxford University Press, New York.

Posner, EA and Vermeule, A 2004, 'Transitional justice as ordinary justice', *Harvard Law Review*, vol. 117, no. 3, pp. 761–825.

Ramji-Nogales, J 2010, 'Designing bespoke transitional justice: A pluralist process approach', *Michigan Journal of International Law,* vol. 32, no. 1, pp. 1–72.

Ratner, SR 1999, 'The United Nations Group of Experts for Cambodia', *The American Journal of International Law*, vol. 93, no. 4, pp. 948–953.

Reisman, WM 1996, 'Legal responses to genocide and other massive violations of human rights', *Law and Contemporary Problems*, vol. 59, no. 4, pp. 75–80.

Rodman, KA 2008, 'Darfur and the limits of legal deterrence', *Human Rights Quarterly*, vol. 30, no. 3, pp. 529–560.

Rosenthal, Am 1995, 'On my mind: Arresting the negotiators', *The New York Times*, July 28.

Ruigrok, N 2005, *Journalism of Attachment: Dutch Newspapers During the Bosnian War*, Het Spinhuis, Amsterdam, The Netherlands.

Saxon, D 2005, 'Exporting justice: Perceptions of the ICTY among the Serbian, Croatian and Muslim communities in the former Yugoslavia', *Journal of Human Rights*, vol. 4, no. 4, pp. 559–572.

Scharf, MP 1996a, 'The prosecutor v Dusko Tadic: An appraisal of the first international war crimes trial since Nuremberg', Albany Law Review, vol. 60, no. 3, pp. 861–882.

Scharf, MP 1996b, 'The case for a permanent international truth commission', *Duke Journal of International and Comparative Law*, vol. 7, pp. 375–410.

Scharf, MP 1997, *Balkan justice: The story behind the first international war crimes trial since Nuremberg*, Carolina Academic Press, Durham, North Carolina).

Schrag, M 2004 'Lessons learned from ICTY Experience', *Journal of International Criminal Justice*, vol. 2, no. 2, pp. 427–434.

Sciolino, E 1995, 'Bosnian talks snag on fate of two Serbs', *The New York Times*, November 17.

Sebastian, S 2010, 'Statebuilding in divided societies: The reform of dayton in Bosnia and Herzegovina', *Journal of Intervention and Statebuilding*, vol. 4, no. 3, pp. 324–344.

Shearing, C and Froestad, J 2007, 'Beyond restorative justice - Zwelethemba, a future-focused model using local capacity conflict resolution' in Mackay, R, Bosnjak, M, Deklerck, J, Pelikan, C, Van Stokkom, B and Wright, M (eds) *Images of Restorative Justice Theory*, Verlag fur Polizeiwissenschaft, Frankfurt, Germany.

Shenon, P 1998a, 'U.S. seeks China's help in arranging Pol Pot trial', *The New York Times*, April 11.

Shenon, P 1998b, 'U.N. plans joint war crimes tribunal for Khmer Rouge', *The New York Times*, August 12.

Shenon, P and Schmitt, E 1998, 'U.S. is planning a move to seize Pol Pot for trial', *The New York Times*, April 9.

Silber, L and Little, A 1997, *Yugoslavia: Death of a nation*, Revised Edition, Penguin, New York.

Simons, M 1995, 'Conflict in the Balkans: War crimes; Tribunal indicts Bosnian Serb leader', *The New York Times*, July 26.

Simons, M 1996a, 'Far from former Yugoslavia, first war crimes trial opens', *The New York Times*, May 8.

Simons, M 1996b, 'A war crimes trial starts', *The New York Times*, May 12.

Simons, M 1998, 'U.N. war crimes tribunal steps up its inquiry into Kosovo', *The New York Times*, August 26.

Simons, M 1998, 'Proud but concerned, tribunal prosecutor leaves', *The New York Times*, September 15.

Simons, M 2001a, 'Tribunal in Hague finds Bosnia Serb guilty of genocide', *The New York Times*, August 3.

Simons, M 2001b, 'Milosevic calls tribunal unfair, infantile and "a farce"', *The New York Times*, October 31.

Simons, M 2002, 'An American With Opinions Steps Down Vocally at War Crimes Court', *The New York Times*, January 24.

Simons, M 2003, 'Bosnian ex-leader sentenced to 11 years for her war role', *The New York Times*, February 28.

Simons, M 2004, 'The Saturday Profile: Weaving the threads of law, war and Shakespeare', *The New York Times*, January 3.

Simons, M 2009, 'International criminal tribunals and the media', *Journal of International Criminal Justice*, vol. 7, no. 1, pp. 83–88.

Simons, M 2016, 'Bosnian Serb leader Karadzic convicted of genocide and war crimes', *The New York Times*, March 25.

Simons, M with Gall, C 2001, 'The handover of Milosevic: The overview; Milosevic is given to U.N. for trial in war-crime case', *The New York Times*, June 29.

Simpson, G 1997, 'Didactic and dissident histories in war crimes trials', *Albany Law* Review, vol. 60, no. 3, pp. 801–839.

Spoerri, M and Freyberg-Inan, A 2008, 'From prosecution to persecution: Perceptions of the International Criminal Tribunal for the Former Yugoslavia (ICTY) in Serbian domestic politics', *Journal of International Relations and Development*, vol. 11, no. 4, pp. 350–384.

Stanley, E 2002, 'What next? The aftermath of organised truth telling', *Race and Class*, vol. 44, no. 1, pp. 1–15.

Stanley, E 2004, 'Torture, silence and recognition', *Current Issues in Criminal Justice*, vol. 16, no. 1, pp. 5–25.

Sunstein, C 1995, 'Incompletely theorized agreements', *Harvard Law Review*, vol. 108, no. 7, pp. 1733–1772.

Sunstein, C 1996, *Legal Reasoning and Political Conflict*, Oxford University Press, New York.

Sykes, GM and Matza, D 1957, 'Techniques of neutralization: A theory of delinquency', *American Sociological Review*, vol. 22, no. 6, pp. 664–670.

'Ta Mok, Khmer Rouge Head Facing Genocide Trial, Dies' 2006, *The New York Times*, July 21.

Teitel, R 2005, 'The law and politics of contemporary transitional justice', *Cornell International Law Journal*, vol. 38, pp. 837–862.

The Human Rights Center and the International Human Rights Law Clinic, University of California Berkeley, and the Centre for Human Rights, Sarajevo, 2000 'Justice, accountability and social reconstruction: An interview study of Bosnian judges and prosecutors', *Berkeley Journal of International Law*, vol. 18, no. 1, pp. 102–164.

Theissen, G 2004, *Supporting justice, co-existence and reconciliation after armed conflict: Strategies for dealing with the past*, Berghof Research Center for Constructive Conflict Management, Berlin.

Un, K and Ledgerwood, J 2010, 'Is the trial of 'Duch' a catalyst for change in Cambodia's courts?', Asia Pacific Issues – Analysis From the East-West Center No 95, East-West Center.

United Nations General Assembly and Security Council, *Identical Letters dated 23 June 1997 from the Secretary General addressed to the President of the General Assembly and the President of the Security Council*, 23 June 1997, UN Doc. A/51/135-s/1997/488 (letter dated 21 June 1997 from the First and Second Prime Ministers of Cambodia addressed to the Secretary-General annexed thereto).

'U.N. Prosecutor Plans Bigger Push in Balkans' 1999, *The New York Times*, December 23.

U.S. Agency for International Development 1998, *Managing Conflict: Lessons from the South African Peace Committees*, USAID Evaluation Special Study Report No. 78.

Verfuss, T 2004, 'Trying poor countries crimes in a rich city: The problems of the press from the former Yugoslavia', *Journal of International Criminal Justice*, vol. 2, no. 2, pp. 509–515.

Villa-Vicencio, C 2000, 'Why perpetrators should not always be prosecuted', *Emory Law Journal*, vol. 49, no. 1, pp. 205–222.

Volcic, Z and Dzihana, A 2011, 'Introduction: Towards peace journalism' in Dzhiana, A and Volcic, Z (eds), *Media and national ideologies: Analysis of reporting on war crime trials in the former Yugoslavia*, Media Centar Sarajevo, Sarajevo, Bosnia and Herzegovina.

Waters, TW 2009, 'Seeking justice decades later: Hear the victims' voices', *The New York Times*, February 4.

Wilson, R 2005, 'Judging history: The historical record of the International Criminal Tribunal for the Former Yugoslavia', *Human Rights Quarterly*, vol. 27, no. 3, pp. 908–942.

Wren, C 1999, 'Judge says Yugoslavia impedes work of war crimes tribunal', *The New York Times*, November 9.

Zehr, H 1995, *Changing lenses: A new focus for crime and justice*, Herald Press, Scottdale, PA.

Zehr, H 2002, *The little book of restorative justice*, Good Books, Intercourse, PA.

Zdravkovic-Zonta, H 2011, 'The case of scorpions: Media, nationalism and war crimes', in Dzhiana, A and Volcic, Z (eds), *Media and national ideologies: Analysis of reporting on war crime trials in the former Yugoslavia*, Media Centar Sarajevo, Sarajevo, Bosnia and Herzegovina.

Zikic, B 2011, 'The Biljana Plavsic case: Nationalist and gender narratives in the service of media (non)reporting on the Plavsic case in Serbia and Bosnia and Herzegovina (The Republika Srspka)', in Dzhiana, A and Volcic, Z (eds), *Media and national ideologies: Analysis of reporting on war crime trials in the former Yugoslavia*, Media Centar Sarajevo, Sarajevo, Bosnia and Herzegovina.

Zoglin, K 2005, 'The future of war crimes prosecutions in the former Yugoslavia: Accountability or junk justice?', *Human Rights Quarterly*, vol. 27, no. 1, pp. 41–77.

Index

R. Nickson and A. Neikirk, *Managing Transitional Justice*,
Palgrave Studies in Compromise after Conflict,
https://doi.org/10.1007/978-3-319-77782-5

The manufacturer's authorised representative in the EU is Springer Nature Customer Service Centre GmbH, Europaplatz 3, 69115 Heidelberg, Germany. If you have any concerns regarding our products, please contact ProductSafety@springernature.com

Printed and bound by CPI Group (UK) Ltd, Croydon, CR0 4YY
25/09/2026
02222647-0004